The New Frontier
N L R B

by

KENNETH C. McGUINESS

Published by

LABOR POLICY ASSOCIATION, INC.
1815 H STREET, N.W.
WASHINGTON 6, D. C.

PRICE $6

July '67

THE AUTHOR

Kenneth C. McGuiness is singularly qualified by an uncommon breadth of experience to write this effective criticism of the current NLRB. Widely known as one of the truly expert labor lawyers practicing today, he has served as an NLRB policy maker, a consultant to Congress, and as an impartial arbitrator. He has also handled labor matters in a corporate law department and as representative of an employers' association.

Mr. McGuiness has been active in the labor law field since 1946, when he joined the California Association of Employers, negotiating labor agreements and advising the members of the Association on a wide variety of labor problems. Later, he joined the staff of U. S. Steel Corporation in San Francisco, handling workmen's compensation cases, wage-hour problems, and arbitration proceedings.

Early in 1954, Mr. McGuiness came to Washington as Associate Chief Counsel for NLRB Member Albert C. Beeson and, after Mr. Beeson's term ended, held similar posts under Chairman Guy Farmer and Member Boyd Leedom. He was then selected by Theophil C. Kammholz, who had recently been appointed General Counsel, as Associate General Counsel in charge of the Board's regional offices and its case handling before the Board. Upon Mr. Kammholz's resignation, Mr. McGuiness received a recess appointment as General Counsel and served in that capacity for several months. Although one of the first lawyers with a management background to serve as a staff member of the National Labor Relations Board in a high-level position in Washington, he won the lasting respect of the career staff of the agency for his fairness and objectivity.

iii

Mr. McGuiness left the Board in 1958 to enter the practice of law in Washington, D. C., and early in 1959 became special consultant to the House Committee on Education and Labor during consideration of the legislation leading to passage of the Landrum-Griffin Act. In this capacity he participated in the hearings on the major labor bills then before the Congress, the Committee executive sessions, and the drafting of Landrum-Griffin. He sat on the floor of the House as an advisor during the debates and participated in the deliberations of the Senate-House Conference Committee, where the final changes in the law were made.

Mr. McGuiness was born in Iowa and is a graduate of Iowa State College and of the School of Law of the University of California at Berkeley, California. He is a member of the State Bar of California, the District of Columbia Bar, and of the Labor Law Section of the American Bar Association. He has also served as arbitrator by appointment of the Federal Mediation and Conciliation Service.

Co-author of a book entitled, "Practice and Procedure before the National Labor Relations Board," published by the American Law Institute, Mr. McGuiness is a frequent speaker on labor matters.

Mr. McGuiness is now the Washington partner of a leading Mid-West law firm.

TABLE OF CONTENTS

ABOUT LABOR POLICY ASSOCIATION

Labor Policy Association, Inc., is a membership society established and maintained for the following purposes, among others, as quoted from the charter:

> "To make and to encourage researches and studies pertaining to government policies affecting labor and labor relations and their effects upon individual liberty, a free competitive market, the welfare of labor and industry, and any or all elements of the social order and economy of the United States; . . . and . . . to publish and distribute such researches and studies . . . ;"

The members of Labor Policy Association, Inc., are a group of far-sighted employers who are earnestly seeking equitable and effective answers to some of the critical questions which arise concerning labor policy.

To foresee needs on specific issues and to prepare in advance of the event in the field of its competence is one of the functions of the Association.

Laws are made for men of ordinary understanding, and should therefore be construed by the
ordinary rules of common sense. Their meaning
is not to be sought for in meta-physical subtleties,
which may make anything mean everything or
nothing, at pleasure.

THOMAS JEFFERSON:
Letter to
William Johnson, 1823

FOREWORD

On April 10, 1962, we took the Floor of the House of Representatives to advise Congress and the American people about a disturbing trend reflected in the National Labor Relations Board decisions which purport to interpret and apply the 1959 labor reform law that bears our names. We found it necessary then to report that, in many instances, the meaning of the Landrum-Griffin Act had been distorted, and that the clear intent of Congress to curb certain abuses had been frustrated.

Since then there has been no reason for a lessening of our concern. Indeed, it has become increasingly apparent that an exhaustive study and analysis of the new Board's decisions would be helpful to provide an over-all appraisal of the extent to which Congressional intent in this field is being frustrated. We are pleased that such an analysis has been made by Mr. Kenneth McGuiness and is now available in this volume.

The result of Mr. McGuiness' exhaustive work is this documented statement of a disturbing situation which is cause for genuine alarm. He makes clear that the distortion and frustration of Congressional intent which we found budding in April, 1962, has now blossomed forth into outright usurpation of the Congressional power to legislate. The new NLRB members are altering not only the 1959 amendments but the entire National Labor Relations Act to replace the will of Congress with their personal views.

With his close acquaintance with the development and intent of the 1959 Act, combined with his experience as a top level NLRB official, Mr. McGuiness is uniquely qualified to place in proper perspective the obvious conflict which exists between Congress and a majority of the present Board.

As Special Counsel to the House Committee on Education and Labor during 1959, Mr. McGuiness provided us with invaluable assistance throughout the development and enactment of the Landrum-Griffin Act. The author's personal participation in the Conference Committee deliberations, where much of the final language of the secondary boycott and picketing amendments were worked out, makes his comments on NLRB action in these areas particularly significant.

When legislative history to support its new theories has been found lacking, the new Board has not hesitated to place its reliance upon legal writers who had no part in the legislative process leading to the Landrum-Griffin Act, or upon others who participated but took the position at the time that Taft-Hartley amendments were not necessary or appropriate for inclusion in the 1959 labor reform bill. It should be noteworthy that Mr. McGuiness counseled those who prevailed in Congress with their position that employees, neutral employers and the public should have protection against such coercive practices as boycotts and blackmail picketing.

If the Constitution made anything clear, surely it was that legislating is primarily the function of Congress. Regardless of the personal inclinations of its members, the NLRB should function to implement and carry out the policies laid down by Congress in this field.

Mr. McGuiness' book, THE NEW FRONTIER NLRB, is interesting and important reading for every member of Congress, for everyone concerned with labor-management relations, and for every citizen who thinks that the laws of our country should be written by the elected representatives of the people.

PHIL M. LANDRUM, M.C.   ROBERT P. GRIFFIN, M.C.
House of Representatives, Washington, D. C.
April, 1963

I

THE KENNEDY BOARD

Any mortal system of law must be administered by human beings. The background, philosophy, strengths and weaknesses of the administrators are inevitably reflected in opinions which, in their eyes, represent an equitable result.

Few informed observers would take exception to the view that the NLRB has been an agency where interpretations of the law have been peculiarly dependent on the predilections of its members. Therefore, an introduction to the "Kennedy Board" before reviewing its decisions will place our study in better focus. Also, present members through published speeches have more clearly defined their approach to the law than did most earlier Boards. Reference to some of their speeches provides both an introduction to their overall viewpoint and an opportunity to compare promise with practice.

Gerald A. Brown, although the newest appointee, was the first to set forth with some specificity the broad outlines of the Kennedy Board approach. An NLRB career employee and the only non-lawyer member of the Board, Brown was sworn in April 14, 1961, and will serve until August 27, 1966. Before joining the Board as Field Examiner in 1942, he taught economics and political science in his native Texas for four years and was an instructor at the University of North Carolina for three years while taking graduate work.

He served in various regional offices of the Board and was Regional Director in San Francisco for 15 years prior to his Board appointment.

Brown's outline of the Kennedy Board approach was first presented in a speech before the Duke University Institute on Labor Law, February 9, 1962. Viewing the role of NLRB as one of translating a general public policy into varied and changing factual situations, he expressed that policy as:

> ". . . the encouragement of collective bargaining as the democratic method of solving labor problems."

And, to him, consistency in applying that policy comes by adhering to the fundamental purposes of the statute rather than by following the same rule inexorably.

Disagreeing with the approach of earlier Board members and particularly with that of Guy Farmer, Chairman during the early days of the Eisenhower Administration, Brown declared that the Board is "unquestionably a policy-making tribunal." He would not hesitate, therefore, to reverse a prior policy when it becomes outmoded, is recognized as having been unsound initially, has not worked out as expected, or when experience indicates a better approach. Forthrightly recognizing that a member's viewpoint may be influenced by his background and philosophy, yet denying this to be political, Brown quoted approvingly the frequently urged theory that an administrative agency should reflect the political climate and thus more effectively express the majority will than would reliance on elected officials acting through the legislative process.

With this background, Brown explained his basic approach to the decision-making process as ". . . independent analysis on a case-by-case basis [which] must be substituted for mechanical rules." He saw the alternative as "rubber stamp approval of 'per se' rules" and, though recognizing that fixed rules are easy to apply and provide the parties with knowledge

[2]

upon which to predicate their actions, he concluded that the resulting "uncertainty" was superficial, destined for disrepute, and actually yielded more uncertainty than certainty. To avoid any possibility of being misunderstood, Brown closed by emphasizing the fact that the choice between the "per se" and the "case-by-case" theories of decision-making is not one of degree but of approach.

Several days after Mr. Brown's speech, Chairman Frank McCulloch echoed his colleague's thinking. McCulloch, the first Kennedy appointee, took office March 7, 1961. At the time of his appointment, he had been Administrative Assistant to Senator Paul Douglas of Illinois for 12 years. McCulloch came from a well-known family of lawyers, both his father and mother having been members of the Chicago Bar. He was educated at Williams College, where he was Phi Beta Kappa, and at Harvard Law School. He was associated with a large Chicago law firm during his first years out of law school but his official resumé, which lists "evening settlement work" during the same period, discloses his own recognition of more abiding interests in other activities.

In 1935, McCulloch became Industrial Relations Secretary for the Congregational-Christian Council for Social Action and, during the next eleven years, was a frequent lecturer at various theological seminaries throughout the country. From 1946-49, before joining Senator Douglas, he was Director, Labor Education Division, Roosevelt University in Chicago.

Enlarging upon Brown's remarks, McCulloch, in an address before the American Management Association in Chicago, February 15, 1962, declared that the arrival of the Kennedy appointees was an obvious ". . . time to pause and take new soundings." In support, he emphasized the recently-amended statute, the findings of the Cox Panel in 1960, the Pucinski Subcommittee in 1961, and a series of recent Supreme Court decisions which he found to be a dictate ". . . to re-examine our approach as well as our end results." Finally, he found the staggered terms of the Board members led to the "obvious conclusion" that Congress recognized the President should have some influence through the appointive process over the broad direction taken by the agencies which execute the law.

McCulloch left no doubt that he fully agreed with Brown's "case-by-case" approach to the decision-making process. In a pungent summation of his thinking, he said,

> "The price of a mechanistic approach is a mechanistic result, and an automaton, give thanks, lacks the delicate perceptiveness necessary to achieve justice."

In another address at Michigan State University about two months later, and after an immediate public reaction to the earlier speeches, the Chairman forcefully reiterated his previous views on the new approach but was careful to note that he did not wish to create the impression of having totally abandoned a per se approach to all problems. He used two examples to illustrate situations where he thought fixed rules appropriate. Both involved employer violations of the Act. The first was an employer grant of super-seniority rights to those who abandoned a strike, i.e. the employer guaranteed that employees who worked during a strike would have greater seniority in case of a reduction in force than those who continued on strike. *Erie Resistor,* 132 NLRB No. 51, 48 LRRM 1379. The second was a unilateral change in conditions of employment by an employer during bargaining, e.g. wage increase granted and sick leave policy liberalized while negotiations are going on, as in *Benne Katz d/b/a/ Williamsburg Steel Products,* 126 NLRB No. 39, 45 LRRM 1300.

The Board member who completes the New Frontier majority is John H. Fanning. Though first appointed by the previous Administration at the suggestion of Secretary of

Labor Mitchell, his views have been consistent throughout his service. Over half of his more than 70 dissents during the days of the Eisenhower Board have been adopted by the Kennedy appointees. In his own words,

"I didn't catch up with the New Frontier. It caught up with me."

Fanning is also a career government employee, although he had no experience with NLRB prior to taking office in December, 1957. A native of Rhode Island, he is a graduate of Catholic University Law School in Washington, D. C. After a brief stint of private practice with a law firm in Pawtucket, R. I., he came to the Solicitor's office at the Department of Labor in 1942, and, a year later, moved to the Industrial Personnel Division of Army Service Forces. The balance of his pre-NLRB career was spent in various positions with the Department of Defense, most having some connection with labor matters. Fanning was reappointed by President Kennedy, and his present term will expire December 16, 1967. Although his public statements have been more restrained than the other majority members, an analysis of his decisions demonstrates Fanning's full acceptance of the case-by-case approach.

The two remaining Board members, the Eisenhower minority, are Philip Ray Rodgers and Boyd Leedom. Rodgers, the senior member of the Board, took office August 28, 1953. His present term will expire August 27, 1963. He came from Utah and is a graduate of the University of Utah in public administration. He has a Ph.D. in the same field from American University and a law degree from George Washington University. After experience as both a college professor and a Senatorial secretary, he became Chief Clerk of the Senate Labor Committee when Senator Taft was Chairman in 1947. Rodgers served in that capacity or as Minority Clerk until his appointment to the Board.

Leedom, the former Chairman, was a practicing attorney in South Dakota from 1929 to 1949, when he was appointed to the Supreme Court of that State. He remained on the Court, though sitting as a referee for the National Railroad Adjustment Board frequently during the same period, until his appointment to NLRB in April, 1955. Like Rodgers, Leedom is now serving a second five-year term which will expire December 16, 1964.

Rodgers has been the most consistent dissenter from the new Board's decisions, with Leedom joining in most instances. Curiously, however, Rodgers has not infrequently expressed approval of a "case-by-case" concept of decision-making and dissastisfaction with "a purely mechanistic" approach, e.g. *Litton Industries,* 125 NLRB 722, 45 LRRM 1166. It is apparent, however, that Rodgers, unlike Brown, views the method as one of degree which requires, rather than removes, the need for standards comprehensible to the parties governed by them, e.g. *American Cyanamid Co.,* 131 NLRB No. 125, 48 LRRM 1152.

As pointed out by McCulloch in one of his speeches, the five Board members collectively have an impressive record of public service. However, except for Brown, with his long tenure with NLRB, and Rodgers' intimate knowledge of the background and drafting of the Taft-Hartley Act, the Board's background in the area of day-to-day labor-management relations is minimal. Leedom has frankly admitted his experience in the field began when he came to the Board. Fanning's years in the Department of Defense brought him into contact with labor problems on many occasions, but, by no stretch of the imagination, could he have been called well-grounded in the Act. McCulloch likewise had considerable contact with labor problems prior to his service with Senator Douglas, but apparently from an academic point of view rather than as a participant.

In any event, none of the five Board members has participated in an organizing drive, either as a union representative or a member of management. None has negotiated a collective bargaining agreement or has been responsible for a decision to strike or take a strike. None has worked as a union representative or an industrial relations director or operated a business. While such experience is not a prerequisite to satisfactory performance as a Board member, its lack may be reflected in some decisions.

The Board staff, with few exceptions, has an even more limited practical background, and legal assistants to Board members rarely have had other significant experience. By far the great majority of the cases are decided on "cold" records, read by the legal assistant only. None of the decision-makers or their assistants see the parties or have any opportunity to hear, first-hand, their arguments. It is consequently not surprising that some Board decisions are (to put it kindly) unrealistic and doctrinaire in their approach to day-to-day realities of labor-management relations.

The background of the members and their published speeches portend the practical impact of the Kennedy Board on labor-management relations. The concept of the Board as a policy-making tribunal is most significant. Unquestionably, the Board has some policy-making functions, e.g. determination of the period a valid labor contract will bar a representation election, the circumstances under which review of a Regional Director's direction of an election will be granted, or flexibility in fashioning an appropriate remedy. These elaborate on the Congressional purpose as embodied in specific provisions of the Act. But, McCulloch and Brown clearly see the Board's role of policy maker as much broader in scope. Their decisions, even more than their speeches, demonstrate a firm belief that the Act's fundamental purposes (as construed by the Board) carry greater weight than the literal language of the statute. Such a view places the Board squarely in conflict with Congress.

Expressed another way, the new Board members apparently feel they have a mandate to re-examine the existing law and shape it to fit their concept of the current political climate. We need go no further than the organizational and recognition picketing amendments (see Chapter XVI) before it is apparent that re-examination to them includes re-writing the law rather than revising policy within the strict confines of the Act as written. The "case-by-case" approach is a logical method of carrying out the New Frontier concept. It obscures the application and simplifies the abandonment of established rules.

Whether from lack of practical experience in day-to-day labor-management relations or from lack of concern, the chaotic effect of such an approach on employees, employers and unions who must conduct themselves within the confines of the Act is overlooked by the new Board. Collective bargaining is not a precise science. Employee rights are not easily defined. Interests must be balanced. Disputes must be settled without waiting for litigation. Even moderate success can be accomplished only if rules of conduct are expressed as clearly as possible. When the Board declares emphatically, both through speeches and decisions, that established rules will not only be changed but will be replaced by "independent analysis" or "delicate perceptiveness," confusion is inevitable.

In support of their purported injunction to re-examine the law, McCulloch, Fanning and Brown have frequently referred to the United States Supreme Court decisions, beginning in 1959, some of which reversed rules adopted by the Eisenhower Board. But the language of the Court in one of these very cases demonstrates the contrary to be more accurate.

> "It is suggested here that the time has come for a re-evaluation of the basic content of collective bargaining as contemplated by the federal legislation. But that is for

Congress. Congress has demonstrated its capacity to adjust the Nation's labor legislation to what, in its legislative judgment, constitutes the statutory pattern appropriate to the developing state of labor relations in the country. Major revisions of the basic statute were enacted in 1947 and 1959. To be sure, then, Congress might be of the opinion that greater stress should be put on the role of 'pure' negotiation in settling labor disputes, to the extent of eliminating more and more economic weapons from the parties' grasp, and perhaps it might start with the ones involved here; or in consideration of the alternatives, it might shrink from such an undertaking. But Congress' policy has not yet moved to this point, and with only §8(b)(3) to lean on, we do not see how the Board can do so on its own." *N.L.R.B. v. Insurance Agents' Union (Prudential Insurance Co.)*, 361 US 477, 45 LRRM 2704.

Finally, it is difficult to ignore the increasing conflict between Congress and the Board as to the Board's function. Congressional dissatisfaction with the Board has erupted many times since 1935, but rarely has the policy issue been drawn as clearly as early last year. After Brown stated his view that ". . . the Board is unquestionably a policy-making tribunal," public reaction was highly critical. Congressional feeling was pointedly set forth by Congressmen Landrum and Griffin, the drafters of the 1959 amendments. On April 10, 1962, in a speech on the floor of the House, Congressman Griffin said:

> "If the Constitution made anything clear, surely it is that policymaking is primarily a function of the Congress. To be effective in the performance of that function, it is essential that Congress at least observe whether, and to what extent, its policies are actually being implemented and carried out.
> "The pattern of recent decisions by the NLRB gives rise to a serious concern that policies laid down by Congress, in the Taft-Hartley and Landrum-Griffin Acts, are being distorted and frustrated, to say the very least.
> "The decisions themselves are startling enough. However,

when viewed in the light of some recent extrajudicial pronouncements by Board members, there is reason to wonder whether the NLRB—which was created by Congress—even concedes the constitutional authority of Congress to formulate and establish policy in the labor-management field."

The same day, Congressman Landrum declared:

"The law spells out in definite terms the conduct which constitutes these unfair labor practices. These unfair labor practices are clearly defined. They are carefully enumerated in the law. This point, Mr. Speaker, is most important. It underscores the fact that the Labor Board has no policy-making authority in these cases. Congress, not the Labor Board, has defined the unfair conduct which the law prohibits. Congress gave to the Labor Board the job of deciding only whether the well-defined terms of the law are violated. This is a judicial role, not a policymaking role. But notwithstanding all this, the Board seems determined to make policy—to legislate, if you please. Board spokesmen now proclaim publicly that theirs is a policymaking function."

These comments are merely the beginning. The new Board is unlikely to change its approach and it is unrealistic to expect Congress will sit idly by as the Board usurps its policy-making prerogative.

The Kennedy appointees are convinced their views are firmly grounded on reason and logic. Although the writer vigorously disagrees, many voices will be heard in support of the new members. Albert Woll, General Counsel of the AFL-CIO, for example, has characterized them as ". . . honest, devoted public servants, honestly trying to interpret a very complex law."

Criticism contained in this volume, both of the Board's approach to decision-making and of its decisions, must not be construed as an attack upon its members. They are not unique. The error is impersonal and needs constantly to be so recognized if acceptable solutions are to be found.

II

POLICY OF THE ACT

Throughout the decisions of the New Frontier Board, many references are made to the policy of the Act. Member Brown has expressed that policy on one occasion as ". . . in essence, the encouragement of collective bargaining as the democratic method of solving labor problems." Another time he said, "It is the stated policy of this country that free collective bargaining is the way of democracy."

Both statements reflect the approach of the Kennedy Board. Both reflect *one* of the policies of the Act, but they also reflect a very common over-simplification. Before commencing our review of the new Board's cases, it may be helpful, therefore, to take a closer look at the policy as expressed by Congress.

Section 1 of the National Labor Relations Act, which is titled "Findings and Policies," includes this paragraph:

> "It is hereby declared to be the policy of the United States to eliminate the causes of certain substantial obstructions to the free flow of commerce *and*
> to mitigate and eliminate these obstructions when they have occurred
>
> > *by* encouraging the practice and procedure of collective bargaining *and*
> > *by* protecting the exercise by workers of full freedom of association, self-organization, and designa-

> tion of representatives of their own choosing, for the purpose of negotiating the terms and conditions of their employment or other mutual aid or protection." (Emphasis supplied)

The paragraph has remained unchanged since the Wagner Act was passed in 1935 and, without question, was meant to include two statements of policy. One was to eliminate the causes of certain obstructions to the free flow of commerce and the other was to mitigate and eliminate these obstructions when they have occurred. Congress, then, incorporated two *ways of accomplishing* the desired result. One was the encouragement of collective bargaining. The other was the protection of the exercise by workers of full freedom of association, self-organization and designation of representatives. Both were equally important in the eyes of the Congress, and neither was subordinated to the other by the language used.

From the outset, the Supreme Court recognized employee protection as of major importance. Chief Justice Hughes, in *N.L.R.B. v Jones & Laughlin Steel Corp.*, 301 US 1, 1 LRRM 703, the landmark decision which upheld the constitutionality of the Wagner Act, said,

> "Thus, in its present application, the statute goes no further than *to safeguard the right of employees* to self-organization and to select representatives of their own choosing for collective bargaining or other mutual protection without restraint or coercion by their employer. That is a fundamental right." (Emphasis supplied)

The lack of balance in the Wagner Act, limited as it was to employer misconduct, together with the Board's early emphasis on encouragement of collective bargaining at the expense of employee freedom of association, led to the Labor Management Relations Act of 1947, the Taft-Hartley Act. There, after adverting to the failure of employers, employees and labor organizations to recognize one another's legitimate rights in their relations with each other and with the public, Congress left its original Wagner Act statement of Findings and Policy intact, but added a new Declaration of Policy (Section 1) as the reason for enacting Taft-Hartley:

> "It is the purpose and policy of this Act, in order to promote the full flow of commerce, to prescribe the legitimate rights of both employees and employers in their relations affecting commerce, to provide orderly and peaceful procedures for preventing the interference by either with the legitimate rights of the other, to protect the rights of individual employees in their relations with labor organizations whose activities affect commerce, to define and proscribe practices on the part of labor and management which affect commerce and are inimical to the general welfare, and to protect the rights of the public in connection with labor disputes affecting commerce."

The dual policies of the Wagner Act were left unchanged, but now five new ways of implementing the policies were added. The first three emphasized the role of the Act in protecting the rights of employees. The fourth demonstrated the intent of Congress to place limitations on some practices of unions and of employers, and the fifth emphasized protection of the public. Also, Section 7 was amended to safeguard specifically the right of employees to refrain from union activities. Thus, although encouragement of collective bargaining remained as a means of carrying out the policy of the Act, the new ways added by Taft-Hartley placed far greater emphasis on protection of full freedom of association to employees and of the public in general.

The third major change in labor legislation, the Landrum-Griffin Act of 1959, again underscored the interest of Congress in protection of employee rights. In Section 2, after finding that it continued to be the responsibility of the Federal Government "to protect employees' rights to organize, choose their own representatives, bargain collectively, and otherwise engage in concerted activities for their mutual aid or protection," Congress said,

> "The Congress, therefore, further finds and declares that the enactment of this Act is necessary to eliminate or prevent improper practices on the part of labor organizations, employers, labor relations consultants, and their officers and representatives which distort and defeat the policies of the Labor Management Relations Act, 1947 . . ."

Thus, the policies of the 1947 Act were emphasized, greater stress was again laid upon protection of employee rights, and new ways of preventing obstructions to the flow of commerce were added.

It is apparent after reviewing the development of Congressional policy that it is inaccurate to state the policy of the present law in terms of the encouragement of collective bargaining. Even in the 1935 Act, it was a way of accomplishing the Congressional policy rather than the policy itself. And not once has Congress since found it necessary to enlarge upon the concept of encouragement of collective bargaining. But, on two different occasions and in several different ways, it has been impelled to strengthen employee right to freedom of choice and to protect employers and the public. It would be more appropriate, if simplification is required, to highlight another statement of Member Brown:

> "Basic to the entire statute and pervading all its provisions is the right of employees freely to select a bargaining representative."

Yet, though recognizing the concern of the Act over the rights of employees, the decisions of the Kennedy Board continue to subordinate those rights to the growth of unionism. Neither in the original Wagner Act nor in any of its amendments did Congress express any concern over the protection of labor organizations as such. Always, its interest has been in the protection of the individual. Protection of unions is a Board-imposed policy, based, unquestionably, on the sincere but mistaken belief that "What is good for the union is good for the individual."

If the Act is interpreted literally, the new Board's misconception of the Congressional intent would be of less significance, for Congress has not stated a broad policy and left its implementation to the NLRB. Instead, it has set forth specific rights of employees. These are contained in Section 7 of the Act. Proscriptions on the conduct of both employers and unions follow in Section 8. The restrictions on interference, restraint and coercion, found in Section 8(a)(1) and 8(b)(1)(A), specifically refer to the exercise of the rights guaranteed in Section 7. Therefore, in interpreting the Act, Section 7 and the rights guaranteed therein, including the "right to refrain" from concerted activities, provide ample direction where the language of Section 8 is not clear.

As we have already seen, the Kennedy appointees view their function as one of policy-making based on the broad declarations of purpose in the 1935 Act. Their apparent claim of wide discretion within these boundaries requires an accurate concept of Congressional policy. Unfortunately, as will be shown by the discussion of their decisions, the essential understanding is missing. They misconstrue the 1935 Act and ignore the declarations quoted above from the 1947 and 1959 amendments. These demonstrate that Congress has subordinated the encouragement of collective bargaining to the protection of the exercise by workers of their full freedom of association, self-organization and designation of representatives.

III

CHANGE-REASONED OR
RATIONALIZED?

The wisdom of the old maxim, "All things change except
the love of change," is demonstrated as clearly in the field
of labor-management relations as in other areas of human
endeavor. In a single generation, union power has grown
from a weak, struggling infant (more of an irritant to management than a serious threat) into a lusty, over-powering
giant, fully capable of bringing our economy to a standstill.
During the same period, the political impact of unions has
swollen from an isolated, local phenomenon to the most
powerful organized influence brought to bear on our legislators, with an effect, frequently undeserved, approaching
the hypnotic.

Union growth, however, has been accompanied by the
public realization that the union label neither automatically
guarantees a selfless interest in the working man nor an
impeccable motive directed toward the public good. The
revelations of the McClellan Committee, exposing corruption
and dishonesty in important segments of the labor movement,
fully demonstrated that labor organizations and labor leaders
are no better and no worse than the rest of our society. The
same forum conclusively established, however, that those

same unions and union officials possess an awesome amount of poorly restrained power.

In the context of such swift changes in the labor movement, it is unreasonable to expect theories of rights protected by the National Labor Relations Act and its amendments to remain static. Some of these concepts have been altered by legislative action. The original Act protected employees in the right to self-organization, to form, join or assist labor organizations, to bargain collectively through freely chosen representatives and to engage in other concerted activities (Section 7). In 1947, Taft-Hartley added a guarantee of the right to refrain from any of the foregoing activities. The unfair labor practices listed in Section 8 of the Wagner Act established, in broad terms, standards for the protection of employee rights from employers only. Taft-Hartley added similar restrictions on union activities and incorporated new protections for employers and the public from union conduct. The 1959 Landrum-Griffin Act extended the limitations on union conduct. The procedures found in Section 9, under which employees may freely express through secret ballot elections their views on a bargaining representative, have steadily been perfected through legislative action. Delegation of authority over representation cases to the Regional Directors, made possible by Landrum-Griffin, is an example.

Substantive rights adapted to changing conditions by the Congress and procedural modification incorporated by administrative and legislative action show the normal evolution expected in any dynamic field. Congressional changes have been thoroughly considered. The rights involved and the political pressures extant assure that labor matters will not be taken lightly by elected officials. The NLRB, however, with the element of responsibility to the electorate missing, has been much less concerned about demonstrating a solid basis for the changes adopted.

Thus, at one end of the scale, we find the new Board altering well-established policies without controversy. In

Leonard Wholesale Meats, Inc., 136 NLRB No. 103, 49 LRRM 1901, the Board abandoned its long-settled rule that an election petition filed more than 150 days prior to termination of an existing contract is premature. In the *Leonard* case, the 150-day period was reduced to 90 days because, as a result of delegation of representation case authority to Regional Directors, the length of time necessary to process a representation petition diminished considerably. The Board felt that reduction of the open period for filing avoided disturbing existing bargaining relationships through a Board election conducted well in advance of the terminal date for an existing contract. In the same case, however, the Board left intact an insulated period of 60 days immediately prior to the expiration of the contract during which election petitions may *not* be filed. The period had been adopted to eliminate rivalry and uncertainty between competing unions during bargaining. The change in policy was well grounded, was not in conflict with the literal language of the Act, and the new rule is as easily followed as the old.

At the opposite end of the scale are the changes made without compelling reason, which seem little more than "change for the sake of change." *A. P. W. Products, Inc.,* 137 NLRB No. 7, 50 LRRM 1042, is an example. There the Kennedy Board reversed the policy of tolling back pay during the period between date of issuance of an intermediate report (the recommended decision of the Trial Examiner who presides over the hearing in an unfair labor practice matter) and the decision of the Board itself in those cases where the Examiner found no violation of the Act but was reversed by the Board. The prior rule was established in 1936 and is reported in a case appearing in the first volume of NLRB reports. *E. R. Haffelfinger Co., Inc.,* 1 NLRB No. 760, 1 LRRM 47. The new Board rationalized that the former rule benefitted the wrongdoer at the expense of the wronged. The Board saw no other legal proceeding as giving a similar benefit to the offending party and argued that, in private suits, damages are not stayed pending appeal. The majority said:

> "In sum, we are convinced, on the basis of our examination of the equities of the situation, an analogy to court procedures, and our experience, that the Board's practice of tolling monetary awards from the date of an intermediate report recommending dismissal of 8(a)(3) allegations to the date of a Board order finding such violation does not effectuate the policies of the Act and should be abandoned."

Dissenters Rodgers and Leedom emphasized that the former practice stemmed from the desirability of striking an equitable balance between a party's reliance on the Trial Examiner and the principle of granting appropriate remedial relief. As they pointed out, the old rule had been followed by the Circuit Courts without critical comment; the Supreme Court had approved the case which initiated the practice, and there had been no criticism of the doctrine by management, unions or Congress. The dissenters did not find the analogy to private litigation persuasive, as a Board proceeding is not a suit at common law nor in the nature of such a suit and the theory had been specifically rejected by the Courts. Finally, they felt the changed rule would weaken the important role of the Trial Examiner in the adjudicative process and penalize a party for reliance on the official recommendations of the public officer charged with making such determination.

Neither the "equities of the situation," which have caused no outcry from any source in 27 years, nor an analogy to court procedure specifically rejected by the courts, form compelling arguments for reversing a long-established rule. Nor does the third factor—the majority's "experience"—carry any greater weight, particularly where no explanation of that background is advanced and the "experience" of the new majority scarcely outweighs that of the other authorities who have spoken on the issue in the last 27 years.

Experience is a valid reason for a revised policy but is not persuasive unless accompanied by an explanation of its substance. Also, it seems obvious that a new rule or policy must be an improvement, demonstrable in theory, at least. *Pacific Tile and Porcelain Co.*, 137 NLRB No. 169, 50 LRRM 1394, illustrates both points. In determining voter eligibility in a representation election, previous Boards followed the rule that discharge of an employee prior to the election would be presumed to have been for cause, making the employee ineligible to vote, unless a charge alleging the discharge to be discriminatory within the meaning of Section 8(a)(3) had been filed with NLRB. The precedent, known as the *Dura Steel* rule, was followed for more than 20 years. See *Dura Steel Products*, 111 NLRB 590, 35 LRRM 1522, and cases cited in the Sixth Annual Report of the NLRB (1941), pages 57-60.

The Kennedy majority decided in *Pacific Tile* that the presumption would not apply where grievances were pending because of discharges. Instead, the Board would wait until the grievances were resolved to rule on the voting eligibility of such employees. Although the new Board claimed problems in its application of the rule, no examples were given. The dissenters pointed out that the new approach was both uncertain and unworkable, and had been repeatedly rejected by previous Boards. In their view, it was ill-defined and could only tend to prolong and confuse the resolution of questions concerning representation. Also, it seems apparent that the *Dura Steel* rule, as applied to discharged strikers, was easy to follow and provided a Board-controlled means of resolving their status as voters. Thus, even in theory, the new rule was not an improvement.

The majority also held in the *Pacific Tile* case that it would facilitate the investigation of challenges to the ballots of economic strikers if it were presumed their status as such continues unless the party challenging their votes could affirmatively show that the challenged voters had abandoned interest in their struck jobs. Acceptance of other employment without informing the new employer that only temporary employment is sought will no longer, of itself, be sufficient evidence of abandonment of a struck job to render the economic striker ineligible to vote.

The new Board relied on the difficulty it had experienced in determining the objective intent of the economic strikers but gave no details. While there may be merit in this comment, such difficulties seem slight in comparison with that of the party challenging a voter under the new rule. To demonstrate affirmatively that the striker has abandoned interest in his struck job, when evidence showing that he has taken a new job without informing the new employer that only temporary employment is sought is insufficient, will require a most resourceful lawyer. The practical effect seems obvious. Choice of status will be completely within the power of the economic striker and, obviously, if he takes the trouble to vote, he will be eligible. Such a result can seriously impair the rights of employees who truly constitute the bargaining unit.

The foregoing examples may seem rather technical. Unfortunately, we are dealing with a highly technical law. But the significance of the cases is that, in neither *A. P. W. Products* nor *Pacific Tile*, was any compelling reason for change shown. Nor was any concern shown for the problems of the parties who must rely on Board decisions and attempt to pattern their conduct within the framework of the established law. Instead, the Board seemed completely absorbed in its somewhat theoretical view of the impact of the statute. The result is rationalized rather than reasoned change.

The examples used dealt with procedural matters. As our analysis of the new Board's decisions develops, a similar approach to substantive problems is apparent. Changing conditions and necessary shifts of interpretation serve to keep this complicated area of the law sufficiently confused without adding modifications which smack more of intellectual exercises than the realities of labor-management relations.

IV

ARRIVAL OF THE NEW
FRONTIER-AMERICAN CYANAMID

The first discernible impact of the New Frontier on Board decisions appeared on May 31, 1961, just seven weeks after Member Brown was confirmed by the Senate. The first glimpse provided a somewhat misleading view, but, looking back, the portent of the future was plainly indicated.

Vehicle for the arrival was *American Cyanamid Co.,* 131 NLRB No. 125, 48 LRRM 1152, a representation proceeding involving the question of the right of maintenance employees to a separate bargaining unit. Pensacola Building and Construction Trades Council had, some time in 1960, petitioned NLRB to be certified as bargaining agent for a unit of maintenance employees at American Cyanamid's Santa Rosa plant near Milton, Florida. The Textile Workers' Union had also filed, seeking a broader unit of both production and maintenance employees, the unit favored by the employer. Two other unions, the Chemical Workers and District 50 of the United Mine Workers, were likewise interested in the larger group. There was no bargaining history at the plant.

When the issue came before the previous Board, Members Rodgers, Jenkins and Kimball held that the unit of maintenance employees was not appropriate, even though it previously had been Board policy to permit separate representation of maintenance employees where there was no bargaining history on a broader scale. Their rationale consisted of little more than a statement that

> ". . . where a question concerning representation has been raised by a labor organization seeking to represent all the production and maintenance employees involved, no sound basis exists for finding that a narrower unit limited to maintenance employees may be appropriate."

The Council's petition, therefore, was dismissed and an election directed in the over-all unit. Chairman Leedom dissented, contending that the majority was changing Board policy of long standing without indicating the need for a change and declaring his unwillingness to let the fact that one union seeks a more comprehensive unit obliterate an otherwise appropriate unit.

Member Fanning also dissented, using language which, in the light of future events, is of particular interest. He said:

> "It is my opinion that the primary advantages in the performance of governmental functions by administrative agencies are flexibility and the capacity of expert specialists to meet new problems in specialized areas with new solutions. However, I am also firmly convinced that an agency such as the National Labor Relations Board has the responsibility of establishing guide posts, which are as clear and understandable as the circumstances and the Board's organic Act permit.
>
> "Once such guides have been established they should not be obliterated without good, sufficient, and carefully weighed reasons . . . Employers and labor organizations alike should be able to follow the Board's guide posts with some degree of assurance that they are on the right road. It should not be a game of chance.****"

The decision issued on February 2, 1961. *American Cyanamid Co.*, 130 NLRB No. 1, 47 LRRM 1231. A few days later, the Council filed a Motion for Reconsideration which was granted March 2, 1961, before either McCulloch or

Brown took office. Oral argument was held May 11, 1961, after the Kennedy appointees had become members.

In the new decision, Chairman McCulloch and Member Brown joined Leedom in his view that the original decision reversed a long-standing policy without rationale and sufficient support in the record. They found the record did not establish an operation so integrated that maintenance had lost its identity as a function separate from production and, as a readily identifiable group (whose similarity of function and skills created a community of interest), a separate election in the maintenance department was warranted.

Thus, the first impact of the Kennedy Board apparently was to re-establish a long-standing precedent which the Eisenhower Board had, for none-too-persuasive reasons, overruled. The result seemed encouraging to those who must decipher Board rules and conduct themselves in conformity to their changing patterns. But a decidedly different picture was revealed on closer inspection.

In the most significant language in the case, the majority said:

> "We specifically do not conclude that an absence of a more comprehensive bargaining history would necessarily establish the appropriateness of a maintenance unit. The Board must hold fast to the objectives of the statute, using an empirical approach to adjust its decisions to the evolving realities of industrial progress and the reflection of that change in organizations of employees. To be effective for that purpose, each unit determination must have a direct relevancy to the circumstances within which collective bargaining is to take place. While many factors may be common to most situations, in an evolving industrial complex the effect of any one factor, and therefore the weight to be given it in making the unit determination, will vary from industry to industry and from plant to plant. We are therefore convinced that collective-bargaining units must be based upon all the relevant evidence in each individual case. Thus we shall continue to examine on a case-by-case basis

the appropriateness of separate maintenance department units, fully cognizant that homogeneity, cohesiveness, and other factors of separate identity are being affected by automation and technological changes and other forms of industrial advancement."

The quoted language was a forthright exposition of the new Board's case-by-case approach. Although easily misread to apply only to the bargaining unit issue involved, the Board's declaration of the necessity of using an empirical approach (defined by one authority as "based entirely on practical experience, without regard to science or theory") was stated in broad terms. Subsequent developments unmistakably show such an intent.

The decision is also misleading in that it does not reflect the "New v. Old" Board split found in most of the cases which will be discussed later. Member Fanning concurred in the results for the reasons stated in his earlier dissent and, apparently, therefore did not adopt the language quoted above. Member Rodgers dissented with the cryptic comment that he agreed with the majority philosophy and procedure but that it failed to apply its own formula to the facts of the case.

The fact that Fanning concurred, rather than joining in the quotation, may have illustrated some reluctance on his part to adopt the case-by-case concept of the decision-making function. If so, his later opinions indicate that any reservations have disappeared.

The real importance of *American Cyanamid* is that it demonstrates that the Kennedy Board, from its very inception, emphasized its determination to make its own policy. No great concern was expressed about the Eisenhower Board's over-ruling a long-standing precedent. Instead, the new appointees, in essence, declared they would look at the objectives of the statute and on the basis of their own experience adjust the Board's decisions to their view of present day labor-management relations. Any doubt of the validity of this conclusion must necessarily be dispelled when one turns to the new Board's decisions.

It would be impossible in a volume of this size to analyze all of the cases decided by the new Board. Instead, our discussion will center on decisions reflecting a split in the members' views of the case, expressed ordinarily in a dissent but, from time to time, by footnoted disagreement. The divided opinions highlight the new Board's approach, include changes in interpretation of the Act, and provide the best guidelines for future conduct.

V

FREE SPEECH

No area of Board law provides a better illustration of the impact of the New Frontier than that dealing with employer freedom of speech—the right of an employer to communicate his views on unions to his employees. Here, as in nearly all areas of Board responsibility, the stamp of the New Frontier is clearly seen. Despite the fundamental nature of the right to free speech, its Constitutional basis, and repeated declarations of Congressional intent to protect employer expressions of opinion, the Kennedy Board has adopted its own notion of what the law should be.

The new approach seems far removed from the principles of free speech generally accepted by the Courts and the public. As Justice Douglas said in "We The Judges":

> "Freedom of speech in America is not reserved for a select few. It extends to labor as well as capital, to farmers as well as merchants, to socialists and communists as well as to Republicans and Democrats, to Catholics as well as to Protestants."

But employers may justifiably contend today that current Board decisions place them among the select few to whom free speech is *not* granted.

Concern about safeguarding employer free speech was expressed in Congress prior to enactment of the Wagner Act in 1935, but an amendment guaranteeing that right was rejected as having no proper place in the statute. The first Board quickly aggravated the problem by taking the position that an employer must remain strictly neutral with respect to his employees' choice of a labor organization. The Board theorized that an employer's superior economic position carried with it an inherent fear of economic reprisal and his slightest suggestion was thus of great weight.

The opposite approach, that an employer might enjoy a guarantee of free speech in the literal sense used in the Constitution, received no support in the Board and little from the courts. But many divergent views between these two extremes developed as courts sought to balance employer free speech against employee freedom from interfernce with union activities. The Supreme Court in *N.L.R.B. v. Virginia Electric & Power Co.*, 314 U.S. 469 (1941), 9 LRRM 405 finally clarified the issue to some extent when it held that an employer is constitutionally protected in expressing his views on labor problems as long as the statements do not amount to "coercion."

The Board reacted by evolving the "compulsory audience" doctrine which held that a speech, though constitutionally protected itself, was unlawful if given to employees during working hours. In support, it was argued that the employees' freedom to determine whether to receive information concerning self-organization was violated when they were compelled to assemble and listen to the speech. *Clark Bros. Co., Inc.*, 70 NLRB 802 (1946), 18 LRRM 1360.

The hostility of Congress was aroused by such obvious and persistent attempts to limit the right of employers to express their views. An overwhelming majority seemed convinced that the Board, while publicly disclaiming any intent to limit free speech, effectively suppressed the right through its decisions. As a result, Section 8(c) was added to the Taft-Hartley Act. It provides:

"The expressing of any views, argument or opinion, or the dissemination thereof, whether in written, printed, graphic, or visual form, shall not constitute or be evidence of an unfair labor practice under any of the provisions of this Act, if such expression contains no threat of reprisal or force or promise of benefit."

The Board was not to be frustrated so easily in its endeavors to deny employers the right to express their views on unions to their employees. The will of Congress was accepted to the limited extent of abandoning the compulsory audience doctrine but other avenues leading to further restrictions on employer expression were immediately developed. In *General Shoe Corp.*, 77 NLRB 124, 21 LRRM 1337, Section 8(c) was held to apply only to unfair labor practice cases. Also, a new concept was evolved which held an employer could not speak against the union on company time and property on the eve of an election without affording a substantially similar opportunity to the union, the "equal opportunity" doctrine. *Bonwit Teller, Inc.*, 96 NLRB 608, 28 LRRM 1547.

Though the Appellate Courts refused to accept the latter theory, the Board persisted in its application until the first Eisenhower appointees issued new rules on employer speech in both representation and unfair labor practice cases. In *Livingston Shirt Corp.*, 107 NLRB 400, 33 LRRM 1156, they held an employer could call his employees together during working hours and express his views on a union, without affording the union an equal opportunity to reply, as long as the employees were permitted to solicit for the union on company premises when they were not working. And, in *Peerless Plywood Co.*, 107 NLRB 427, 33 LRRM 1151, they adopted a rule in election cases which prohibited both unions and employers from making election speeches to massed assemblies of employees on company time within 24 hours before the scheduled hour of the election.

Another method utilized by the Board immediately after Section 8(c) was passed, to weaken the impact of the amendment, was set forth in *Alliance Rubber Co.*, 76 NLRB 514, 21 LRRM 1221. Although accepting the principle that speech, otherwise privileged, did not become coercive because the employer had committed other unfair labor practices, the Board found unlawful words and conduct ". . . so intertwined as to be considered a single coercive act." This technique precluded real substance being given to the "threat of reprisal . . . or promise of benefit" language in Section 8(c) until the Eisenhower Board began to distinguish between illegal "threats" or "promises" and privileged "predictions," "prophecies" or "expressions of legal position."

Current decisions make it abundantly clear that the Kennedy Board has reverted to the policies of the Wagner Act Boards with little concern shown for Section 8(c). It seems determined to nullify that section of the law and to deprive employers of their constitutional and statutory rights to state their views on union matters vitally affecting their interests and the welfare of their employees.

On August 2, 1959, the International Union of Electrical Workers filed a petition to represent a unit of production and maintenance employees at the Dallas plant of Dal-Tex Optical Company, Inc. An election was held October 30, 1959, and the union lost by a vote of 96 to 88. The union filed objections and, later, unfair labor practice charges. More than a year afterward, on March 14, 1961, the objections were sustained, unfair labor practices consisting of an attempt to prevent unionization by threats and promises of benefits were found, and a second election was directed. This election was held on September 22, 1961, and again the union lost, 101 to 96, with 10 ballots challenged. In ruling on objections which the union again filed, the Kennedy Board gave the clearest insight yet provided to its policies on free speech.

Dal-Tex Optical Co., Inc., 137 NLRB No. 189, 50 LRRM 1489.

The objections ruled upon by the Board involved three speeches given by the employer during the week immediately preceding the election. Unquestionably, they were vigorous and tough, presenting the employer's views in unmistakable terms and in language the employees could understand. The first, quoted in part in the Board decision, explained the history of the union's organizing effort and the employer's firm belief that the Board was in error in setting aside the first election. The employer stated positively that the matter was going to the courts, predicted it would be another "couple of years" before the question was settled, and explained he was giving the employees the information so that they would understand the "wild promises by this Union of what is going to happen here if the Union wins don't mean a thing." He also emphasized, "When the courts decide the matter, I will abide by the decision of the courts." Finally, after detailing some of the benefits the employees were receiving and explaining his current practice of reflecting efficiency gains in increased wages, he said,

> "Do you want to gamble all of these things? If I am required by the Court to bargain with this Union, whenever that may be, I will bargain in good faith, but I will have to bargain on a cold-blooded business basis. You may come out with a lot less than you have now. Why gamble because agitators make wild promises to you? If I am required to bargain and I cannot agree there is no power on earth that can make me sign a contract with this Union, so what will probably happen is the Union will call a strike. I will go right along running this business and replace the strikers... I am not afraid of a strike. It won't hurt the company. I will replace the strikers. They will lose all of their benefits. Strikers will draw no wages, no unemployment compensation and be out of a job. The Union won't pay you wages.

The Union has nothing to lose. You do all of the losing. No employee is so important that he or she cannot be replaced."

The second speech, also quoted at some length, talked again about merit wage increases and the company's wage position as the highest in the industry. After promising to maintain the merit system even though the union came in, the employer said,

"It is the system I have operated on from the beginning. I do not have to, nor will I, change it."

No reference is made in the decision to the third speech given the day before the election.

The case was decided by a panel consisting of McCulloch, Leedom and Fanning. McCulloch and Fanning characterized the speeches as couched in language calculated to convey to the employees the danger and futility of their designating the Union. The references to "gamble all of these things," bargaining on a "cold-blooded business basis," and "may come out with a lot less than you have now," were said to emphasize the employer's control over wages and were a "clear-cut readily understandable threat, that the employer would bargain 'from scratch' . . . and the employees would suffer economic loss and reprisal if they selected the Union." The references to the probability of a strike and the threat to replace strikers were found to have been calculated to create fear of loss of employment if the union won, particularly because of the background of unfair labor practices. In addition, the majority found the employer conveyed the idea he would not sign a contract even if required to engage in bargaining which, though innocuous on the surface, was coupled with the prediction of a strike, the threat to bargain "from scratch," and the graphic description of the results of replacement during a strike. The entire import, in their view, was a clear message that the employer would not sign a contract, even if required to negotiate.

[33]

No reference was made to the employer's promise to abide by the decisions of the courts and to bargain in good faith. Nor was it acknowledged that the threat not to sign a contract was conditioned on inability to agree with the Union on contract terms.

The majority members then made three important rulings. First, after adverting to cases which held statements similar to those made by Dal-Tex to be mere expressions of "legal position," they found it "well settled" that the same type of statement was not within the free speech protection of Section 8(c) and was thus unlawful interference, restraint and coercion within the meaning of Section 8(a)(1). Finding no logic or reason in this distinction, they ruled that conduct which violates Section 8(a)(1) is *automatically* conduct which interferes with an election because the "laboratory conditions" for an election are considerably more restrictive than the test for conduct amounting to interference, restraint and coercion. *National Furniture Mfg. Co., Inc.*, 106 NLRB 1300, 33 LRRM 1004, and similar cases were over-ruled.

Such a rule confuses the issue. Section 8(a)(1) bans interference, restraint and coercion with the employees' right to organize and bargain collectively, and violations of the section are found if that right has been impaired. But validity of pre-election conduct in a representation proceeding should be determined by whether or not it interferes with the employees' ability to exercise a free choice in the election. In some instances, free choice may be exercised despite interference. For example, conduct violative of 8(a)(1), occurring long before the date of balloting in an election, might well have no impact whatsoever on the ability of the employees to exercise their independent judgment in a secret ballot election.

Second, untroubled by the "per se" character of a rule that conduct violative of Section 8(a)(1) necessarily is sufficiently objectionable to require setting aside an election, the Kennedy appointees announced the "case-by-case" policy, which they propose to follow in similar matters in the future. The exact language is worth repeating because it demonstrates the lack of guidelines upon which employers and their representatives must predicate their future conduct in this highly important area:

> "To adhere to those (the "legal positions") decisions would be to sanction implied threats couched in the guise of statements of legal position. Such an approach is too mechanical, fails to consider all the surrounding circumstances, and is inconsistent with the duty of this Board to enforce and advance the statutory policy of encouraging the practice and procedure of collective bargaining by protecting the full freedom of employees to select representatives of their own choosing. Rather, we shall look to the economic realities of the employer-employee relationship and shall set aside an election where we find that the employer's conduct has resulted in substantial interference with the election, regardless of the form in which the statement was made."

Finally, the majority returned to the 1948 *General Shoe* rule that Section 8(c) is limited to unfair labor practice proceedings, specifically over-ruling those cases which suggested that it was also applicable to pre-election statements. The First Amendment was dismissed with one sentence in a footnote which read, "The strictures of the First Amendment, to be sure, must be considered in all cases." No explanation was offered as to the substance of these strictures, or the reason for their inapplicability to *Dal-Tex*.

In another footnote, the majority characterized the employer's statements as going far beyond a bare announcement that it would test the legality of the Board's action in setting aside the previous election. The majority then carefully pointed out that it was unnecessary to decide whether such an announcement, standing alone, would exceed the permissible bounds of electioneering. Thus, an election could be declared invalid because the employer did no more than announce he would appeal the results of an *earlier* vote.

Dal-Tex might have been predicted from the Kennedy Board's result, if not its language, in *Somismo, Inc.,* 133 NLRB No. 131, 49 LRRM 1030. The Teamsters, after losing an election 28 to 26 at Somismo's Chicago plant, objected because of a speech which the employer made the day before the election. He said, in part:

> ". . . Now what I mean to bring out to you is simply this: that if by chance the Union were to be voted into this shop, there is no doubt in my mind, because of the terrific demands that they are showing, there is no doubt in my mind that there will be a strike. Somismo will not be able to cope with that problem; there will be a strike; whether we go out of business or not I am not saying right now. Use your own judgment. Most of you, as I have said, have been here a long time, and you know what we can withstand.
> ". . . This (sic) tremendous demands that the Union has shown is going to fight to get for you if you sign a contract with Somismo are so out of proportion, so ridiculous that I hope some of you men who are entertaining such thoughts can realize how utterly impossible it is. As it is now, we've laid off a number of men already and you all know it . . .
> ". . . Once more, I want to say that the demands of the Union cannot and will not be met. . . ."

McCulloch, Leedom and Brown disagreed with the Regional Director, who thought the speech a mere prediction of the dire consequences which would result from the union's demands, and held that the remarks conveyed to the employees the threat it would go out of business if it had to deal with the union, thereby interfering with the employees' freedom of choice. No explanation or rationale was given by the majority, but the result fits the test used in the *Dal-Tex* case.

Dal-Tex, viewed as a whole, approaches a test for employer speech turning on whether the statements are favorable to unionism. Each assertion made by the employer (with the possible exception of his single comment that he would not change his merit system) represented a position clearly permissible to an employer dealing with a union. Not only was *Dal-Tex* entitled to test the validity of the first election by court proceedings, an employer has no other method of doing so. Moreover, *Dal-Tex* promised, it would abide by the court decision if the test was lost. The statute provides that an employer need only bargain in good faith—not that he must agree to any specific contractual terms—and the statute contains no requirement that bargaining start from existing terms and conditions of employment. Dal-Tex was under no compulsion to sign a contract unless agreement was reached with the union and, if it intended to bargain hard (as it was fully entitled to do), a strike was probable, if not inevitable. Finally, if a strike occurred, Dal-Tex was completely within its rights to continue operating and replace the strikers.

The majority view, in essence, comes very close to a rule that employees should not be informed of the disadvantages of union organization. Such a position is a travesty on the purposes of the Act. Are employees to be given only the union's glowing promises on which to make their decisions? It is fallacious to argue that employees are protected in their free choice of a bargaining representative if they do not have *all* available facts as to the results which will flow from their selection. There are some harsh realities in the world of collective bargaining and, while persuasion plays an important role, it is of little value unless backed by power and willingness to exert economic force. Employees are entitled to know the consequences of strike action and its impact on them personally. If they are to have the free and untrammeled right to choose a bargaining agent or *to refrain from doing so* (as the Act also provides), it seems implicit that they must hear the cons as well as the pros. The union has ample incentive to present the benefits of unionism. Only the employer has sufficient interest to explain the other side.

Another case which throws light on the Kennedy Board's approach to free speech is that of *Trane Co.*, 137 NLRB No. 165, 50 LRRM 1434. The International Association of Machinists lost an election among the Trane Employees by a vote of 85-79. The union objected on several grounds, including the employer's distribution on election day of paychecks to employees from which $5.00 had been deducted. Five dollar bills were enclosed in a separate envelope containing the following statement:

"THIS ENVELOPE CONTAINS $5.00 OF YOUR MONEY. This is the estimate (sic) amount the union would want you to take out of your pay check every month and hand over

TO THEM!

The money in this envelope does not include fines, assessments and other charges that you may be forced to pay to the union * * *"

McCulloch and Fanning found the distribution involved a "material misrepresentation" as to dues and important requirements which the employees were incapable of evaluating. The union's dues were actually $4.00 and not $5.00 per month, and the union argued that the company was located in a "right to work" state, so that an employee could not be forced to join the union and pay dues. Reference was made to the fact the employer had ample opportunity to raise such points earlier in the campaign and, had he done so several days before the election, the union could have correctly pointed out both the dues obligation as $4.00 and rebutted the right to work point. *Gummed Products,* 112 NLRB 1092, 36 LRRM 1156, was cited. (Brown did not rule upon this issue.)

Rodgers and Leedom dissented, finding no misrepresentation, as the $5.00 was said to be only an estimated amount,
and the statement contained no language that union membership would be compulsory. They found nothing that intelligent employees could not evaluate and pointed out that the
majority's reliance on *Gummed Products* was in error, as
that case is applicable when a material misrepresentation
has been made by a party with specialized and authoritative
knowledge of the facts.

McCulloch, Fanning and Brown also found objectionable
a letter of the employer which stated that it would continue
to review the benefit program in effect, "union or no union,"
that its wage policy was to pay equal or better than the
average, and that this policy would continue "union or no
union." The employer made other similar comments, emphasizing the benefits which the employees had received without
a union and making such statements as: "We have done
this without a union. We suggest that you can judge the
future by the past." The Kennedy majority considered these
remarks as conveying that the employer had a unilateral wage
and benefit policy, that it would be continued without inter-
vention of the union, and that the policy would not be
changed even if a union were selected. Therefore, it would
be an unnecessary expense and futile for the employees to
select a union. The majority found such an attitude inconsistent with good faith bargaining and reasonably calculated to have a coercive effect, as there is no more effective
way to dissuade employees from voting for a bargaining
representative than by telling them that their votes will avail
them nothing.

Rodgers and Leedom dissented, arguing that the statements were merely an effort to show the employer's basic
policy and to assure the employees that, regardless of the
election results, the company did not contemplate any change
in its future policy. There was neither a threat to discontinue

benefits nor a promise of increase, and there was no implication that the employer would not engage in good faith bargaining.

The Kennedy Board's approach to "material misrepresentation" is also shown in *Haynes Stellite Company, Division of Union Carbide Corp.*, 136 NLRB No. 3, 49 LRRM 1711. There Fanning and Brown found interference, misrepresentation and coercion within the meaning of Section 8(a)(1) and thus an unfair labor practice, where an employer who had engaged in an active, though lawful, anti-union campaign read at each of 33 employee meetings the following statement:

> "Customers are buying products on the basis of prices, delivery and dependability. The facts are that in some cases we are the sole source of supply at present for some of our customers. We have been told that we would not continue to be the sole source of supply if we became unionized, due to the ever present possibility of a work stoppage due to strikes or walkouts."

The majority members concluded that the employer

> ". . . had materially misrepresented the facts when it stated that 'some of [its] customers' would seek other sources of supply, whereas only *one* customer had so informed the Respondent."

They also found it significant that the employer had failed to name the customers involved or to supply other information and that the statements were made by high-ranking supervisors. Leedom, the remaining member of the panel, dissented, pointing out that the statement was not made in the context of other interference and that it merely informed employees of what others meant to do if a union was selected.

An earlier case, *R. D. Cole Mfg. Co.*, 133 NLRB No. 130, 49 LRRM 1033, appears to go even further and places a duty upon the employer of "supporting" assertions made in speeches. The speech in question was made on the day before the election by the company's president. He told the employees that after the union had lost an election conducted two years previously, the employer had received more contracts for work because customers, who were unnamed, had confidence in it. Now, he said, since these customers learned that the union had started up its "agitation" again, the employer had been having difficulty obtaining contracts and his business had declined. The employees were then told that if the employer could demonstrate to his customers there were be no interference from the union or other labor trouble at the plant, he could obtain more contracts and thereby better conditions in the shop. The remainder of the speech contained statements to the effect that unionization would result in hard bargaining, strikes, and lack of steady work; that unionization, generally, meant less business for companies with operations similar to the employer's and that the employer regarded a union as a serious obstacle to the advancement and progress of the Company.

McCulloch, Fanning and Brown found that the "burden of the speech was the employer's *unsupported* assertion that the recent decline in his business was attributable to . . ." the union's organizing effort and that business would increase and employee conditions improve if the union was defeated. Under all of the circumstances (if there were circumstances other than the speech outlined above, they were not mentioned in the decision), the majority decided that the election atmosphere was such as to prevent the exercise of a free choice. Rodgers, in agreement with the Regional Director, would have dismissed the objections.

Fanning and Brown also found a Section 8(a)(1) violation in a statement by an employer that, if the plant did go union, he would probably have to shut it down in 45 days because he couldn't pay union wages. *T. E. Mercer Trucking Co.,* 134 NLRB No. 85, 49 LRRM 1300. The employer testified he had talked about exorbitant wages demanded by some unions, "up to $3.50 an hour," and that, if he had to pay such wages, the Company would be out of business. The employer was unable to identify the source of the $3.50 figure. The majority finding was based on the employer's lack of factual basis for his prediction. Leedom disagreed on the theory that the statement was privileged under Section 8(c). He pointed out that the Trial Examiner did not resolve the conflict in the testimony as to what was said and the evidence "does not preponderate to establish a violation."

In another early decision of the new Board, *Central Freight Lines, Inc.*, 133 NLRB No. 32, 48 LRRM 1669, a panel consisting of McCulloch, Rodgers and Fanning found the employer had violated Section 8(a)(1) of the Act by granting wage increases during the union campaign to influence the employees' union sentiments, soliciting withdrawals of union membership applications, and threatening broad shutdowns or sale of the business if the union came in. McCulloch and Fanning also found a violation in a letter written by the employer after he had heard that some 640 employees had signed a petition stating that they did not want the union to represent them. The employer had nothing to do with the distribution and signing of the petition or its transmittal to NLRB, but merely wrote the employees, saying the company had heard of the petition and "we certainly appreciate this show of loyalty and confidence that we have had. . . ." Rodgers found nothing unlawful in a mere announcement of the employer's appreciation.

The foregoing cases show the new Board restricting free speech by foreclosing declarations of the employer's legal position, by eliminating speculation as to the practical consequences of unionism if unfavorable to the union, and by requiring absolute accuracy in employer statements and support for all assertions made. Even expressions of employer gratitude are suspect. If these rulings do not demonstrate the desire of the new Board to repeal Section 8(c) administratively, any doubt is eliminated by the majority's clear return to the *Bonwit Teller* doctrine on employer speeches to captive audiences in *May Department Stores Co.,* 136 NLRB No. 71, 49 LRRM 1862.

Generally, an employer may prohibit outsiders from soliciting for the union on company property at all times, but employees may be so restricted only during working time. Broader restrictions have been upheld in retail stores because of their semi-public nature. The May Department Stores Company had a broad no-solicitation rule in its two stores in the Cleveland area. These rules prohibited union solicitation at all times in selling areas, a type of rule which has been held privileged in retail stores. Shortly before a representation election, the employer spoke to employee meetings on company time and property. The speeches were anti-union but contained no promise of benefits or threat of reprisals. A union request for an equal opportunity to address the employees was denied by the Company. When the union lost the election, it filed Section 8(a)(1) charges and objections to the election.

McCulloch, Fanning and Brown viewed the issue in such a case as whether the employer's conduct ". . . to any considerable degree created an imbalance in the opportunities for organizational communication," citing *Steel Workers v. N.L.R.B. (Nutone, Inc.),* 357 U.S. 357, 42 LRRM 2324. They found a "glaring imbalance" created by the employer's use of company time and property for its speeches while the union had only "catch-as-catch can" methods such as home visits, meetings on employees' time, telephone calls, letters, and various mass media of communication. Unfair labor practices were found and the election set aside.

Rodgers dissented, declaring the majority decision contrary to the First Amendment and to Section 8(c) (which the majority did not even mention). He believed the majority failed to make any findings, as required by *Nutone,* to show an "imbalance" and predicated their result solely on the denial to the union of a channel of communication used by the employer. Leedom also dissented, relying on *Nutone,* because a true diminution in the ability of the union to carry its message was not established merely by showing that, as a general principle, department store employees can be more easily reached through the avenues of communication open to their employer than through avenues open to the union.

The Supreme Court, in the *Nutone, Inc.,* case, specifically held that an employer who engages in anti-union solicitation is *not* automatically barred from enforcing his own no-solicitation rule. The Court reasoned that nothing in the Act gives a union the right to a medium of communication merely because used by the employer. Yet, the results of the *May Department Stores* case amounts to a rule that, in a retail store, the union does have such a right. In effect, the majority adopted a per se rule, contrary both to its announced policy and, in this instance, to the ruling of the Supreme Court in the closely related *Nutone, Inc.* case.

Another disturbing aspect of the *May Department Stores* case is that, in a speech at Michigan State University on April 19, 1962, McCulloch characterized the decision as reflecting a recommendation of the Pucinski Subcommittee of the House Committee on Education and Labor made the previous year. The Subcommittee report included a very strong statement urging the Board to re-examine the *Livingston Shirt* doctrine and provide "equal opportunity in presentation of issues." The Subcommittee specifically would require an employer who spoke to his employees on company time to provide the union with equal time. It was precisely such extreme restrictions on free speech which led Congress, in 1947, to add Section 8(c). When the 1959 amendments were adopted, no attempt was made through revisions of

Section 8(c) or in any other way to place greater restraint on employer expression than that imposed by the Eisenhower Board. As the minority members of the Subcommittee vigorously disagreed with the majority view, the "recommendation" was that of only four members out of the entire Congress. To consider such a report as supplying either Congressional approval or impetus for a changed interpretation of the free speech rules is to make a mockery of the legislative process. Yet, Chairman McCulloch not only fails to disagree with the Subcommittee report but one gains the impression that he looks upon the *May* case as but the first step in carrying out the entire recommendation. Certainly, the language used in *May* does not preclude application of the principle beyond the retail field.

Another innovation adopted by the Kennedy Board in the free speech area, bound to be labelled political, is a policy that "racial appeals" will provide grounds for setting aside representation elections. The Act contains no reference to race or color, the rights protected being limited to concerted activity for the purpose of dealing collectively. Previous Boards, while careful not to condone appeals to racial prejudice, did not find them a basis for setting aside an election unless misrepresentation, fraud, violence or coercion was involved.

The new rules were set down in two cases, *Sewell Mfg. Co.*, 138 NLRB No. 12, 50 LRRM 1532, and *Allen-Morrison Sign Co., Inc.*, 138 NLRB No. 11, 50 LRRM 1535. A racial appeal was found in the *Sewell* case, and the election set aside, because the appeal was viewed as deliberately seeking to over-stress and exacerbate racial feelings by irrelevant and inflammatory language. The employer circulated a widely-publicized picture of James Carey, President of the Electrical Workers, dancing with a Negro woman and also sent letters to employees about paying assessments to a union which promoted the N.A.A.C.P. Copies of letters by union officials praising "freedom riders" and other material sought to identify the union with "race-mixing" and organizations promoting integration. The Board felt that, as a result of the propaganda, the "uninhibited desires" of the employees could not be determined.

The election was upheld in *Allen-Morrison,* however, as the employer's racial appeal was moderate in tone and contained in a long letter discussing matters "indisputably germane to the election." The Board made it clear in the two cases that the burden will be on the party making use of a racial appeal to establish that it is truthful and germane. Any doubt as to whether the conduct is within permissible limits will be resolved against the party using it.

Rodgers did not join in the *Sewell* case but did not dissent. Brown dissented in *Allen-Morrison* and would have set aside the election there, also.

The new Board's incorporation of the race issue, desirable as it may seem to many, is a clear example of law-making by presidential appointees. Congress has had ample opportunity to include language foreclosing racial discrimination in the Act. Such an amendment was offered and rejected during the debate on the Landrum-Griffin Bill. But the new Board, without reference to this legislative background, in effect has written a racial provision into the statute.

One final and most serious problem in connection with future speech cases arises because of the delegation of representation matters to the Regional Directors. Most free speech issues stem from employer statements prior to elections and are brought to the Board as objections to elections, though some come through the unfair labor practice channel as alleged violations of Section 8(a)(1). Under the delegation, the objections cases will be decided by Regional Directors. The Directors are now faced with the very difficult task of applying the vague standards of the *Dal-Tex* case and will be unable to turn to the pre-Kennedy Board decisions for additional guidance in this difficult area. While the rules provide the parties may request leave to appeal decisions of the Regional Directors, including objections cases, experience has demonstrated this to be an infrequently afforded privilege. The requests are given only the most cursory treatment by the Board's staff and, absent a glaring error or novel issue, leave to appeal is rarely granted. Free speech cases are primarily factual in nature, though often resting on inferences drawn from those facts, and the party attempting to reverse a Director faces a most difficult task.

Few case histories need be reviewed before one questions why the term "free speech" is used at all. If an employer cannot tell his employees what he thinks about a union and, indeed, cannot even state his legal position with respect to such an organization, it is a misnomer to suggest that he has any right of free speech whatsoever. Or, if the test of employer speech turns on whether the words used "tell employees their votes will avail them nothing," can any argument against the union be voiced? Does not every anti-union statement show the disadvantages of unionism and, consequently, the futility of securing gains through union organization? The answer seems obvious. The inescapable conclusion is that the Kennedy appointees are swiftly moving toward the position held by the first NLRB—the employer must remain a strict neutral, saying nothing to his employees. While this may seem a reasonable position to those convinced of the value of union organization in every instance, it is completely incompatible with freedom of employee choice and has been thoroughly rejected by Congress.

Fundamental to the free enterprise system is the employer's interest in making a success of his business. The employer's relationship with his employees, his ability to negotiate terms and conditions of employment compatible with his profit margins, his assurance of production uninterrupted by strikes —all are of primary importance to sound management. To restrict the employer's right to voice his views on union organization, therefore, directly weakens his capacity to protect the interests of his business and impairs the success of the enterprise, the very foundation on which the employees rely for their livelihood and without which their rights are meaningless.

CHAPTER VI

EMPLOYER RESISTANCE TO
UNION ACTIVITY

Although the free speech area has witnessed the most persistent Board efforts to restrict employer activity, resulting in the marked conflict with Congress discussed in the previous chapter, the Board has been equally partisan in condemning other types of employer interference and in finding unlawful discrimination. As a consequence, an employer must now watch his conduct as carefully as his comments. The obstacles he faces when required to deal with a union today are innumerable and their impact unpredictable.

Restrictions on employer activity are found in Section 8(a) of the Act, where the employer unfair labor practices are set out. The sections most frequently applied are 8(a)(1), which prohibits an employer from interfering with, restraining or coercing employees in the exercise of their right to organize and bargain collectively or to refrain from doing so, and 8(a)(3), which forbids an employer to discriminate in regard to hire or tenure of employment because of union activities. Board cases involving these sections highlight the enigma facing an employer when he tries to resist a union organizing drive.

During an organizing campaign conducted by the Retail Clerks at the W. T. Grant Company store in Sacramento,

California, the employer discharged an employee who was soliciting union memberships from fellow employees during working hours. The store manager called the employee into his office when he heard reports of the activity, advising her that he would not tolerate such conduct and that she would be discharged if it continued. The following day, the manager learned of two more instances occurring after his warning and, when they were admitted by the employee, she was terminated. Another employee, who was circulating an anti-union petition and was also instructed not to solicit during working hours, obeyed the manager's instructions.

Fanning and Brown held the discharge discriminatory in violation of Section 8(a)(3), as an invalid application of a no-solicitation rule. Rodgers dissented, finding the employer's conduct to be the lawful discharge of an employee for violation of a valid instruction to refrain from union solicitation during working time. In the past, an employer has been permitted to ban union solicitation on company property during working hours if the rule was uniformly applied. The majority accepted the claim of the W. T. Grant employee that she was seeking to counter the effects of an anti-union petition being circulated without hindrance of the employer. However, as pointed out by Rodgers, the record showed that, upon hearing a report that such a petition was being circulated, the manager gave an identical warning against solicitation to the employee involved and, unlike the union adherent, the latter employee observed the instruction. *W. T. Grant Co.*, 136 NLRB No. 12, 49 LRRM 1727.

Drawing a conclusion as to the law of such a case, with a view to following it as a binding precedent, is hazardous. It is a "fact" case. Its value lies in the impression given of the new majority's approach. It demonstrates that any discipline of a union adherent, particularly for engaging in union activities, must be scrutinized more carefully than ever before by the employer before he acts.

Essential to the discrimination cases is a finding of anti-union motivation on the part of the employer. Not all employer conduct is unlawful; only that which prevents employees from exercising the rights guaranteed by the statute is proscribed. Union considerations for an employer act are not always easily demonstrated and, when the Board draws inferences from questionable facts or places the burden upon the employer to prove he is not motivated by union activity, highly questionable results follow.

At Electric Steam Radiator Corporation in Paris, Kentucky, the employer did not give a Christmas bonus after a union was certified on December 17, 1959. The bonus had been paid regularly for the previous ten years. The General Counsel alleged anti-union motivation was shown by a statement of a supervisor on December 23 that the bonus would not be paid because the union had organized the plant and that this was what employees got for voting for the "damn union." The General Counsel also argued that specific anti-union motivation need not be shown, because the employer's conduct *inherently* discouraged union membership, and that the employer had the burden of proof to establish an economic justification for withholding the bonus.

The Trial Examiner disagreed, finding the supervisor's statement did not establish anti-union motivation because it did not show the bonus was withheld in retaliation for the union activity. He ruled the bonus was not paid because of: (1) advice of counsel that payment might be considered an unfair labor practice; (2) realization that unionization could result in additional labor costs, and (3) economic considerations which indicated a declining profit position.

McCulloch and Leedom reversed the Trial Examiner and found a violation. They considered the "damn union" statement as demonstrating the bonus was denied because of the vote for the union. They decided the employer had conditioned payment of the bonus on withdrawal of an unfair labor practice charge, even though there were other conditions to the offer and the union refused the complete proposal. The majority found it apparent from the foregoing that payment was not withheld because of any fear of an unfair labor practice but because the employer intended to use the bonus as an economic weapon in future bargaining. *Electric Steam Radiator Corp.*, 136 NLRB No. 85, 49 LRRM 1893. Rodgers dissented, stating merely that he would affirm the Trial Examiner.

The majority holding, in effect, rests upon no firmer foundation than an inference of union motivation from a single statement of the plant superintendent and one questionable bargaining demand. The Trial Examiner found the statement merely an explanation to inquirers that the bonus was withheld as a *consequence* of organization, not in retaliation. If the bargaining demand was an adequate basis, it seems peculiar that it was raised for the first time in the Board decision. The General Counsel made no such contention and the Trial Examiner neither included findings of fact on the point nor mentioned that the demand had been made. Characterization of the union as the "damn union" was meaningless.

The majority did not speak to the "inherent anti-union motivation" argument of the General Counsel, but the case clearly illustrates the slight evidence necessary to find an improper motive on the part of an employer and the majority's disregard for the dilemma in which the employer was placed. Payment of the bonus during negotiations without union agreement might well have been considered an attempt to undercut the union and a refusal to bargain in good faith. Yet, non-payment was discrimination. The employer demonstrated he had acted upon advice of counsel and convinced the Trial Examiner of valid economic considerations. When such proof was offset by dubious inferences, the employer was not only required to prove his innocence but to prove it beyond a reasonable doubt. Also, see *Tru-Line Metal Products Co.*, 138 NLRB No. 98, 51 LRRM 1159, where McCulloch and Brown, with Leedom dissenting, found anti-union motivation from a single statement of a supervisor.

A similar shift of burden of proof appears in *Murray Ohio Mfg. Co.*, 134 NLRB No. 19, 49 LRRM 1118. The company, a manufacturer of bicycles, window-cooling fans and other products, moved its operations from Cleveland to Lawrenceburg, Tennessee, in 1956. In both cities, the company operated on a seasonal basis, with peak production during the late spring and summer, and substantial layoffs at the end of the season. The employees in Cleveland were represented by the United Auto Workers, but the union was unsuccessful in its attempts to organize the new plant.

In 1957, about a month after the Auto Workers lost a representation election at Lawrenceburg, the employer adopted an employee-evaluation program, under which department heads rated all employees on various aspects of their work performance and assigned a numerical rating to each employee. At the beginning of the 1958 season, 100 employees were not recalled, 22 of whom filed charges. All of the 22 were known union adherents with sufficient seniority for recall. The employer justified the failure to recall on the basis of the evaluation sheets and certain "incident" reports.

McCulloch, Fanning and Brown found the employer guilty of discrimination by his failure to recall the 22 persons who filed charges. Rodgers and Leedom dissented because, though the General Counsel had adduced considerable testimony establishing the union activity of the 22 and the employer's knowledge, he failed to produce any information with respect to the 78 who did not file unfair labor practice charges. In their view, discrimination implies disparate treatment. Without any background against which treatment can be compared or contrasted, disparate treatment cannot be shown to have existed. The majority took the position that it was up to the employer to rebut the General Counsel's case. This, of course, amounts to a shift of burden, requiring the employer to prove that he is not guilty rather than our usual concept of justice, where the prosecutor must prove guilt.

The same principle is found in cases holding that employer knowledge of union activity may be inferred from the small size of the plant or bargaining unit, the working area, or the community. The Board infers knowledge from the small size of the plant, and the employer must prove he did *not* have the knowledge with which he is charged. Examples are: *Flora Construction Co.*, 132 NLRB No. 55, 48 LRRM 1417, construction project employing about 10 men; *Standard Data and Rating Service, Inc.*, 133 NLRB No. 39, 48 LRRM 1651, a 28-man composing room at a publishing plant; *Syracuse Tank & Manufacturing Co.*, 133 NLRB No. 53, 48 LRRM 1723, plant of 57 employees; *Fairbanks Knitting Mills, Inc.*, 134 NLRB No. 65, 49 LRRM 1299, plant of 40-45 employees, of whom 35 were women; *Sheidow Bronze Corp.*, 135 NLRB No. 66, 49 LRRM 1582, 7 employees; *Cowlitz Veneer Co.*, 135 NLRB No. 31, 49 LRRM 1475, 29 employees at a plant located in a community of 200-400 inhabitants; and the *Niagara Chemical Division, F.M.C. Corp.*, 137 NLRB No. 40, 50 LRRM 1176, 14 employees. Also, see *Sachs & Sons*, 135 NLRB No. 111, 49 LRRM 1681, and *Duval Engineering & Contr. Co.*, 132 NLRB No. 65, 48 LRRM 1449, where an employer's refusal to reinstate known union adherents proved to Fanning and Brown that they had been discriminatorily discharged when laid off previously along with others for economic reasons. Rodgers usually footnotes disagreement in the small plant cases, but Leedom more often goes along with the Kennedy majority.

The small plant theory, which purportedly rests on the

"case-by-case" approach, is slowly evolving into a per se rule. The only missing factor is a precise definition of "small." The most extreme example found thus far is *Texas Bolt Co.*, 135 NLRB No. 116, 49 LRRM 1662, where McCulloch and Fanning, Rodgers dissenting, decided that the employer must have known of the union activities of the employees because of a small plant, although there were 100-150 production and maintenance employees in the bargaining unit.

Board willingness to infer employer misconduct is also seen in interrogation cases where, for many years, the Board found unlawful interference in employer questioning of employees about their union activities. The courts were unwilling to follow the Board in its highly restrictive view of such conduct and, in the 1954 *Blue Flash* Express decision (*Blue Flash Express*, 109 NLRB No. 85, 34 LRRM 1384), the Eisenhower Board adopted an approach reflecting that of the courts. *Blue Flash* held that interrogation of employees as to their union activities was not in itself unlawful, if the employer showed his intent was only to determine whether the union actually represented an employee majority, the employees interrogated were assured against retaliation, and there was no background of hostility to unions.

The Kennedy Board has already indicated the *Blue Flash* case will be found easily distinguishable, if not specifically over-ruled. In *T. E. Mercer Trucking Co.*, 134 NLRB No. 85, 49 LRRM 1300, a Leedom-Fanning-Brown panel found an employer had violated Section 8(a)(1) of the Act by asking certain employees if they had seen or signed authorization cards. The interrogation occurred *after* the union began organizing but *before* it had filed a representation petition. *Blue Flash* was distinguished on the ground that the Blue Flash employees had been questioned to determine how to answer a union letter requesting recognition, while Mercer was not legally concerned with whether the union represented a majority at the time the Mercer employees were interrogated. Also, see *J. Weingarten, Inc.*, 137 NLRB No. 81, 50 LRRM 1237, and *P-M Garages, Inc.*, 139 NLRB No. 84, 51 LRRM 1449.

Formerly, *Blue Flash* was used as authority for dismissing charges of unlawful employer interference with union activities when the conduct was isolated in nature. Substantial doubt has been cast on the continuing validity of the rule by *Hilton Hotels Corp.*, 138 NLRB No. 15, 50 LRRM 1556. There, McCulloch and Brown found the employer guilty of such interference because a single supervisor, on but two occasions, conveyed a threat to two employees. The supervisor told both that a former part-time employee would not work at the hotel again and "She isn't going to come down here and organize this hotel." (Although the record is not specific, the organizing drive was apparently directed at all the employees in one of the largest hotels in Dallas, Texas.) Leedom, dissenting in part, would have upheld the Trial Examiner who viewed the remarks as "less than clear in their meaning," and, at most, isolated in character.

It is apparent from the foregoing cases that the majority-minority split is less consistent in interference and discrimination cases than in most of the current Board decisions. As a result, the problems of predicting Board reaction to employer conduct in a specific case become even more complex. *Offner Electronics, Inc.*, 134 NLRB No. 89, 49 LRRM 1307, is an illustration. Offner, on September 15, 1959, consented to an election with the International Brotherhood of Electrical Workers. The election was scheduled for October 23. The company president, at an employee meeting September 29, expressed his opinion that company policies had worked to the benefit of all employees and stated it was the employees' choice whether they wanted to place their best interests in the trust of the union or of the company. To that end, he asked the employees to express, in a secret ballot, their feelings on the need for union representation and the type of union desired, in order that the company might have some guide as to its actions with the petitioning union or in some other way.

To conduct the poll, ballots were placed in employees' pay envelopes. Space was provided to show whether they favored continuing the present employee relationship without a union or being represented by a union. A preference for the IBEW, an independent union of Offner employees, or some other union was also requested. A substantial majority of the 95 employees eligible to vote expressed their wish to continue without a union.

An employee, who was active on behalf of the union in organizing the company's employees and who acted as an observer at the election, was discharged on November 6 for the asserted reason that she circulated an anonymous note containing untrue gossip. Immediately after the discharge, she was caught attempting to take certain confidential company records without authorization.

The NLRB election was held as scheduled, the vote was secret, the ballots not being identified in any way, and the union lost by a vote of 53 to 35. Objections were filed, and the Eisenhower Board, with Rodgers dissenting, set aside the election on the basis that the poll was an intrusion upon the Board's responsibility. *Offner Electronics*, 127 NLRB 991, 46 LRRM 1136.

When the same conduct came before a McCulloch-Leedom-Rodgers panel of the new Board in an unfair labor practice proceeding, the split of opinion highlighted the present confusion. Leedom found the poll unlawful only because it occurred in the context of other coercive conduct, i.e. a somewhat ambiguous reference to improvements in the group insurance plan. McCulloch, on the other hand, adopted a "per se" approach, finding the poll coercive without regard to the existence of other violations. In his view, an employer may lawfully poll his employees concerning their wishes regarding representation, if his purpose is to determine whether a union actually represents a majority of the employees in order that the employer may recognize the union voluntarily. The employer had no such intention here, but chose to intrude by raising new issues and new solutions, such as whether the employees might prefer an independent union or a union other than the IBEW. Thus, the poll was an unwarranted inquiry into the state of the employees' desire for representation and was reasonably calculated to intimidate and coerce them. McCulloch and Leedom also found the discharge to be discriminatory but denied reinstatement because of the post-discharge conduct of the employee.

Rodgers dissented, as he considered a "dry run" or "open poll" to be like those in political elections, and employees could make up their own minds on how to vote when the official balloting took place. He also dissented as to the discharge, maintaining that neither the Intermediate Report nor the majority decision alluded to any evidence that the employee's union activities were known to the employer. The employer knew she was a union observer at the election but this did not immunize her from discharge for cause, and the other union observer was not discriminated against but was, in fact, promoted.

Another example is *General Dynamics Telecommunication*, 137 NLRB No. 183, 50 LRRM 1475, where McCulloch joined Rodgers and Leedom to form a majority. They found no interference, restraint or coercion when an employer prohibited distribution of union literature on a privately owned and maintained street by non-employee union organizers, since other means of communication were readily available to the union, which the union used. No disparity of treatment existed, though employees distributed literature favorable to the incumbent union on company property during their non-working time. The majority relied on the Supreme Court decision in *Babcock & Wilcox*, 351

U.S. 105, 38 LRRM 2001, where it was held that an employer may validly post his property against non-employee distribution of union literature, if reasonable efforts by the union through other available channels will enable it to reach the employees with its message, and if the employer's notice or order does not discriminate against the union by allowing other distribution. The majority also found no disparity of treatment existed, despite employee distribution of literature favorable to the incumbent union on company property during non-working hours, because the employer, as a matter of law, could not deny employees the right to distribute literature on company property on non-working time.

Brown dissented on the theory that the majority unduly extended *Babcock & Wilcox,* because there the court was concerned over property from which the general public is excluded. In the *General Dynamics* case, though title to the street was vested in the company, it was open to the public except for one day of the year. Brown expressed no concern as to whether or not the outside union was denied an opportunity to communicate with the employees but would have adopted a fixed rule that company denial of union solicitation by non-union employees on company property open to the public is a violation of the Act.

The same division of opinion on a similar issue is seen in *Stoddard-Quirk Mfg. Co.,* 138 NLRB No. 75, 51 LRRM 1110, where McCulloch, Rodgers and Leedom ruled that an employer may ban distribution of union literature in working areas at all times but must permit employees to carry on such activity in non-working areas of the plant premises on their own time. Fanning and Brown dissented and would have permitted the literature to be distributed throughout the plant. Also, see *Minneapolis-Honeywell Regulator Co.,* 139 NLRB No. 65, 51 LRRM 1400, and Brown's comment in *Ryder Truck Rental, Inc.,* 135 NLRB No. 8, 49 LRRM

1438 and in *Young Spring & Wire Corp.,* 138 NLRB No. 76, 51 LRRM 1119.

It would appear that, of the five Board members, Brown has the most noticeable penchant for finding employer interference or discrimination. For example, McCulloch and Leedom in *Russell-Newman Mfg. Co., Inc.,* 135 NLRB No. 6, 49 LRRM 1421, upheld the Trial Examiner and dismissed a discrimination charge arising out of the termination of an employee, shortly after an election which the union lost by a vote of 157 to 58. Although the employee served on the union's organizing committee, they found discharge to have been caused by the use of vulgar language when the employee swore at a fellow employee who said she was not going to vote for the union. They also found the use of profanity to be against a plant rule; there was no showing the employer was aware of or tolerated use of profane language by other plant employees, and another employee had been disciplined for a similar offense. The majority pointed out there was no direct evidence showing the employer was motivated by any reason other than the profanity and no evidence of any additional questionable conduct by the employer. Three other employees on the union organizing committee were neither discharged nor discriminated against in any way.

Brown, in his dissent, argued that the employee discharged was an efficient worker with 13 years service and a known union leader, and that profanity was commonplace and the employee addressed with the profane language made no complaint. He emphasized the penalty was more severe than that used in the similar instance and found union animus demonstrated by visits of company officers to employees' homes during which the employees were interrogated concerning their union affiliations. However, the Trial Examiner found no evidence whatsoever of any threats or promises of benefits made to the employees during the visits. Instead, the employees were assured that their vote on election day would be secret, that no one would know how anyone voted, and that it was their right to vote as they saw fit. In any event, these visits occurred more than six months prior to the filing of the charge and were not alleged as violations. Also, see *Texas Industries, Inc.*, 139 NLRB No. 22, 51 LRRM 1306.

The "protected activity" cases supply another example of an unpredictable area of Board law. Since an early Supreme Court decision (*N.L.R.B. v. Sands Mfg. Co.*, 306 U.S. 332, 4 LRRM 530), it has been clear that an employer need not reinstate employees who strike in violation of their contract. Several years later, however, the Board decided strikers retained their protection and were entitled to reinstatement, regardless of a "no-strike" clause in their contract, if they struck in protest over their employer's "serious" and "flagrant" unfair labor practices. The decision was upheld by the Supreme Court without mentioning the flagrant nature of the unfair labor practices involved. *Mastro Plastics Corp. v. N.L.R.B.*, 350 U.S. 270, 37 LRRM 2587.

In a decision which deviates from the usual Kennedy Board pattern, McCulloch and Leedom adopted an exception to the *Mastro Plastics* rule. They held that an unfair labor practice strike was not protected where, in the face of a no-strike clause and an arbitration and grievance procedure which would have permitted reasonably swift settlement, the employees struck to protest the unlawful discharge of a union steward. The unfair labor practice, in their view, was not so serious as to be "destructive of the foundation on which collective bargaining must rest." The employer's discharge of the strikers was, therefore, upheld. Fanning dissented and would have found an unfair labor practice strike of whatever kind or nature a protected activity. *Arlan's Department Store of Michigan, Inc.*, 133 NLRB No. 56, 48 LRRM 1731.

The difference between the two views is important because

of the limitation which Fanning's approach would place on an employer's ability to discipline employees. A strike in violation of a contract is a proper basis for a damage action but, in the light of recent Supreme Court opinions, it cannot be enjoined. *Sinclair Refining Co. v. Atkinson,* 370 U.S. 195, 50 LRRM 2420. Discharge is the employer's sole method of putting pressure on the strikers to stop their illegal activity immediately. Where the union includes a general protest against the employer's unfair labor practices on its picket signs, the Fanning view requires the employer to ascertain, at his peril, whether any such practices have occurred before he acts. The difficulties in making such a judgment when the Board is changing its rules as rapidly as at present is shown by cases such as *New England Tank Industries,* 133 NLRB No. 25, 48 LRRM 1605.

Three individuals, formerly employed by a pipeline operator whose function had been taken over by New England Tank, turned down an offer of employment and picketed instead. McCulloch, Leedom and Fanning found the picketing to be in protest over New England Tank's refusal to "rehire" their former co-workers; therefore, the three were unfair labor practice strikers and all were entitled to jobs upon their unconditional offer to abandon their strike. Rodgers dissented. A striker, in his view, must be an employee of the employer against whom the strike is directed and must cease work. Because the three men refused New England Tank's offer of employment, no employment relationship was ever established, and they could not cease work.

Although Fanning's theory that any unfair labor practice strike is protected did not prevail in *Arlan's,* it cannot be disregarded. The Board has not defined the meaning of "serious" unfair labor practices, and it would not be surprising to find a strike in protest over a discharge protected because the grievance procedure operated more slowly than in *Arlan's.* In an earlier case, a suspension and discharge for leadership of an "unauthorized" meeting legalized a breach of contract strike in the view of Rodgers, Leedom and Fanning. *Ford Motor Co.*, 131 NLRB No. 174, 48 LRRM 1280. And, in *Young Spring & Wire Corp.*, 138 NLRB No. 76, 51 LRRM 1119, McCulloch, Leedom and Brown held that a contract clause banning strikes in connection with any "grievance or complaint arising under" the contract did not bar a strike over the disciplinary suspension of an employee, because the contract contained no provision covering such a suspension. Also, see *Paul Biazevich et al.*, 136 NLRB No. 1, 49 LRRM 1700. Taken as a whole, these decisions show little interest in restricting breach of contract strikes.

A final example of the confusion facing an employer is found in the "lock out" cases. Since the United States Supreme Court decision in *Buffalo Linen Supply Company* (*N.L.R.B. v. Truck Drivers' Local 449*, 353 U.S. 87, 39 LRRM 2603), the right of members of a multi-employer bargaining association to "lock out" their employees as a defense to a strike by a union against a single member has been clear. The Supreme Court recognized the right to strike as not so absolute as to deny self-help by employers when legitimate interests of employees and employers are involved. In the *Buffalo Linen* case, the interest was that of small employers in preserving a multi-employer unit as a means of bargaining on an equal basis with a large union. The *Buffalo Linen* rule appears to be narrowed by another interpretation of the new Board, although in this instance Leedom joined the Kennedy appointees to form the majority.

Five employers operating retail food stores constituted a multi-employer bargaining unit. On March 16, 1960, the union struck and picketed one employer, Food Jet. As they had previously advised the union they would do, the remaining four employers locked out their employees and told them they would be returned to work at the conclusion of the strike. All of the stores attempted to continue operating, Food Jet by hiring replacements and the others by using supervisors, relatives of management and *temporary* replacements. The strike ended April 22, and all employers immediately recalled their employees.

McCulloch, Leedom and Brown found a violation, distinguishing *Buffalo Linen*. The majority reasoned that locking out employees in order to replace them with other workers is not equivalent to a shutdown to preserve the solidarity of the association unit. By continuing to operate, they, in effect, temporarily replaced their employees solely because they were engaged in a protected, concerted activity. *Brown Food Store*, 137 NLRB No. 6, 50 LRRM 1046.

Rodgers and Fanning dissented, declaring the majority position illogical. The lockout was permissible under *Buffalo Linen*, and temporary replacements did not affect the strikers' employment or their union adherence. In their view, performance of a non-discriminatory act cannot "make unlawful something which was theretofore privileged."

Not all lockouts are unlawful. In *Building Contractors' Ass'n. of Rockford, Inc.*, 138 NLRB No. 143, 51 LRRM 1211, the contractors suspended operations after the Operating Engineers refused to promise they would not call a "quickie" strike. When charged with an unlawful lockout, the employers convinced the Board that a "quickie" strike would cause substantial losses, because of the need for continuous pouring of concrete and for continuous operations in the construction of bridges, overpasses and roads, and would create a serious danger to the health and safety of the public. Refusing to find the lockout discriminatory, the Board, with Brown dissenting, relied on *Betts Cadillac-Olds, Inc.*, 96 NLRB 268, 28 LRRM 1509, which held an employer is not prohibited from closing down his plant where necessary to avoid economic loss or business disruption attendant upon a strike. Brown distinguished the *Betts* case and saw the facts as demonstrating the lockout was to force acceptance of the employers' contract proposals. He viewed the majority rationale as justifying every lockout in a bargaining context. Also, see *Publishers' Ass'n. of New York City,* 139 NLRB No. 107, 51 LRRM 1434.

The foregoing examples of Board rulings on interference and discrimination demonstrate two significant factors. First, though precedent is rarely specifically over-ruled, a clear change of direction is apparent. Second, the alignment of majority and minority members defies precise analysis and makes prediction of results in future cases extremely difficult. Certainly, employers may be sure their conduct will be more carefully scrutinized than it has been previously. Discipline of union adherents will be increasingly difficult. Discipline of strikers who violate a no-strike clause must be handled with caution. In litigating any interference or discrimination case, realism requires that the employer be prepared to prove affirmatively lack of union knowledge or anti-union motivation. *Building Contractors of Rockford* provides some hope in lockout cases but, in the light of the other decisions discussed, it is apparent that employers will receive little assistance from the NLRB in resisting unlawful union activity.

CHAPTER VII

EMPLOYEE RIGHTS
v. UNION SECURITY

Regardless of its membership, every Board has seemed far more willing to protect employees from employer unfair labor practices than from those committed by union representatives. Reasons are difficult to bring into focus, though "pro-union bias" is the most frequent charge levelled by Board critics. A partial explanation is a statutory distinction. Employers may not "interfere with, restrain or coerce employees" in the exercise of their rights [Sec. 8(a)(1)], while unions may "interfere" but not "restrain or coerce" [Sec. 8(b)(1)(A)]. But the language variation does not require the Board to condone violence or to be hesitant about suppressing unlawful union security practices. Too often this has been true.

Whatever the reason, the Kennedy Board has shown noticeably less concern for employee rights where union security is involved than did the Eisenhower Board. As in the employer interference and discrimination cases, few precedents are overturned but there is a decided shift in result.

In *Operating Engineers, Local 825 (H. John Homan Co.)*, 137 NLRB No. 118, 50 LRRM 1310, Local 825 and the employer had a collective bargaining agreement which contained no union security provision but made the union exclusive source of referrals for employment. The contract also provided that Local 825 should maintain at its hiring hall an open employment list of men available for work. Placement on the list was not based on union criteria. Registrants who were not members of the union were required to share the cost and expenses of the hiring hall. Non-union registrants paid $9.00 per month, with payments made quarterly in advance. Members of Local 825 paid $10.00 in the form of monthly dues. Of that amount, $1.10 was specifically allocated to the International Union as a per capita tax. They paid no hiring hall registration fee as such. Members of sister locals paid $2.00 per month as "travel service dues," but payment was not required prior to being registered on the hiring list. They paid no other fee to Local 825. The monies collected went into the union's general fund, from which all union expenses were paid, including those completely unrelated to operation of the hiring hall.

Individuals filed charges alleging fees paid by non-union members to be discriminatory. McCulloch, Fanning and Brown dismissed. Even though only $8.90 per month was retained at the local level from members' dues for all union expenses, they decided the higher monthly charge of $9.00 per month (paid by non-union members solely for the hiring hall) was offset by a requirement that members pay an initiation fee of $360, plus six months dues in advance. The majority noted, also, that the responsibilities of the union members subjected them to payment of assessments and other continuing monetary obligations. In the majority's view, it would be difficult to distinguish between costs of operating a referral system that guaranteed each applicant union wages and conditions of employment and those costs which might be said to have no relation to the applicant's job opportunities before, during, and after his employment at a particular job site. Because the General Counsel did no more than recite a number of expenses which appeared to him "totally unrelated" to the operation of the hiring hall and did not attempt to specify the fair cost of the referral procedures or a registrant's pro rata share, he was found not to have proven discrimination.

Rodgers and Leedom dissented, arguing that, even though it was assumed all dues received from union members were allocated to defray the cost of operating a hiring hall, it was apparent that non-union applicants paid ten cents more per month than union members. After listing a variety of items, ranging from convention expenses to refreshments at union meetings, which clearly had nothing to do with the hiring hall, they pointed out that fees for members of sister locals were different from either of the other two categories and all registrants were required to contribute $1.00 to a Defense and Education Fund, in no way related to the hiring hall. The dissenters believed "a preponderance of testimony" showed that a discriminatory practice existed. In any event, the General Counsel made at least a *prima facie* case showing discrimination and the union had the burden of offering some explanation for its practices.

The result not only shows little concern for registrants who chose to remain non-union but also provides an interesting contrast with the burden of proof placed on the employer who failed to pay a Christmas bonus in *Electric Steam Radiator* (see Chapter VI). There, the mere withholding of the bonus forced the employer to prove the validity of his conduct and he was found to have been motivated by union considerations, even though he had sound economic reasons and acted upon advice of counsel that payment of the bonus would have been unlawful. But here, where non-union registrants admittedly were forced to pay more than union members, the Kennedy Board could not find a *prima facie* case requiring the union to defend its registration system. Also, see *Hod Carriers, Local 7 (Yonkers Contracting Co.)*, 135 NLRB No. 88, 49 LRRM 1593.

Similar reluctance to impinge upon union security appears in other cases. The Glass Container Manufacturers Institute and the Plate Glass Workers' Union maintained contracts providing that "the employer must request journeymen mould makers whenever he has a vacancy," and, if the union was unable to comply within thirty days, the employer might obtain labor from any source. The General Counsel contended that "journeymen mould makers" meant members of the union and that the contract gave the union the exclusive right to provide such workmen during the 30-day period, in violation of Section 8(b)(2). McCulloch, Leedom and Brown found the term in question synonymous with the word "craftsmen" and that nothing in the contract itself, in the practices or in the interpretations of the parties, though the contract had been in existence for twelve years, indicated the contrary. *American Flint Glass Workers' Union (Glass Container Manufacturers' Institute)*, 133 NLRB No. 47, 48 LRRM 1640.

Rodgers dissented, arguing that the 1959 bargaining demonstrated that "journeymen mould makers" meant union members. As Rodgers emphasized, the employer's spokesman had repeatedly stated that he construed the phrase to mean members of the union and the clause in question would, therefore, provide for a closed shop. The union neither denied nor explained away the accuracy of the interpretation but took the position that it was only fair the union should have thirty days in which to supply journeymen in order that the union could keep the industry supplied with union mould makers. Rodgers also emphasized that the majority, by merely stating that *Ebasco Services Incorporated*, 107 NLRB 617, 33 LRRM 1214, was distinguishable and at the same time carefully noting neither agreement nor disagreement, cast doubt on the continuing validity of that decision. *Ebasco* reached a contrary result under very similar circumstances. It seems clear the law has been changed, but the treatment of *Ebasco* leaves parties with guidelines which, at best, are difficult to follow.

Also, see *Local 694, Carpenters' Union (Jervis B. Webb Co.)*, 133 NLRB No. 9, 48 LRRM 1569, where Fanning and Brown, Rodgers dissenting, refused to find an unlawful hiring arrangement, even though the union's answer to the complaint specifically admitted an exclusive hiring arrangement and the testimony of the union business agent admitted that preference was given in referrals to union members. Compare *Animated Displays Co.*, 137 NLRB No. 99, 50 LRRM 1297.

A case stemming from the widely publicized strike of the two principal newspapers in Portland, Oregon, the "Oregon Daily Journal" and "The Oregonian," provides another illustration of the new Board's reluctance to find any illegality in union attempts to strengthen union security. *Portland Stereotypers' Union No. 48 (Journal Publishing Co.)*, 137 NLRB No. 97, 50 LRRM 1259. The employers charged the Stereotypers with violations of the Act by demanding and, eventually, striking for certain terms and conditions in a new agreement. These included insistence that foremen of the Stereotypers Department, who acted for the employers in early stages of the grievance procedure, be union members, though the demand apparently was tempered by a willingness that the foremen not be subject to union discipline for carrying out the publishers' instructions in accordance with the contract. The union also insisted that the contract incorporate the union constitution and by-laws, which contained provisions requiring its members, including foremen, to favor hiring union members in preference to others.

The Board found unlawful coercion of the employers in violation of Section 8(b)(1)(B) in their choice of a bargaining agent when the union insisted that foremen be union members because they concededly handled grievances. However, the Kennedy majority, with Leedom not participating and Rodgers dissenting, refused to find any coercion or restraint of *employees* in this requirement. Also, they found no illegality in the demand for incorporation of the union constitution and by-laws because of a savings clause, which stated that the union proposal went only to the extent these rules would not conflict with the Act. *N.L.R.B. v. News Syndicate Co., Inc.*, 365 U.S. 695, 47 LRRM 2916, was cited as authority and its holding was said to indicate ". . . that savings clauses are to be given their face value." In addition, the majority considered union membership for foremen as a proper objective, inasmuch as the latter were not to be subject to union discipline.

Rodgers apparently agreed with the majority's reliance on the *News Syndicate* case, which held that incorporation of an unlawful union constitution was not "per se" unlawful where coupled with a savings clause, but only to that extent. He pointed out that the same day the Supreme Court decided *News Syndicate*, it affirmed, because equally divided, a decision of the First Circuit that a strike to obtain a foreman membership clause would violate the Act. *International Typographical Union v. N.L.R.B. (Haverhill Gazette)*, 365 U.S. 705, 47 LRRM 2920. Rodgers noted that the majority relied upon the *Haverhill Gazette* case in finding the Section 8(b)(1)(B) violation but did not mention it in reaching a contrary conclusion on the foreman membership issue.

In each of the foregoing cases, if the Board had found a violation, its customary remedy would have been a simple cease and desist order. The one possible exception is *H. John Homan*, where some type of reimbursement for the fees paid by the non-union members would have been warranted. Because of the Board's broad authority over its remedies, a mere order to cease and desist from charging the non-union registrants a discriminatory amount would have been upheld by the courts. It is extremely difficult to understand the majority's aversion to finding a violation when the remedy causes no hardship other than the correction of an existing condition, highly vulnerable to discrimination against employees.

As will be shown later, the majority has no hesitation in inferring union motivation even though it may require an employer to resume a discontinued operation or re-open an uneconomic plant. Nor does it hesitate to wipe out the employees' right to a secret ballot election. But it does refuse to draw the inferences necessary to support a finding which will protect employees from unlawful union security arrangements, it closes its eyes to proven discriminatory payments, and it is willing to excuse an admitted violation in a case such as *Jervis B. Webb Co.*

The contrast with Board willingness to infer employer misconduct is obvious. Curiously, the new Board has seen fit to illustrate both aspects of the comparison in a single case. The Philadelphia Sheraton Corporation had a valid union shop agreement with the Hotel Employees' Union which required the employer to "register" the name and hiring date of each new employee not obtained through the union within twenty-four hours after employment. The new employees were given a slip of paper by the employer which said, among other things, that they would be required to apply for membership "immediately." Also, they were required to report to the union hall at once, where they were given a "work slip" which was taken back to the employer.

McCulloch, Fanning and Brown found the *employer* maintained an unlawful hiring procedure in that it required new employees to make immediate application for union membership, depriving them of the statutory thirty-day period. But, they refused to hold the *union* liable because there was no evidence that the "work slip" was a prerequisite for employment or that the union had knowledge of the employer's requirement of immediate application. The majority based its decision largely upon an ambiguous stipulation by the counsel for the union and the General Counsel, and disregarded (as pointed out in Rodgers' dissent) a statement which effectively admitted an unlawful practice. Rodgers also would have held the union liable on the basis that the "work slip" procedure was nothing less than a "clearance" requirement. Leedom agreed with the majority result. *Philadelphia Sheraton Corp.*, 136 NLRB No. 75, 49 LRRM 1874.

Another method of subordinating employee rights to those of the union is found in the delinquent dues cases. The statute provides that, where a valid union shop agreement exists, a union may request and an employer must discharge an employee who has failed to tender periodic dues and initiation fees uniformly required as a condition of acquiring or retaining membership. Section 8(a)(3).

In two such cases, McCulloch, Leedom, Fanning and Brown have held that neither the employer nor the union violates the Act by an employee's discharge for dues delinquency, even though the employee tenders dues after the union request for discharge but prior to actual dismissal. According to the majority, the foregoing facts standing alone are not sufficient to warrant an inference that the union's refusal to accept the employee's offer of payment is due to some reason other than his prior dues delinquency. *General Motors Corp., Packard Electrical Div.*, 134 NLRB No. 116, 49 LRRM 1283; *Acme Fast Freight, Inc.*, 134 NLRB No. 98, 49 LRRM 1286. *Aluminum Workers*, 112 NLRB 619, 36 LRRM 1077, which held that a full and unqualified tender of delinquent dues made at any time prior to actual discharge (and without regard to when the request for discharge may have been made) is a proper tender, was overruled. The majority viewed the *Aluminum Workers* rule as permitting dissident employees to frustrate the orderly administration of lawful union security agreements. Rodgers did not participate in either decision.

The new Board's rule ignores the fact that the statute permits discharge only for non-tender of dues. There is no requirement that the tender be timely and where it had, in fact, been made prior to the discharge, the literal language is ignored. Brown was careful to footnote in both cases that the decision did not decide whether the validity of the discharge turned on the fact that the request for discharge was made before the belated tender. His reservation indicates he would permit the union to request, and the employer to discharge, whenever an employee fails to pay his dues on time, even though the union sought his dismissal after tender had been made.

Employee rights again suffered at the expense of the union's security in interpretation of the statutory waiting period before a new employee must become a union member. The previous Board, Member Fanning dissenting, had ruled in *Chun King Sales*, 126 NLRB 851, 45 LRRM 1392, that a union security clause requiring all new employees to become union members "within 30 days from the date of their employment" was unlawful because it did not afford the employees the full 30-day grace period prescribed in the Act. This decision was over-ruled in *New York Electric and Gas Corp.*, 135 NLRB No. 42, 49 LRRM 1487, where McCulloch, Fanning and Brown held that such a clause is lawful. They found "within 30 days" is equivalent to the statutory requirement of "on or after the 30th day." No explanation was offered for the difference in view. Rodgers and Leedom dissented, declaring that the two clauses are not the same and pointing out that their view had been endorsed by a Court of Appeals in *N.L.R.B. v. Industrial Rayon Corp.*, 297 F2d 62 (CA 6), 49 LRRM 2265.

Leedom joined the majority, however, in another "grace period" case, *State Packing Co.*, 137 NLRB No. 157, 50 LRRM 1406. There no violation was found where an employer, upon demand by the union, discharged a man who had been employed by the company for only 32 days at various times during the previous year. Though he had been a full time employee at one point, he was an "extra" when discharged, being called upon only when needed. He was similarly employed by other companies. The majority found a "within 30 days" union security clause lawful in view of the *New York Electric* decision and, though the employee's work was intermittent, he had worked for the employer in excess of 30 days, entitling the union to insist that he pay a reinstatement fee before the company could hire him. Rodgers dissented, reiterating his position that "within 30 days" is not equivalent to "on or after the 30th day." Furthermore, even assuming the clause was lawful, he did not feel the union security provision could be enforced to obligate the employee to pay dues for long periods of unemployment. He pointed to a long line of cases where it had been held unlawful to demand, as a condition of rehire, dues which had accrued while the applicant was unemployed. Though termed a "reinstatement fee," the union was actually attempting to effect payment of dues for a period during which the employee was not obligated to pay.

In their dissent in *Colgate-Palmolive Co.*, 138 NLRB No. 108, 51 LRRM 1176, McCulloch and Brown go even further and would have found a discharge for dues delinquency, even though the union *had accepted* a belated tender of the dues.

Board emphasis on protection of union rather than employee rights is illustrated in a different way by *Duralite Co., Inc.*, 132 NLRB No. 28, 48 LRRM 1371. There, McCulloch, Leedom and Fanning found violations of the Act by both the company and the International Union of Electrical Workers, where the employer withdrew recognition from the contracting union, an unaffiliated group, and recognized the rival I.U.E. He then enforced an arrangement whereby all employees were required to join the I.U.E. and permitted I.U.E. to collect union dues on company time and premises. McCulloch and Fanning, however, refused to order disgorgement of dues because the record did not indicate that the employees were, in fact, coerced into joining the I.U.E. or paying dues, in spite of the arrangement described. They distinguished *Virginia Electric and Power Co. v. N.L.R.B.*, 319 U.S. 533, 12 LRRM 739, which required such a remedy because the Virginia Electric union was "a company union whose very existence was unlawful" and the return of the dues was one means of disestablishing the union. In *Duralite*, the I.U.E. was not company dominated. Leedom would have followed *Virginia Electric*, finding no difference in principle. In his view, the unlawful arrangement between Duralite and the I.U.E., requiring membership in the union as a condition of employment, coerced the employees into supporting a union which was unlawfully imposed upon them.

Viewed in the light of the statutory intent, the *Duralite* case discloses no problem of encouragement of collective bargaining. Thus, even from the majority point of view, the Congressional objective of protecting the exercise of full freedom of association to workers should have free rein. It seems obvious that an employee does not have such freedom if he can be forced to join a labor organization by an employer and an unwanted union, be forced to pay dues to the union and then, even though the arrangement is found unlawful, be prevented from recovering the money extracted from him by the union.

Little can be added to comments already made in discussing the union security cases. As a whole, they disclose a significant lack of concern for employee rights and, in addition, an unwarranted disparity in the vigor with which the law is enforced against employers on the one hand and unions on the other. Employees have never received the protection from union conduct envisioned by the Congress. The cases discussed, therefore, represent a difference in degree, rather than approach. Nevertheless, the result is a marked infringement of employee rights and a failure to carry out the intent of Congress.

The disparity in the Kennedy majority's treatment of unions and employers is not explained by statutory differences for these involve slightly different standards of conduct —not the rights of the employees. Nor are problems of proof the answer, for the new Board has excused union misconduct where the facts necessary to establish a violation were admitted. Instead, we must conclude that the current union security cases reflect the common misconception of early Boards, i.e. the primary protection extended by the Act is to the instrument of collective bargaining—the labor organization—rather than to the employees.

CHAPTER VIII

VIOLENCE

The public, and particularly those individuals who have not become calloused to the oddities of the labor-management arena, must find it difficult to understand the apathy with which governmental authorities view violent conduct in labor disputes. The Board, regardless of membership, has consistently found restraint and coercion of employees in violation of Section 8(b)(1)(A) of the Act where picket line violence, threats of violence and mass picketing exist. But the concept of particular activities falling within these categories and the remedies prescribed leave much to be desired.

If the limited number of Section 8(b)(1)(A) cases decided by the new Board are any indication, the apathy of previous administrations will continue. One case, however, the *Gabriel Company, Automotive Division,* 137 NLRB No. 130, 50 LRRM 1369, demonstrates a different approach but in unusual circumstances. There the full Board set aside a Teamster victory in an election because of anonymous and persistent telephone calls threatening five officials of a rival union, the Machinists. The Board found the calls, which consisted of numerous instances where IAM Committee members were threatened with death and assault, comprised a systematic plan to inhibit IAM officials from asserting their leadership. There were also threats of reprisals by Teamsters against the same officials, tampering with the machinery and work of the IAM adherents, and the reckless operation of a tow-motor by a Teamster which endangered an IAM officer. The Board found it need not assess the actual impact of the conduct upon the quality of leadership asserted by the affected IAM officials or upon individual employees who voted. The vice of the conduct was the threat and actual use of strong arm methods to still opposition as such tactics have a tendency to coerce free choice.

In other contexts, the new Board has not been so meticulous about employee rights. During a strike at the plant of I. Posner Inc., a New York cosmetics manufacturer, violence erupted the first day a picket line was established. On one occasion, four strikers surrounded a non-striker and told him if he kept on working he should not be surprised if he got hurt. Another striker threatened to push in a non-striker's face. A union agent made a similar threat and told a non-striker he would lose his job if the union won. Strikers threatened to beat up the company manager and, on one occasion, the union agent in charge of strike activities punched the employer's general manager with a clenched fist when the manager urged a truck driver to make delivery of materials. Other similar incidents occurred.

Leedom, Fanning and Brown found the described conduct a violation of Section 8(b)(1)(A) of the Act but, with Leedom dissenting, refused to find a threat where a striker told a non-striker ". . . you just might get hurt." The majority also declined to hold the union responsible for threats made by an individual not wearing a picket sign at the time though he was later identified as a picket. Even Leedom saw nothing illegal in the business agent striking the employer. As the Board viewed the matter, the employer threw a union card on the floor, which the union representative had placed on a shelf below a telephone, and the employer's unwarranted conduct was a "personal affront" to the union official and did not arise out of the labor controversy. *District 65 RWDSU (I. Posner, Inc.)*, 133 NLRB No. 141, 49 LRRM 1062.

The principal holding of the case is proper but it is difficult to understand why such fine lines as the distinction between a threat to push in a non-striker's face and a statement ". . . you might just get hurt," need to be drawn in violence cases. Furthermore, it is inconsistent to allow wide latitude in "name calling" and language used on picket line, as the Board has done, and then to excuse violent conduct because of a so-called "personal affront."

Another instance of excusing violence by weighing the gravity of employee misconduct against employer provocation was adopted by the Kennedy Board in *Trumbull Asphalt Co.*, 139 NLRB No. 97, 51 LRRM 1478. Trumbull refused to reinstate two strikers who had made threatening statements to non-strikers, at least one of which was convincing enough to keep an employee from working for 5 weeks. Fanning and Brown, with Rodgers dissenting, decided the strikers were entitled to reinstatement with backpay because of the employer's unfair labor practices and the fact the threats had never been carried out. (cf. an employer threat to close his plant if a union should win an election).

McCulloch, Brown and Leedom found a violation of Section 8(b)(1)(A) where pickets at Vulcan Cincinnati, Inc., took license numbers of automobiles approaching the plant, threatened to "get" the drivers, and threatened to push an employee's car into the ditch and "jerk" him out of the car. McCulloch and Brown, however, dismissed an allegation of mass picketing and blocking of ingress and egress because, though the pickets situated themselves across the roadway of the plant and obstructed automobiles, photographers who were apparently present during most of the strike were never able to take a picture of such an incident. Movies showed that, though many vehicles were considerably retarded, it was always possible for a vehicle to enter or leave. *Local 2772, Steel Workers Union* (Vulcan-Cincinatti Inc.), 137 NLRB No. 9, 50 LRRM 1085.

Leedom dissented as to the majority holding on mass picketing. In his view the pickets sought to deter persons from entering the plant by their physical presence in superior numbers accompanied by threats of bodily harm and property damage. Because picketing which blocks ingress and egress is a violation, it does not follow that picketing which *does not* have this effect *is not* a violation. In Leedom's opinion, the question turns on whether the picketing was intended, or necessarily intended, to restrain or coerce. In this instance, it did.

The majority cited *H. N. Thayer Co.,* 99 NLRB 1122, 30 LRRM 1184, in support of its dismissal of the mass picketing allegations. There, as pointed out by Leedom, the pickets were specifically instructed to permit non-strikers to enter and leave. Citation of a case in this manner serves to alter the meaning of precedent without actually overruling it.

In *Continental Can Company,* 136 NLRB No. 98, 49 LRRM 1951, Continental and the Paper Makers' Union reached an impasse in bargaining and the union voted to strike July 25th, 1960. On July 21st, the company made a new offer and, the following day, granted the Regional Director of the union permission to hold a meeting in the plant cafeteria to consider the offer. At the meeting, a group of employees opposing reconsideration of the strike vote became so vehement that a fight started. Minor injuries resulted. During the scuffle the Regional Director fled the cafeteria but, before leaving the plant, spoke to the plant manager. After the Director identified the man who caused the disturbance, the manager, accompanied by police, went to the cafeteria and discharged him. The company later offered to reinstate all who would sign a statement showing they were not involved in the fight and took back two who did so. The others filed charges and the Trial Examiner found the discharges were "purely pretextuous," the Company having discharged the individuals for engaging in concerted activity.

Rodgers and Leedom overruled the Trial Examiner and dismissed the charges. In their view the Act does not protect violence, and fighting is not protected even if it arises from union activity. McCulloch dissented, finding the issues factual and no basis to overrule the Trial Examiner.

McCulloch had no hesitation, however, in overruling the Trial Examiner where it was the employer who engaged in the unruly conduct. Salyer Stay Ready Filter Corp. had a valid rule banning union solicitation by non-employees on company property. When the employer's son discovered an organizer passing out cards he ordered him off the property. The organizer resisted and attempted to hand out additional cards. The son called his father and, after repeatedly but unsuccessfully ordering the organizer off the property, the employer seized him by the arm and shoved him out into the street. The altercation continued in the middle of the street with the employer finally striking the organizer twice and causing his sunglasses to fall to the ground.

Rodgers and Fanning, in agreement with the Trial Examiner, dismissed charges of interference, restraint and coercion in violation of Section 8(a)(1). The employer was enforcing a valid no-solicitation rule and the controversy which occurred in the street was a continuance of lawful action begun on the employer's property. The employer's expressed dislike for the union did not alter his right to enforce the valid rule. *Salyer Stay Ready Filter Corporation,* 136 NLRB No. 116, 49 LRRM 1957. McCulloch dissented, viewing the eviction as a mere pretext to cloak the employer's anti-union designs.

Again, to the public it is difficult to understand why any

violence should be condoned whether engaged in by a union or an employer. Here, because the union agent refused to leave the property, it may have been necessary for the employer to eject him forcibly but there was no necessity that he be knocked down after his ejection.

The Board's indifference to violence is also demonstrated by its reluctance to seek injunctions in such cases. Section 10(j) of the Act permits the Board, at its discretion, to go into the District Court and seek temporary relief whenever a complaint is issued in an unfair labor practice case. The power was used most sparingly for many years but, in one of his early speeches, Chairman McCulloch announced his belief that a broader use was warranted. In April, 1962, reporting on implementation of his view, McCulloch said Section 10(j) injunctions had been sought on nine occasions in the previous year. The power was used in only one violence case but twice to halt employer discharge of union leaders and three times to require an employer to bargain. No records are available from which one can readily determine cases in which the discretionary relief has been authorized. There is no reason to believe its rate of use in violence cases has been increased. In the writer's own experience, the Board refused to act where massed pickets completely blocked ingress and egress at a plant for more than a month. There had been continual violence but, fortunately, only one incident was sufficiently serious to require hospitalization of the victim.

Violence, mass picketing, physical blocking of ingress and egress, and threats have no place in the concept of picketing as a means of publicizing a labor dispute. None of these techniques can be justified as encouraging collective bargaining or eliminating industrial strife. When condoned, regardless of degree, they are nothing more nor less than a license aiding a wrongdoer to coerce acceptance of his position. It may be arguable that their use augments the bargaining strength of the employees engaging in the physical coercion. If this were a valid argument, then bargaining should be conducted between industrial armies, not negotiators. There is no support whatsoever for the view that Congress intended such a result, and it is obviously in derogation of the rights of employees who are victims of the conduct.

Perhaps the answer to the Board's unconcern about violence is found in statements such as ". . . some disorder is not unusual in any extensive strike." *Redwing Carriers, Inc.,* 130 NLRB 1208, 47 LRRM 1471. With the multitude of protections now afforded strikers, it is inconceivable that a right to violence or other physical coercion, though minor, must also be included.

CHAPTER IX

REFUSAL TO BARGAIN-ORGANIZING

Early in February, 1960, Local 512 of the Hod Carriers began an organizational campaign at Pinellas Paving Co., Inc., in St. Petersburg, Florida. On February 8, Business Agent T. J. Guthrie, sent a telegram to the employer, advising that his organization represented a majority of the Pinellas employees and asking for immediate negotiations. Guthrie had in his possession at the time cards designating the union as bargaining agent signed by 28 or 29 production and maintenance employees out of a unit of some 55 employees.

Receiving no reply to his telegram, Guthrie called J. W. Hayes, Pinellas' General Manager, on February 9 and asked if he was ready to begin bargaining. Hayes acknowledged receipt of the telegram but stated that he wanted to obtain legal counsel who would contact Guthrie. Guthrie expressed approval and said he would be looking for the call.

Hayes tried to call Guthrie about 4:30 p.m. on Friday, February 12, and again the following morning but was unable to reach him. Before leaving on a business trip to Chicago that same morning, Hayes called Beck, his dispatcher, from the airport, explained his inability to reach Guthrie, and let Beck know where he could be contacted in Chicago. When Beck found Guthrie later in the day and relayed the message, Guthrie said he saw no reason to call

Hayes but would go ahead with an NLRB petition. The petition was placed in the mail that afternoon with 33 authorization cards and was received and filed by the Board the following Monday morning, February 15. The Board subsequently directed an election, which was cancelled after the union, on April 18, 1960, filed charges of a refusal to bargain in violation of Section 8(a)(5) of the Act.

A Board panel, consisting of Fanning and Brown with Leedom dissenting, adopted the Intermediate Report of the Trial Examiner and found a violation. The panel held that the union represented a majority of the employees and the employer had refused to bargain with the union in order to dissipate its majority. The Hod Carriers were designated as bargaining agent, the employer ordered to bargain, and the employees were deprived of their right to vote. *Pinellas Paving Co., Inc.*, 132 NLRB No. 85, 48 LRRM 1475.

The employer's principal defense was that the union never offered to prove its majority status. The majority answered that the union's claim was not challenged until the hearing in the unfair labor practice case more than three months later, long after the employer embarked upon a deliberate program to dissipate the union's majority by unlawful interrogations and threats. The employer's efforts to contact the union were said to be inadequate and, under the circumstances, to show that the company had no intention of recognizing or bargaining.

The "program" to dissipate the union's majority, as found by Fanning and Brown, consisted primarily of one meeting on February 5, prior to the union's first telegram to the employer. They decided the Plant Superintendent threatened to discharge any one who signed a union card or mentioned the union, stating at the meeting that it was his job to prevent the union from coming in and to stop it in any way he could. [The finding was based on the testimony of four employees, three of whom alleged discriminatory discharges which were dismissed by the Trial Examiner and the Board, while the Plant Superintendent's denial that he made the remarks was corroborated by three other employees and a foreman.] The balance of the "program" was comprised of two instances where the Plant Superintendent allegedly asked employees if they knew anything about the union and threatened to fire those who talked about joining, the questioning of two employees as to whether they had signed union cards and a question to another as to his attendance at a union meeting. There were no findings of any interference of any sort after mid-February.

Leedom, agreeing that there had been interference as found by the majority, refused to find a refusal to bargain. He found the employer evinced willingness to bargain by Hayes' assurance he would retain a lawyer and his attempt to communicate with the business agent. When the union became impatient only five days after its initial request and shifted its tactics from seeking voluntary recognition to use of the NLRB election procedure, it was only reasonable for the employer to conclude that, until the Board resolved the representation case, it was unnecessary to communicate further with the union. In Leedom's opinion, the majority's theory that the employer's conduct demonstrated no intent to bargain with the union, is in reality a theory that a violation of Section 8(a)(1) of the Act automatically constitutes a refusal to bargain. He did not believe it could be inferred from the 8(a)(1) activity, none of which occurred after the union filed its petition, that the employer did not intend to bargain in good faith.

Leedom might also have pointed out that, in finding the employer did not challenge the majority status until the unfair labor practice hearing, the majority was obviously incorrect. It is evident that a hearing was held in the representation case, probably early in March since the direction of election issued on April 11. There the employer unquestionably denied the union's claim of a majority or no question of representation would have existed and the direction of election could not have issued.

Without specifically reversing any precedents, the case accomplishes a major shift of policy, going back to pre-Taft-Hartley days when the employees' right to an election was frequently denied in favor of a direct order to bargain. The underlying theory of such cases is that the employer's unfair labor practices are so serious that the employees are incapable of exercising a free and uncoerced choice of a bargaining agent. It is unbelievable that, under the circumstances of this case where no unfair labor practices were found after the election petition was filed, four or five isolated instances of employer threats were so serious that the employees could not evaluate the conduct and express a free choice in a secret ballot election held two months later.

The majority's approach puts an impossible burden on the employer. A skillful organizer should have little difficulty in entrapping most small employers into sufficient inadvertent conduct to apply the standard deemed sufficient to require a bargaining order in the *Pinellas* case.

Having bargaining authorization cards from 31 of approximately 52 employees of Snow and Sons, a Yakima, Washington, packer of corn and asparagus, representatives of Local 760 of the Teamsters demanded recognition. The employer requested that an NLRB election be held with a "normal" posting of 30 days but the union demanded that any election take place within 72 hours. The union representatives refused to show the employer either the signed cards or a blank card indicating the nature of those signed.

When the union threatened an immediate strike, the son of the employer agreed to a check of the cards by an impartial person, undisputedly "to ascertain if the union representatives were representing any substantial number of employees." A local minister conducted the check the same day, finding 31 employees out of a list of 49 had signed. At a further meeting later in the day, the union would agree to the election only if held that night, refusing both to wait for an NLRB petition and to call the regional office to learn how quickly an election could be held.

Shortly after the meeting broke up, 12 employees walked off the job in protest. That evening, still another meeting was held at which the union withdrew its offer to have a union-conducted election and insisted that bargaining be carried out on the basis of the card check. When the employer persisted in his efforts to secure an NLRB election, a picket line was established the following morning and 7 more employees refused to cross it.

At the hearing on the union's charges of refusal to bargain, two employees testified they were induced to sign cards to aid the union in securing an election and did not authorize it to act as bargaining agent. Viewing the testimony as casting serious doubt on the validity of the balance of the cards, the Trial Examiner held the majority status of the union was not established. In addition, he found no evidence that the employer's insistence on an election was for the purpose of dissipating the union's majority *and no evidence of interference, restraint or coercion by the employer.*

The Kennedy Board, with Leedom joining, held the employer guilty of a refusal to bargain and designated the Teamsters as bargaining agent, denying the employees any right to vote on the question. *Snow & Sons,* 134 NLRB No. 57, 49 LRRM 1228. The Board reasoned that, even though the two cards were tainted, there was no evidence that other employees had signed only to obtain an election and elimination of the two cards did not destroy the majority. (The opinion made no reference to the fact that only 19 of the employees, substantially less than a majority, honored the union's picket line.) In addition, the Board held that the employer had agreed to a card check (but omitted to mention the fact that "undisputedly" this was done to see if a "substantial" number had signed and not as a substitute for an election), which indicated that a majority of the employees had applied for membership. The Board emphasized that the right of an employer to insist on an election is not absolute. Rodgers footnoted disagreement because there was no evidence that the employer was motivated by bad faith.

At no place in the Board's opinion is any concern expressed for the right of employees to exercise a free choice as to their bargaining agent. There is no evidence whatsoever to show that the employer had any intention of dissipating the union's claimed majority or even that he inadvertently committed any act which might be so construed. Therefore, it cannot be argued there was any conduct which prevented the employees from expressing a free and uncoerced choice in a secret election.

Here, on one side, was an employer who insisted on a secret ballot election, conducted by the agency designated under the law to handle such matters, and who was willing that the election be held as quickly as possible. On the other side was a union (in the context of testimony of two employees showing the union had misrepresented the purpose of the cards), which adamantly insisted on no election or one which the union itself conducted. In the middle were the employees. The rights of those employees as guaranteed in the Act are fragile indeed if, under such circumstances, they may be set aside by their employer because of a technical mistake in his handling of the union demand.

Kennedy Board abuse of authorization cards to deprive employees of their vote is also found in *Koehler's Wholesale Restaurant Supply*, 139 NLRB No. 74, 51 LRRM 1427. There the Teamsters were able to demonstrate a majority to the satisfaction of McCulloch and Fanning where they obtained cards from 22 employees in a bargaining unit of

38. In its opinion the majority makes this surprising statement:

> "This is not the type of case, as our dissenting colleague (Rodgers) apparently believes, where employees have been beguiled by a union into signing authorization cards with the assurance that the only purpose in doing so was to obtain an election. . . . Knowing that the employees feared Respondent's reprisal for moving away from the dominated KEU, (the union organizers) assured them that (the cards) would be used *to obtain a secret election* in which the Respondent would be unaware who had signed the cards or who had voted for the Union."

If such language has any meaning the majority must be drawing a distinction between cards signed for the sole purpose of obtaining an election and those signed for the purpose of demonstrating a majority through a secret election. Such a distinction is meaningless and serves only to provide a rationale for depriving the employees of their right to vote.

Employee rights suffered a similar fate in *Madsen Wholesale Co.*, 139 NLRB No. 58, 51 LRRM 1411, where Fanning and Brown, as pointed out by dissenter Rodgers, disregarded the usual rules on inclusion of seasonal employees in a bargaining unit. By excluding three such employees, who would undoubtedly have been permitted to vote if an election had been held, the majority allowed a Teamster local to be designated as bargaining agent because 8 of 13 employees had signed cards.

Also, see *Al Tatti, Inc.*, 136 NLRB No. 17, 49 LRRM 1738, where, though the Board established a majority by a card showing, it did add that failure to reply to a union's request for negotiations, *standing alone,* is not persuasive as to bad faith. And see *Webb Fuel Co.*, 135 NLRB No. 30, 49 LRRM 1484; and *Greystone Knitwear Corp.*, 136 NLRB No. 53, 49 LRRM 1834.

In *Porter County Farm Bureau Co-operative Assn.*, 133

NLRB No. 105, 48 LRRM 1760, the Teamsters had represented the employer's truck drivers for several years. Bargaining had been on a multi-employer basis but individual contracts were signed. Prior to expiration of the current agreement on June 30, 1958, the employer notified the union it wanted individual, rather than group bargaining. When the contract expired, the employer stopped making payments to a union insurance fund. At the first negotiating session, July 14, only economic issues were discussed and no reference was made either to the appropriate bargaining unit, the union's majority status, or the cessation of payments to the fund. A week later, without notice to the union, the employer filed an election petition for a production and maintenance unit. The union followed with a refusal to bargain charge which was subsequently withdrawn.

On September 16, 1958, in response to inquiries by employees as to their union insurance coverage, the employer offered to cover them in a plan for employees not in the bargaining unit effective immediately, if they voted for it unanimously, which they did. The employer advised them the plan would remain in effect until the election petition was determined.

After settling with other employers in the multi-employer group, the union met again with Porter County Co-op on October 1. Economic issues were discussed, but the principal subject was the employer's request and the union's refusal to agree to an election to clarify the unit and the union's majority status. Eventually, the union called a strike which was honored by only part of the drivers. Some of the strikers advised the employer they wished to return to work but were afraid of violence from the union if they did so. At their request, the employer assisted in preparing a form of resignation from the union, which was later sent to the union. Also, because of the employees' fear of violence, the employer called a group of farmers who accompanied the strikers to the union hall and waited outside while the employer discussed the removal of the pickets with the business agent in order that the strike might end. When the business agent refused, the meeting broke up and the strikers returned to work. The picketing continued.

The Trial Examiner found he could not say the employer did not entertain an honest doubt of the union's majority status in the new ill-defined unit. He also felt the unilateral action on insurance was not improper, because the employer had no obligation to bargain. Assistance as to the withdrawals was ministerial and assembling the farmers was not to interfere with the employees' activities in any way. Rodgers agreed with the Trial Examiner, but Leedom and Brown reversed, finding that the unit consisted of the employees previously represented and the union's majority was demonstrated by the check-off of dues. Action on the insurance demonstrated lack of good faith and calling the farmers was a device to undermine the union and discourage the strikers from changing their minds, not to protect them. Bargaining was ordered without an election.

Once again, it is difficult to understand the reluctance to let the employees vote. Surely a secret ballot is a more accurate means of determining employee preference than a check-off authorized months before. An employee might readily fear reprisal if he sought to revoke the check-off. The fear of violence expressed by the employees demonstrated concern about the union's conduct. There was no hint that the employees would have been unable to exercise a free choice in a secret ballot election. But their rights were ignored and the identity of their bargaining agent dictated by their employer's misconception of a course of conduct which would pass an unpredictable Board test.

A mistake by the union also may cause a meaningful change in the extent to which employee rights are protected and in the remedy against the employer. In *Orkin Exter-*

minating Co., 136 NLRB No. 59, 49 LRRM 1821, Rodgers and Fanning held an employer had not refused to bargain in good faith, even though he had committed serious unfair labor practices during an organizing drive, because the union's request for a bargaining unit was somewhat ambiguous and, even after the employer became aware of the unit sought, he had good faith doubts as to its appropriateness. McCulloch dissented and would have found a refusal to bargain because the employer's conduct was to forestall union activity.

As pointed out before, Congress established employee rights and then prescribed certain standards of employer and union conduct to protect those rights. One such standard was the duty of an employer to bargain in good faith. Thus, when placed in proper context, it is apparent that the duty is a part of the protection of employee rights. By concentrating on the employer's good faith, the Board has effectively elevated one of the standards of conduct to a position of greater importance than the employee rights which those standards were designed to protect.

The Board views each case in the light of all the circumstances and determines whether the employer has demonstrated a lack of good faith by refusing to bargain in order to gain time to dissipate the union's majority. This, of course, is what every employer is doing when he puts the slightest stumblingblock into the path of an immediate election. The Board's rules, not the law, in practical effect give controlling weight to whether or not the employer successfully avoids committing any unfair labor practices prior to an election. If he fails, either because of bad advice, inadvertence, or his own willful misconduct, his employees lose their chance to vote. It is inescapable that the rights of the employees, therefore, hinge on the technical competency of the employer and his advisors in treading the intricate paths of permissible employer conduct.

Difficult as these trails have been in the past, the case-by-case approach of the Kennedy Board will, of necessity, make them more obscure. If there is doubt on this score, consider the statement of the majority in *Snow & Sons* and of McCulloch in *Orkin Exterminating* to the effect that the Board will not be limited by the *Joy Silk Mills* doctrine (*Joy Silk Mills, Inc.*, 85 NLRB 1263, 24 LRRM 1548; enfd. sub. nom. *Joy Silk Mills, Inc. v. N.L.R.B.*, 185 F2d 732, 27 LRRM 2012, cert. den. 341 U.S. 914, 27 LRRM 2633). In that landmark case, decided in 1950, the "Truman" Board held that an employer cannot insist on a union proving its majority status in an election if the employer is seeking to gain time to undermine the union's majority status. The implications of *Snow & Sons* and of McCulloch's comments are that the employer's motive in insisting upon an election may no longer be controlling.

Where the policy of the Act and the rights to be protected demand that employees be given a free and uncoerced choice of bargaining agent, the test of employer misconduct during organizing should turn on that factor. By April, when the election was to be held, could not the Pinellas employees have exercised a free choice? The unfair labor practices committed by their employer, if any, were minor and his conduct had been above reproach for some two months. Could not the Snow employees have exercised a free choice if the union had been forced to wait several days for an NLRB election? Their employer had not committed a single unfair labor practice.

Yet, these cases discuss only the good faith of the employer, making no attempt to protect the employees' rights. Nothing in the Act requires that an election be held when the union's strength is at its highest level or prior to any opportunity for the employees to hear arguments adverse to unionism. The free and uncoerced choice of the employees is the right to be protected. It has limited practical meaning when it can be eliminated by the Board without comment because of an employer's mistakes or minor misconduct.

The final vice of Board-imposed bargaining is that it invariably rests on a majority showing demonstrated by union authorization cards. It is inconceivable that those who claim expertise in labor-management matters can equate a union authorization card with a secret ballot as a true expression of employee free choice. The cards are often signed at a union meeting where "everybody's doing it," or at the request of a fellow employee "in order to get an election," or just to get rid of an aggressive organizer.

The unreliability of cards is best demonstrated by the Board's own experience. According to Chairman McCulloch, a study made of elections in the Board's Atlanta Region showed that petitioning unions which had authorization cards from 50-70% of the employees won only 52% of the elections. Thus, even though a majority had signed cards, the employees rejected the union almost half the time. The card showing in both the *Pinellas* and *Snow* cases fitted the foregoing figures. In both instances, therefore, the probabilities of employee rejection or acceptance of the union were almost identical. To wipe out the former and arbitrarily impose the union on the employees is plainly inconsistent with the protection of employee rights.

CHAPTER X

BARGAINING UNITS

Representation proceedings—the Congressionally provided means for employees to select or reject a bargaining agent—are the heart of the Act. The vital part of each representation case is the bargaining unit—the particular assortment of employees who will vote in the election. Unfortunately, bargaining units have a quality common to at least one area of every science or profession. Though fascinating to the initiated in the field, they are virtually incomprehensible to the layman and defy simplification. The necessity for discussing bargaining unit problems in a study of this kind is clear, however, for they provide another illustration of the Kennedy Board's encouragement of union objectives. The unit decisions consistently encourage the growth of unionism as such, rather than protect the rights of employees.

One of the key, though little publicized, provisions of the Landrum-Griffin Act gave the Board authority to delegate its powers in representation cases to its Regional Directors. The language found in the final version of the Act first appeared in a bill introduced by Congressman Kearns (H.R. 7265) as a part of a plan to increase the capacity of the Board and provide faster processing of cases. It was incorporated in the House Committee bill and finally used as an integral part of the Senate-House compromise on the very troublesome issue which had arisen out of the so-called "no-man's land" in Board jurisdiction. In explaining this portion of his bill, Mr. Kearns said:

> "Such (representation) cases account for more than 50% of the Board's workload. During the early years of NLRB, the Board undoubtedly needed to handle these cases itself. More than 20 years later, the rules of decision are well established and nearly all of the cases are decided on established precedent."

Mr. Kearns' theory was sound and his comment accurately reflected the stability which had come to characterize issues in election cases, with predictability of result as its desirable outgrowth. Unfortunately, the theory had not yet received a practical test when the Kennedy appointees took over. The Landrum-Griffin Act was passed September 14, 1959, but the Eisenhower Board did not exercise the authority to delegate. The delay was promptly resolved when the Kennedy members took office, the present delegation of authority becoming effective May 15, 1961.

Predictability is slowly but surely beginning to disappear. *American Cyanamid,* as explained above, was the keynote. Its emphasis on the case-by-case approach immediately served notice that previously well-established rules could no longer be relied upon. The "empirical" method effectively placed a cloud over each accepted precedent.

As further decisions of the new Board in representation matters have issued, there can be no doubt of its consistent reliance on the empirical approach and its complete lack of concern for precedent or predictability. Analysis of actual cases, however, is exceedingly difficult for it must be limited to published decisions and statements of the new Board. The great majority of representation matters are now handled by Regional Directors, and Board action on requests for leave to appeal these decisions are unpublished.

Analysis is further hampered by the curious approach of the Board in publishing only selected representation case decisions. Prior to the delegation, the use of "short form" unpublished decisions in routine cases was understandable. The drafters of the authority to delegate assumed that, after its exercise, any matter sufficiently important for Board consideration would be incorporated in the Board's printed decisions for the guidance of Regional Directors and the public. Nevertheless, as explained more fully in Chapter XV, the Board does not always publish its representation decisions even in cases of first impression.

Incomplete though the material may be, sufficient examples are available to show the direction in which the Board is moving. *American Cyanamid* must again be a starting point, though more for the language used than the result. The Eisenhower Board, in the original *American Cyanamid* decision, had changed the long-standing rule which precluded establishment of a separate bargaining unit of maintenance employees if a more comprehensive unit was sought by another union, regardless of the absence of bargaining history. The reconsidered decision substantially restored the original policy, permitting maintenance employees to be represented separately in the absence of a bargaining history for a broader unit of production and maintenance employees. The majority was careful to note, however, that absence of bargaining history does not *necessarily* establish the appropriateness of the maintenance unit.

Elections were directed in separate units of maintenance and of production employees but, if the Building Trades Council, which was interested only in the former group, lost, the votes of that unit were ordered pooled with those of the production employees and a single over-all bargaining unit established. In other words, a self-determination election was granted to the maintenance employees and, if rejected, they were then considered a part of one broad unit. This result appears to give the employees an adequate opportunity to express their preference.

The self-determination theory has not been followed in other cases, however. Thus, in *Ballentine Packing Co., Inc.,* 132 NLRB No. 75, 48 LRRM 1451, the Meat Cutters petitioned for a production and maintenance unit excluding truck drivers, while the Teamsters sought the truck drivers only. McCulloch, Fanning and Brown ordered separate elections in each unit in view of the homogeneity of each group, the absence of bargaining history, and the fact that no union sought a larger unit. In their view, because a union is not required to seek representation in the largest possible unit, there was no objection to the drivers remaining unrepresented if they rejected the Teamsters, and the placement of the Meat Cutters on the driver unit ballot would have created unnecessary confusion and would have been an obstacle to organization of the employees.

Rodgers and Leedom were of the opinion that the drivers should have been placed in an over-all unit if they rejected separate representation. They pointed out that, if a single union sought a production and maintenance unit excluding truck drivers, the Board would require their inclusion. (The majority indicated that, perhaps, this rule should be reconsidered.) They felt the theory of the majority's argument is applicable to every craft or departmental group and that it would defeat the purpose of self-determination elections, which is to provide for separate representation, not fragmentation of a broad unit into small groups of unrepresented employees. Finally, they took exception to the majority's failure to give weight to the employer's unit position. They viewed the employer as having some appreciation of an effective bargaining unit and he, too, has the duty to bargain in the unit certified.

The effect of the *Ballentine Packing* approach is, as pointed out by the dissent, to set the stage for residual unrepresented units in many situations where they would formerly have become a part of a single broad unit. This would be less significant if the new Board continued to follow the *Zia Company* rule (108 NLRB 1134, 34 LRRM 1133), which provided for self-determination elections for fringe or residual groups before their inclusion in a larger historical unit. The *Zia* rule, however, has also been changed by the new Board. *D. V. Displays Corp.*, 134 NLRB No. 55, 49 LRRM 1199. There McCulloch, Fanning and Brown decided that, where there is a question of representation in the historical unit and the incumbent union seeks to add an unrepresented fringe group (which no other union wants on another basis), a single election will be directed in which the fringe group will be included with the historical unit. They theorized that the *Zia* rule was in derogation of the responsibility of the Board to determine the appropriate unit. If the placement of the fringe employees had arisen at the time the historical unit was established, they would have been included in the over-all bargaining. Thus their exclusion was an historical accident. The majority felt a self-determination election perpetuated the "fringe defect" in the unit and the new approach was more democratic because all employees would have an equal voice. Rodgers and Leedom dissented, arguing that the *Zia* rule protected both groups, as the votes of each were not adulterated by any outside groups. Also, see *South-East Coal Co.*, 138 NLRB No. 71, 51 LRRM 1100.

The *Ballentine* and *D. V. Displays* cases, considered together, produce a curious result. The "historical accident" resulting in a fringe group, of which the majority complains in the latter case, is exactly the situation which will be produced by the *Ballentine* rule whenever a separate group (truck drivers, in that instance) vote against representation. In any subsequent election, they would constitute a "fringe defect" and, unless some union other than that which represented the balance of the employees wished to represent them separately, the majority then feels it would have become a more "democratic approach" to vote them as a part of a single broad unit. Thus, the truck drivers might reject a bargaining agent, while the production employees were selecting a representative. The following year, under the rule of these cases, the production workers' union would be entitled to petition for an election at which the truck drivers would no longer have an opportunity to express a separate opinion. If entitled to do so in the first instance, why not at the second election?

The *Ballentine* case is also difficult to square with *Felix Half & Brothers, Inc.*, 132 NLRB No. 135, 48 LRRM 1528. There the new Board, reversing an existing rule, held that, where separate elections are directed in voting groups of represented and unrepresented employees, the votes must be pooled in a manner which gives the incumbent union the maximum opportunity to represent the entire group. Here the Teamsters sought a unit of office employees and a porter-clerk of a carpeting wholesaler. The employer and an incumbent union, the Office Employees, contended the existing unit, limited to office employees and excluding the porter-clerk and an inside salesman, was appropriate. The majority directed an election in the existing unit and another election among the unrepresented employees, with the votes to be counted as follows: If a majority in the "existing unit" voting group selected the Intervenor, that would be an appropriate unit. If a majority in the "unrepresented group" selected the Petitioner, that would also be an appropriate unit. However, and this is the departure from Board precedent, if a majority of employees in the "existing unit" voting group did not vote for the Intervenor, then the votes in that unit would be pooled with those cast by the non-represented group. This pooling arrangement over-ruled *Waikiki Biltmore, Inc.*, 127 NLRB No. 23, 45 LRRM 1511, and makes it extremely difficult to unseat an incumbent union. Votes of the "unrepresented group" give the incumbent union a second chance at retaining its status in the "existing unit," but votes of the "unrepresented group" have no effect in unseating the incumbent union in the "existing unit."

Ballentine Packing was followed in non-truck driver cases, indicating that the minority's prediction as to its application to any craft or departmental unit was accurate. In *Trevellyan Oldsmobile Co.*, 133 NLRB No. 111, 48 LRRM 1814, the Machinists sought a unit of mechanics, helpers and apprentices in an automobile sales and service agency and the Teamsters sought a separate unit of all other service department employees. The employer asked for a single over-all unit. McCulloch, Fanning and Brown directed an election in the two separate units, in view of the homogeneity of each group, the absence of bargaining history, and the fact that no labor organization sought to represent the larger unit. No facts establishing such homogeneity were given. Also, see *Metropolitan Imprinters Corp.*, 133 NLRB No. 126, 49 LRRM 1041.

Ballentine was also followed in other cases involving drivers. For example, in *Giordano Lumber Co., Inc.*, 133 NLRB No. 22, 48 LRRM 1629, the Carpenters sought a production and maintenance unit, excluding truck drivers, the Teamsters asked for the truck drivers, and the employer argued for a plant-wide unit. Separate elections were ordered, and the truck drivers' ballots were not pooled.

After *Ballentine Packing* was decided, the Board, for a time, avoided the problem of where to place truck drivers when a single union petitioned for a production and maintenance unit but asked that the drivers be excluded and the employer urged their inclusion. In *Ben Pearson's, Inc.*, 133 NLRB No. 84, 48 LRRM 1708, the Board, rather than delay the voting, went ahead with an election in the unit requested and permitted the truck drivers to vote, subject to challenge. The same approach was followed in *Intercontinental Engineering Mfg. Co.*, 134 NLRB No. 93, 49

LRRM 1280. In this case, the majority, with Rodgers and Leedom dissenting, also ordered a separate election in a unit of Machinists but refused to pool their ballots in a broad unit in the event they rejected the union.

The majority finally came to a decision on the truck driver issue in *E. H. Koester Bakery Co., Inc.*, 136 NLRB No. 100, 49 LRRM 1925. As might be expected, they were convinced that the application of the present automatic rule, i.e. where the parties are in disagreement, there is no bargaining history, and no union is seeking to represent the drivers separately, they should be placed in the production and maintenance unit, was improper. They viewed such a rule as a refusal to consider on its merits an issue which is basic to the determination of the unit placement of truck drivers—their community of interest. The factors to be considered include whether they have related or diverse duties, mode of compensation, hours, supervision, other conditions of employment, and whether they are engaged in the same or related operations or are spending a substantial portion of their time in such operations.

Rodgers and Leedom dissented, emphasizing that the true basis of the majority opinion was to make the inclusion or exclusion of the truck drivers depend on the desires of the petitioning union because it was clear they would have been included in the unit had the union so requested. They believed the logic used by the majority is equally applicable in cases involving other craft and departmental groups and, in fact, appeared to have been applied in excluding garage mechanics from the unit in the *Koester Bakery* case. The dissent again, as in a number of previous cases, expressed serious concern about the failure of the majority to establish a measure of certainty in an area where certainty is desired because of the delegation to Regional Directors. Also, see *Ideal Laundry & Dry Cleaning Co.*, 137 NLRB No. 147,

50 LRRM 1413, and *Tops Chemical Co.*, 137 NLRB No. 94, 50 LRRM 1247.

The difficulties which truck drivers have caused the new Board are also illustrated by *Kalamazoo Paper Box Corp.*, 136 NLRB No. 10, 49 LRRM 1715. There the Teamsters attempted to sever a unit of truck drivers from the existing production and maintenance unit currently represented by the Paper Mill Workers. According to McCulloch, Fanning and Brown, who denied severance, the truck drivers were under the same supervision, received the same benefits, worked the same hours, were paid on the same basis, were on the same seniority list as other employees, and regularly and frequently interchanged with other employees. The majority ruled that truck drivers would not be severed automatically from a unit merely on the basis of their traditional job classification and request for separate unit. Before severance is allowed, determination must be made as to whether in reality such employees constitute a functionally distinct group and whether as a group they have over-riding special interests. This determination must be based upon factual situations existing in each case and not upon title, tradition or practice.

Rodgers and Leedom dissented, pointing out that the Board has consistently recognized the separate identity and interests of truck drivers since the earliest days of the NLRB. These precedents were based on the fact that truck drivers constitute a functionally distinct group of employees engaged in a traditional occupation. Their interests are identified with the function of transportation rather than the particular business or industry which they serve. According to Rodgers and Leedom, the majority reversed settled Board policy, allegedly because it disregarded the community of interest which truck drivers have with other employees, but neither the Teamsters' Union (the traditional representative of truck drivers) nor the truck drivers themselves ever protested the

Board practice. In the view of the dissenters, an employee's "predominant community of interest" is a reflection of his "predominant" duties and responsibilities. The "predominant" duties of the Kalamazoo Paper Box drivers were the driving of trucks, not the manufacturing of paper boxes. Therefore, their predominant community of interest lay with one another and not with other employees in the plant. Also, see *Sylvania Electric Products, Inc.,* 135 NLRB No. 69, 49 LRRM 1564.

The Kennedy Board has been equally free in changing rules governing other types of bargaining unit issues. In at least one instance, though a well-established precedent was reversed and the result is not without question, the new rule was supported with valid reasons and an easily applied formula was set forth. In 1944, the Board adopted the policy of denying requests for bargaining units of insurance agents which were less than state- or company-wide in scope. *Metropolitan Life Insurance Co.,* 56 NLRB 1635, 14 LRRM 187. This long-standing policy was over-ruled and an election directed in a unit consisting of only the employees in a district office. *Quaker City Life Insurance Co.,* 134 NLRB No. 114, 49 LRRM 1281. The majority found the sole reason for the *Metropolitan Life* rule was anticipation of union organizing in the insurance field on a company- or a state-wide basis. As a practical matter, such a pattern did not materialize. "Obviously, when the purpose for which a rule has been established fails, the rule should also fail," especially when the rule unfairly prejudices the collective bargaining rights of the employees. Rodgers and Leedom dissented because they could see no valid reason for departing from the *Metropolitan Life* rule. Also, see *Equitable Life Ins. Co.,* 138 NLRB No. 70, 51 LRRM 1079; *Quaker City Life Ins. Co.,* 138 NLRB No. 5, 50 LRRM 1537; *Metropolitan Life Ins. Co.,* 138 NLRB No. 73, 51 LRRM 1095,

138 NLRB No. 87, 51 LRRM 1148; *The Western and Southern Life Ins. Co.*, 138 NLRB No. 74, 51 LRRM 1093.

Validity of a rule change is much more obscure in another instance. In *Crumley Hotel, Inc.*, 134 NLRB No. 15, 49 LRRM 1095, the Hotel and Motel Service Employees' Union petitioned for separate residual units of all unrepresented employees of four hotels in Reno, Nevada. There was no bargaining history as to the employees sought, but the four hotels had bargained on a multi-employer basis as to their culinary and fountain employees, waiters, bartenders, and "front help." In a decision issued April 14, 1961, a Rodgers-Leedom-Fanning panel unanimously dismissed the petitions, finding the units requested inappropriate on the authority of *Los Angeles Statler Hilton Hotel*, 129 NLRB 1349, 47 LRRM 1194, because each petition sought merely a segment of the residual group.

On its second attempt, the union was granted reconsideration, and a new panel (McCulloch and Fanning, with Leedom dissenting) reversed. The majority distinguished *Los Angeles Statler Hilton* because the employers there were members of an association of hotels dealing with various labor organizations, while in the *Crumley* case the hotels were members only of the Reno Employers' Council, which is composed of six hotels and more than 50 restaurants, coffee shops and bars. They found the Reno hotels had never bargained exclusively on a multi-employer basis for employees working only at hotels.

Leedom, in his dissent, noted that, prior to 1952, the Board rule was that a history of multi-employer or multi-plant bargaining was controlling as to other categories of employees of the employer. The rule was then modified in *Joseph E. Seagram and Sons, Inc.*, 101 NLRB No. 101, 31 LRRM 1022, to permit a single plant unit for employees as to whom there was no bargaining history. Later this was extended to cover multi-employer as well as multi-plant units. In *Los*

Angeles Statler Hilton, the *Seagram* line of cases was distinguished as involving categories of employees, such as salesmen and office clericals, having "internal homogeneity and cohesiveness." Because residual units consist of unrepresented employees lacking in homogeneity and, to be appropriate, must include *all* unrepresented employees omitted from the group, the petitions were dismissed in *Los Angeles Statler Hilton.* The majority's distinction in *Crumley,* according to Leedom, is invalid because it turns on the difference between restaurant-hotel and hotel employees, not on whether the residual units are of a type granted by the Board.

The importance of the case lies in its implications for the future. The thrust of the majority view is that it will be more liberal in approving residual units in multi-employer groups and, presumably therefore, in multi-plant units also. It would seem to follow that small groups of unrepresented employees in multi-plant units will be more vulnerable to organizational attempts by outside unions than in the past, providing a foothold for a competing union in some instances. Also, if the holding of the *Crumley* case is placed alongside that of *Ballentine Packing,* it seems apparent that increased fragmentation of bargaining units is in the offing.

A far more important unanswered question in the same general area is the new Board's approach to craft severance. This is the well-established doctrine under which the Board has permitted a traditional craft or departmental bargaining unit to vote on severance from an established broad production and maintenance unit. When the Board heard oral argument in *Kennecott Copper Corp.,* 138 NLRB No. 3, 50 LRRM 1540, there were widespread rumors a new approach to craft severance would be forthcoming. The decision issued in August, 1962, following established rules. Sole indication of a possible change was Fanning's concurrence, in which he urged a re-examination of craft severance policies. As of this writing, no definitive craft severance decision has been issued. Another clue, though not readily apparent because most of the cases are not published, is the fact that McCulloch and Brown are not participating in craft severance matters.

Another case containing an inkling for the future is *Taunton Supply Corp.*, 137 NLRB No. 22, 50 LRRM 1154. The Meat Cutters' Union sought an over-all unit in the employer's two hardware and sporting goods stores, but excluding office clericals. The latter had considerable contact with sales clerks (who were in the unit), worked near the selling areas, but did no sales work. The union argument for their exclusion was based on the established precedent of excluding office clericals from units of shipping, receiving and warehousing employees at a typical wholesale operation. Rodgers, Leedom and Fanning found the business essentially retail in nature and, therefore, included the clerical workers in the unit. Brown footnoted that he would include them regardless of their occupational title because of their community of interest with the other employees. His position can be construed as indicating a willingness to look at the community of interest of office clericals in other types of units, breaking down the long-standing exclusion of such employees from production and maintenance units. Such an approach would obviously be consistent with the "empirical" standard of *American Cyanamid*.

Multi-employer units have come to the attention of the new Board, but the cases in which there have been differences of opinion provide little guidance for the future. In *Sea-Land Service, Inc.*, 137 NLRB No. 65, 50 LRRM 1200, an independent union petitioned for a unit comprised of the employer's stevedoring employees at Ponce, Puerto Rico. There was no valid controlling bargaining history in a larger unit because, though there had been bargaining in a unit which included the employer's stevedores in San Juan, it had been tainted by unlawful assistance to the International Longshoremen's Association. McCulloch, Leedom and Fanning directed an election in the unit sought. Rodgers and Brown would have dismissed on the basis of *Puerto Rico Steamship Association*, 116 NLRB 418, 38 LRRM 1271, which thoroughly examined appropriate unit policy with respect to stevedoring employees on the Puerto Rico waterfront and found a single port unit inappropriate because of the salutary effect of the established pattern of island-wide bargaining.

Another instance of majority refusal to recognize a multi-employer bargaining relationship is found in *U. S. Pillow Corp.*, 137 NLRB No. 272, 50 LRRM 1216. The effect of the decision is to permit a rival union to file a petition for a single employer unit if timely filed in accordance with the last individual contract, even though the employer has unequivocally agreed to be bound by a multi-employer contract which would otherwise be a bar.

Another forerunner of future decisions is application of the case-by-case approach in the unit placement of various types of employees. *Plaza Provision Co.*, 134 NLRB No. 101, 49 LRRM 1295, excluded driver-salesmen, where the sales function predominates, from units of truck drivers and warehousemen. The full Board, Rodgers dissenting, overruled *Valley of Virginia Milk Producers*, 127 NLRB No. 95, 46 LRRM 1096, in which it was held that driver-salesmen should be included in production and maintenance units unless the parties agree to their exclusion or some other labor organization seeks to represent them separately. For rationale, the majority pointed to its "experience" from which it concluded that, if the sales function predominates, drivers have interests more closely allied to sales than to production and maintenance employees. Rodgers viewed the majority decision as giving controlling weight to extent of organization. It is noteworthy that the majority's unit placement once more was in accord with the desire of the union and that the decision reversed a prior determination of the Board involving the same operations of the employer.

Also, surprisingly, Rodgers joined with McCulloch and Brown to reverse a long-standing policy on the unit placement of technical employees. In *The Sheffield Corp.*, 134 NLRB No. 122, 49 LRRM 1265, they over-ruled *Litton Industries*, 125 NLRB 722, 45 LRRM 1166, and decided that technical employees would no longer automatically be excluded from bargaining units of production and maintenance employees whenever their placement was in dispute. The old rule went back to *Chrysler Corp.*, 1 NLRB 164, 1 LRRM 363, and was based on the theory that the distinctive training, experience and functions of technical employees gave them different interests from other employees. As a rationale, the panel contended the *Litton* approach was not a "salutary way of achieving the purposes of the Act," because it gave priority in unit placement to the parties' disagreement. In abandoning the automatic placement formula, the Board stated a "pragmatic judgment" would be used in each case, based on ten different factors which were listed in broad terms. Brown, in his Duke Law School speech, viewed the *Sheffield* case as one of the most significant contributions to modification of the "per se" approach. *Dewey Portland Cement*, 137 NLRB No. 107, 50 LRRM 1302, and *Meramec Mining Co.*, 134 NLRB No. 167, 49 LRRM 1386, provide examples of the application of the *Sheffield* case and leave the unmistakable impression that the desires of the petitioning union have a great deal to do with determining the community of interest of such employees. In *Dewey*, the union wanted the technicals in the unit, and they were found to have interests closely allied with employees in the unit. In *Meramec*, the union wanted a separate unit of technicals and there they were found *not* to have such an interest with other employees at the site, permitting the direction of an election as desired by the union.

Most of the foregoing cases convey an impression that the Kennedy Board has demonstrated greater concern for the objectives of the union than for the intent of Congress. Doubt as to the validity of the impression is eliminated by *Sav-On Drugs, Inc.,* 138 NLRB No. 61, 51 LRRM 1152 and *Knoxville News-Sentinel Co., Inc.,* 138 NLRB No. 91, 51 LRRM 1143. Both cases, as Rodgers points out in his dissents, show that, contrary to Section 9(c)(5) of the Act, the extent of the union's organization has become a decisive factor in determining the appropriateness of a bargaining unit.

In *Sav-On Drugs,* an election was directed in a unit consisting of a single store in a drug chain. The majority abandoned the long-established rule that the appropriate bargaining unit in retail chain store operations should embrace the employees of all stores within an employer's administrative or geographical area. The rule was based on the centralized control of chain store operations, the affinity between stores in a geographical area, common personnel affairs and frequent interchange of employees. As Rodgers pointed out, the majority's sole reason for the new position was "our experience" that the old rule operated to impede the employees' right to self-organization. In his words, "Established precedent ought not to be overturned on the basis of such conclusionary generalizations."

The *Knoxville News-Sentinel* case directed an election in a unit of mailroom employees at a publishing plant. The mailroom was a small segment of the Circulation Department, functionally integrated with that Department. In Rodgers' view, ". . . it is clear to me that my colleagues are making the Union's extent of organization the controlling factor in this case—contrary to the specific prohibition of Section 9(c)(5) of the Act." In addition, the majority followed the union's request and excluded approximately half the employees in the mailroom because they worked only part-time. Part-time employees who work regularly, as did these, have consistently been included in bargaining units with related full-time workers. Also, see *Dixie Belle Mills, Inc.*, 139 NLRB No. 61, 51 LRRM 1344.

A review of bargaining units is heavy going at best and even the rapidly changing rules of the game provided by the New Frontier add little zest to the experience. Nevertheless, once accomplished, the unit cases add to the all-important "feel" of the new Board's approach. They make it apparent that reliance on precedent during the coming years will be speculative, to say the least. The case-by-case approach is being followed, and the new Board has no hesitation in changing well-established rules. Precise patterns are difficult to discern, but it seems clear that the desires of the union on unit questions will carry an inordinate amount of weight and far greater fragmentation of units will, therefore, be permitted.

CHAPTER XI

REPRESENTATION CASES AND
FREEDOM OF CHOICE

With bargaining unit problems out of the way, the remainder of the Kennedy Board's innovations in representation matters are more easily brought into focus. Their "contract bar" revisions will probably have the broadest practical effect.

From its earliest decisions to the present day, the Board has been attempting to weigh the effect of an outstanding labor agreement on a representation proceeding. Termed the "contract bar" doctrine, the problem has been to balance the right of employees to change or reject their bargaining agent with the industrial stability represented by an existing collective bargaining agreement. Because the resulting rules have no statutory background but are "self-imposed and discretionary in application," they have been peculiarly subject to modification as they have reflected the views of individual Board members.

William Feldesman, the present Solicitor of the Board, in an able article in the December, 1960, issue of *The George Washington Law Review*, said:

> "It is apparent at a glance that the Board has formulated its contract bar principles after careful study and weighty deliberation. Rules which have been evolved reflect an earnest effort to reconcile stability and freedom of choice in

terms of industrial reality, with due regard for the sanctity of contracts that are in consonance with the letter and spirit of the collective bargaining statute, and with appropriate safeguards for the protection of the individual employee's right to voice his desires and the democratic concept of majority rule. To the Board's further credit, the enunciated principles are clear and intelligible, informing contracting parties, and those seeking elections despite existing collective agreements, precisely where they stand and how they may act."

Mr. Feldesman then went on to emphasize the need for examination of the rules after an opportunity for fair testing to assure they "do justice," thus avoiding the danger of "blind application of inelastic principles."

The principles stated by Mr. Feldesman are sound and practical. The Kennedy Board has examined most of the important contract bar principles and has made important changes. The question thus becomes whether the established precedents have been demonstrated to be outmoded and the revisions offer, even in theory, better solutions.

Most important of the contract bar rules is that applicable to long term contracts. In 1947 the Board decided that a period of two years was a reasonable time during which employees, in the interest of bargaining stability, must forego voting on a bargaining representative. Previously a one year rule had been used. Long term contracts therefore were a bar to an election proceeding for no more than two years. In a policy change widely supported by interested parties, the Kennedy Board recently extended the rule to three years. *General Cable Corp.*, 139 NLRB No. 111, 51 LRRM 1444.

An early decision by the new members, however, adopted a much more questionable policy. In effect they decided that contract bar rules should be applied in some instances but not in others with the controlling factor to be the identity of the party seeking the election. *Montgomery Ward & Co., Inc.*, 137 NLRB No. 26, 50 LRRM 1137. Although not entirely clear from the decision, it appears that Local 1594 of the Retail Clerks had a five year contract with Montgomery Ward covering employees at its Covington, Kentucky, catalog store. During the third year of the contract, the employer filed an election petition asserting a question of representation existed because Local 1099, with which Local 1594 had merged, was not a legal successor to the contracting union. The employer also alleged a substantial change in its operations and in the character of the unit.

An unpublished decision of the Board, issued November 22, 1961, directed an election, finding the contract not a bar because the petition was filed during its third year. Local 1099 petitioned for reconsideration, contending the Board's decision would unfairly permit the employer to escape its contract obligations. The Kennedy Board reconsidered the case and dismissed the petition in accordance with the union's request. McCulloch, Fanning and Brown decided the contract bar doctrine should be modified to provide that, where the incumbent union is the certified bargaining agent, a current contract will bar a petition by either of the contracting parties during the entire term of the contract. They then stated the new rule to be:

> "Accordingly, we hold that absent a conflicting timely claim by a rival union, a petition by either of (the) parties to a contract is timely only when filed at the proper time with respect to the contract's expiration date."

After stressing the balancing of interests underlying the whole contract bar doctrine, the majority found no necessity for striking a balance where parties to the contract were involved. They were not rival claimants and a petition by either did not indicate possible employee dissatisfaction, which would be shown only by a timely petition filed by a rival union or by employees seeking decertification supported by at least a 30% showing of interest. The old rule, according to the *Montgomery Ward* decision, permitted employers or certified unions to take advantage of whatever benefits might accrue from the contract with the knowledge that they could avoid their contractual obligations by petitioning for an election. Finally, the majority declared the new rule was not contrary to Sec. 9(c)(2), which requires that the same rules of decision apply regardless of who files the petition, because the legislative history showed the section was enacted to assure equal treatment as between affiliated and independent unions. Rodgers and Leedom dissented, maintaining the majority position was in violation of Section 9(c)(2). In their view a rule which makes a contract a bar for its full term if a petition is filed by a certified union or an employer, but only for a limited period if a rival union petitions, clearly fixes different rules depending on the identity of the party filing.

The *Montgomery Ward* rule was extended in *The Absorbent Cotton Co.*, 137 NLRB No. 93, 50 LRRM 1258, to bar an employer petition filed during the third year of a contract with an *uncertified* union. It seems clear that a petition filed by the union would have been processed in order to give the union the benefit of certification.

Returning to the question posed earlier in the chapter, have the majority members demonstrated that the prior long-established contract bar rules failed to "do justice"? They obviously believe an affirmative answer is warranted because, from the language of *Montgomery Ward,* no balancing of interests is involved and the old rule permitted either party to avoid its contractural obligations. Although this reasoning would appear to apply with equal force whether the contracting union was certified or uncertified, the majority has distinguished the two situations. An election would be as effective in avoiding the contractual obligations of the former as the latter and the advantages of certification to an incumbent union during the term of a valid bargaining agreement are more theoretical than practical.

The avoidance of contractual obligation argument is questionable in any event. For the employer to accomplish this goal, he must not only file a petition but he must also convince his employees to vote the union out, no mean accomplishment if the employees are satisfied with their union or their contract. The union which petitions, on the other hand, can avoid its obligations only if the employees vote against the union and it loses its status as bargaining agent, a rather drastic procedure. If the employees themselves are sufficiently interested in avoiding the contract, they need only form a new organization, file a petition, and it will be processed because it is a "rival" claim. In either instance, if the employees vote against the union it is apparent that they are dissatisfied with their representative and, by having been given the opportunity to vote, their freedom to select or reject their bargaining agent has been protected.

The new rule raises doubt in another way as to whether the conflicting interests involved are being properly balanced. The majority asserted that possible employee dissatisfaction would be shown only by a timely petition filed by a rival union or by employees seeking decertification. But the *Montgomery Ward* rule, as quoted above, excepts only a claim "by a rival union." Does this mean that a decertification petition will therefore be dismissed if filed at any time prior to the expiration date of the long term contract? If so, the employees' freedom of choice is clearly subordinated to industrial stability *unless a rival union enters the picture.* As of this writing, no published cases provide an answer.

Although the balancing-of-interest principle is the fundamental reason for the contract bar doctrine, the Board has also used the device as a means of implementing proscriptions on conduct listed in the unfair labor practice sections of the Act. In *Keystone Coat, Apron and Towel Supply Co.*, 121 NLRB 880, 42 LRRM 1456, 43 LRRM 1251, the Eisenhower Board held that a contract containing a union security provision which, on its face, does not conform to the Act will not bar an election, for example.

Keystone was reversed by the new Board in *Paragon Products Corp.*, 134 NLRB No. 86, 49 LRRM 1160, and the new rule is that only those contractual union security clauses which are clearly unlawful, or which have been held unlawful in an unfair labor practice proceeding, will not bar an election. Such clauses include those which specifically require an employer to give preference to union members in hiring, laying off, or for seniority purposes; those which specifically withhold from non-union or new employees the statutory 30 day grace period; and those which specifically require, as a condition of employment, payment of money other than periodic dues and initiation fees uniformly required. Contracts containing ambiguous, though not clearly unlawful, union security provisions will bar representation proceedings in the absence of a Board or court determination of their illegality. No evidence will be admissible in a representation proceeding to show the practice under the union security provisions in question. The majority observed that the *Keystone* case required a "presumption of illegality" and that such presumptions had recently been sharply circumscribed by the Supreme Court. It was believed unsound administrative practice in the face of such language to continue applying a rule with respect to union security provisions indulging in precisely the type of presumption frowned upon by the court.

Rodgers and Leedom dissented, pointing out that the rules of the *Keystone* case were not based upon a presumption of illegality and that they were established for contract bar purposes only, an area where the board has broad discretion. They also took exception to the majority finding that the *Keystone* rules had an "extremely unsettling impact upon established collective bargaining relations," and that "a substantial bulk of the contracts containing perfectly legal union-security provisions cannot meet the strict test required by Keystone," declaring that the majority offered no support for its "categorical pronouncement."

A similar departure from precedent is found in *Food Haulers, Inc.,* 136 NLRB No. 36, 49 LRRM 1774. There McCulloch, Fanning and Brown found a contract to be a bar, even though it contained an alleged "hot-cargo" provision, over-ruling *Pilgrim Furniture Co., Inc.,* 128 NLRB 910, 46 LRRM 1427. They distinguished unlawful union security clauses as a contract bar because the existence of such provisions acts as a restraint upon those desiring to refrain from union activities, interfering with one of the objectives sought to be balanced by the contract bar rules. In their view, a hot-cargo clause does not in any sense act as a restraint upon an employee's choice of a bargaining representative. Rodgers and Leedom dissented, expressing the belief that the only difference between an unlawful hot-cargo clause and an unlawful union security clause is one of form. The important factor is that both violate the Act and are in conflict with it. Congress did not distinguish between the gravity of unfair labor practice provisions and neither should the Board.

In *Hebron Brick Co.,* 135 NLRB No. 16, 49 LRRM 1463, a Teamsters' petition was barred by a contract between the employer and the Clay Workers which provided specifically that it applied only to members of the union. The majority, relying on extrinsic evidence, ruled that the contract did not mean what it said and that the intent and practice of the parties was to apply it to all production and maintenance employees. Rodgers dissented (Leedom did not participate), pointing out that the decision was inconsistent with *Appalachian Shale Products Co.,* 121 NLRB 1160, 42 LRRM 1506, in which the Board said, "to serve as a bar, a contract must clearly, by its terms, encompass the employees sought in the petition." The majority's willingness to accept extrinsic evidence in the *Hebron Brick* case is in sharp contrast to its emphatic refusal to do so in the illegal union security clause cases, such as *Paragon Products.*

New Laxton Coal Co., 134 NLRB No. 92, 49 LRRM 1287, illustrates the difficulties a successor employer may have in asserting a contract bar. In April, 1960, the United Mine Workers petitioned for a unit of employees of C. & P. Coal Company, which operated a mine under a lease arrangement with the owner. While the petition was pending, C. & P. Coal ceased operations and surrendered all rights under its lease to the owner. In October, 1960, New Laxton entered into a similar lease arrangement and, when its employees joined Southern Labor Union, a collective bargaining agreement was executed. In September, 1961, eleven months after it began operations, and without ever having been made a party to the Mine Workers' petition or receiving any notice of it, New Laxton was ordered by the Board to show cause why it should not be substituted for C. & P. Coal in the Mine Workers' proceedings.

Leedom, Fanning and Brown found New Laxton to be a successor because, though there was no relation between it and C. & P. Coal, it used the same equipment and hired many of the same employees. Therefore, the contract was not a bar and an election was directed without the Mine Workers being required to obtain a new showing of interest. Rodgers dissented, pointing out that, though the Mine Workers' petition was pending while New Laxton was entering into the lease and its employees joining Southern Labor Union, it was never made a party to that proceeding. Now, without New Laxton or Southern Labor Union having been afforded a hearing, an election was directed. He viewed such an action as unsound, unfair, and as depriving both of due process of law.

One more contract bar rule changed by the new Board is that involving guard units. In *Columbia-Southern Chem-*

ical Corp., 110 NLRB 1189, 35 LRRM 1212, a unanimous
Board, consisting of Eisenhower appointees Farmer, Rodgers
and Beeson, as well as Abe Murdock and Ivar Peterson,
who had been appointed by Truman, found that a contract
between an employer and a non-guard union covering a
guard unit was not an effective bar. They reasoned that
a contrary result would be inconsistent with Sec. 9(b)(3)
of the Act which proscribes certification of a union for a
guard unit if the union also admits non-guards to membership.

In *The Burns Detective Agency,* 134 NLRB No. 36, 49
LRRM 1145, McCulloch, Fanning, Brown and Rodgers
(who was also a member when *Columbia-Southern* was decided) found such a contract to be a bar. They decided
Section 9(b)(3) precludes units containing both guards and
non-guards and prohibits certification of a union representing
guards which also admits non-guards to membership, but
it does *not* declare the latter units to be inappropriate. They
believed it followed that a unit of guards exclusively is not
invalidated because the union admits non-guards to membership and there is no reason not to apply usual contract bar
rules. Leedom, dissenting, would have adhered to the previous rule on the ground the legislative history demonstrated
guards could have the protection of the act only if they had
a union separate and apart from a union of general employees. It is an interesting sidelight that the Building Service
Employees' Union, which was party to the contract with
Burns, acquired its status by employer voluntary recognition
after an election in which it did not appear on the ballot
(even though then the incumbent) and a majority voted
"no union."

Eligibility to vote in a Board conducted election has been
considered in depth by the new Board and, as indicated in
our earlier discussion of *Pacific Tile and Porcelain Co.,* 137
NLRB No. 169, 50 LRRM 1394, some decisive changes in

policy have been made. During the early days of NLRB strikers were permitted to vote but their replacements, even though permanent, were not allowed to do so. Later the rule was changed to allow both strikers and replacements to participate in the election and, in Taft-Hartley, Congress took a further step and specifically eliminated voting by replaced strikers. Landrum-Griffin included a shift in the other direction and once more the replaced strikers were given a vote but only for 12 months after commencement of the strike.

The Eisenhower Board issued several cases interpreting the amendment, making clear, for example, that replacements will continue to be permitted to vote. Among the policy changes of the Kennedy Board are the adoption of the presumption in *Pacific Tile,* that an economic striker retains his interest in his job and is therefore eligible to vote. The party challenging his status has the burden of proof to show the contrary and it is not met, even though it is proven that the striker has taken a new job without informing his new employer that he only wanted a temporary job. The same case placed a similar burden on the party challenging the permanent status of a replacement, but employees hired as permanent replacements who, unknown to the employer were students on summer vacation, were not eligible.

In *American Metal Products Co.,* 139 NLRB No. 60, 51 LRRM 1338, the Board decided that former employees who had been replaced were strikers and eligible to vote, despite the fact that the union had announced the strike was ended and the strikers had unconditionally sought reinstatement. And in *Greenspan Engraving Corp.,* 137 NLRB No. 135, 50 LRRM 1380, the new Board over-ruled *Tampa Sand & Material Co.,* 129 NLRB 1275, 47 LRRM 1166, and found permanent replacements hired after the election eligibility date but before election day may vote only if the strike started after the Board's direction of election issued. Between 1947 and 1959, the problem caused little difficulty as neither economic strikers nor replacements hired *after* the eligibility date voted. When the 1959 amendments were added and strikers given the right to vote, the Eisenhower Board found that Congress did not intend to disenfranchise replacements. They therefore decided the only equitable solution was to make eligibility of both replacements and economic strikers dependent on their status on election day. McCulloch, Fanning and Brown could see no reason why replacements hired after the eligibility date needed special treatment, unless the strike commenced after that date and there was no opportunity to hire replacements. Rodgers and Leedom dissented, following *Tampa Sand*.

In each instance the direction of the new eligibility rules aids the striker at the expense of the employees who will constitute the bargaining unit. The employer's burden of proving that the striker who has taken other employment is no longer interested in the struck job leaves the choice of status largely to the striker. A striker is entitled to vote for a year even though the strike is over and his job has been permanently filled by another. Individuals who have been discharged, regardless of the reason, apparently can vote if a grievance is filed. And, elimination of recently hired replacements from the voting aids the strikers, particularly where it has been difficult to hire replacements whether because of respect for the picket line or fear of union reprisals.

Another major change of approach in representation matters is found in *Great Western Sugar Co.*, 137 NLRB No. 73, 50 LRRM 1186. There McCulloch, Fanning and Brown decided that "seasonal supervisors" should be permitted to vote in representation elections. They ruled such individuals are supervisors when in that status and rank-and-file employees the balance of the time. If an election occurs while they are in the supervisory status, they will be permitted to vote. Otherwise they are denied the right to bargain collectively. "Part-time" supervisors were distinguished and will continue to be excluded.

Rodgers and Leedom dissented, arguing that Congress specifically excluded supervisors from the Act in 1947 because of its concern over their interference with and domination of rank-and-file employees and the employers' loss of loyalty and control over such individuals. In their view, the same considerations apply whether an individual is a full-time supervisor, a supervisor for several months out of the year and a rank-and-file employee the rest of the time, or a part-time supervisor employed elsewhere most of the year. The majority answered the interference argument by dropping a footnote declaring the Board's decision was not to be taken as a license to seasonal supervisors to interfere with, restrain or coerce other employees.

If McCulloch's dissent in *Rohr Aircraft Corporation*, 136 NLRB No. 102, 49 LRRM 1886, becomes the law another interesting change in election case procedure will take place. There 45 votes were cast for an independent union and 44 for the Machinists. The latter objected because the Board agent failed to notify certain temporarily laid-off employees (who may have been eligible voters) of the time, date and place of election. Rodgers, Leedom and Fanning dismissed the objections, declaring it would place an impossible burden on the Board agent to uncover all conceivable voters. The agent was not apprised by the Machinists or anyone else of the existence of such employees until after the election. The Machinists had checked the eligibility list and certified it as accurate.

McCulloch dissented, arguing that the election result might have been different if any of the employees in question had voted. He did not view the question as one of whether the Board agent was remiss in not notifying the eligible voters or the union was remiss in carrying out its obligations. The issue was whether the employees had a full and free opportunity to participate in the election. Here, wherever the fault lay, they did not. While McCulloch's approach may be sound in theory, its practical effect would be to open the door for objections in a multitude of cases. Furthermore, the permanency of lay-off status is frequently controversial and, where a losing union can obtain another chance at an election by producing former employees who did not receive adequate notice, a fertile field for litigation is established.

When compared with the Board's former policies, the new revisions are less, rather than more, effective in reducing industrial strife and in protecting the rights of employees. The contract bar rules which were "clear and intelligible" now leave a number of questions unanswered. Presumably, the status of decertification petitions will be clarified, but the determination of a "clearly unlawful" union security contract, sufficient to remove a contract as a bar, is more complex and will require many interpretations before clear guidelines appear. Revised voting eligibility requirements may result in some increase in predictability of result but at the expense of the employees' freedom of choice. Permitting seasonal supervisors to vote is another direct infringement on employee rights.

Many of the cases discussed in this and the previous chapter reflect reversed precedents. Very few present compelling reasons for a revised rule. Individually, they frequently seem of minor importance but, taken as a whole, they represent a major agitation of long-established labor management relationships. As such, they are bound to have a disrupting impact on industrial peace.

CHAPTER XII

NLRB AT THE BARGAINING TABLE

In bargaining cases, where the duty of the employer and the union is to bargain in good faith, the case-by-case approach might be expected to have an important application. "Good faith" is difficult to define and it would seem particularly appropriate to look at all the facts and circumstances of each situation. It is in this area, however, that the Kennedy Board has not only failed to follow its announced policy but has applied a per se rule with highly questionable results.

In *Mar-Jac Poultry Co., Inc.*, 136 NLRB No. 73, 49 LRRM 1854, the Meat Cutters' Union had been certified on November 17, 1959 as bargaining agent of the employees of McKibbon Bros. Mar-Jac bought the McKibbon equipment and leased its property on February 1, 1960. The union requested Mar-Jac to bargain on March 1 and, on June 8, 1960, filed a refusal to bargain charge. Mar-Jac entered into a settlement agreement under which it promised to bargain in good faith with the union, a commitment which it apparently carried out, as the Regional Director issued a letter of compliance November 7, 1960.

Bargaining sessions at which considerable progress was made continued until February 2, 1961. About three weeks later, the union again filed refusal to bargain charges which were investigated and then dismissed by the Regional Director on March 29, 1961, the same day the employer filed a petition for an election.

A panel consisting of McCulloch, Fanning and Brown (Rodgers and Leedom did not participate) refused to direct an election, applying the rule that, absent unusual circumstances, an employer will be required to honor a certification for a period of one year. One reason for the rule, according to the majority is to give the union "ample time for carrying out its mandate" and, another, is to prevent an employer from knowing that if he "dilly dallies" he may erode the union's strength and relieve himself of the duty to bargain. The employer was found to have negotiated with the union for only six months, rather than twelve, since the date of the settlement agreement. Therefore, Mar-Jac was ordered to bargain an additional six months. *Daily Press, Inc.*, 112 NLRB 1434, 36 LRRM 1228, where the Eisenhower Board, including Murdock and Peterson, reached the opposite conclusion under similar circumstances, was over-ruled. That Board rested its decision on the rights of the employees, feeling it would be inequitable to deprive them of their franchise in view of the substantial lapse in time since an election held about eighteen months earlier.

The majority members made no reference in the *Mar-Jac* case to the period from mid-November, 1959, until March 1, 1960, during which the union apparently did not attempt to bargain. They also ignored the Regional Director's dismissal of charges on March 29, 1961, the day the petition was filed, which indicated no lack of good faith as of that date. If these periods were added, the union's alloted twelve months would have virtually expired. More important, the majority said nothing of the validity of the employer's reason for breaking off negotiations and filing the petition in 1961, and was silent as to the rights of the employees. It is apparent that, had an election been directed, the employees could have exercised their free choice by giving the union a vote of approval, thereby strengthening its bargaining position, or voting it out if that was their desire. An arbitrary order to bargain for six months is a blind application of a "per se" rule, reflecting more interest in form than substance, and in noticeable contrast to the Kennedy Board's stated policy.

The other case is *Lamar Hotel*, 137 NLRB No. 136, 50 LRRM 1366. There the Hotel Employees' Union was certified on September 23, 1960, as bargaining agent in a unit consisting of all of the Lamar employees with certain exceptions. Bargaining commenced but a dispute arose over the unit placement of eleven out of approximately 220 employees. The union filed a refusal to bargain charge on March 28, 1961, but withdrew it "pursuant to the advice of the Regional Director" on May 18, 1961, and filed a motion for clarification of the certified unit. Prior to a hearing on the motion, but after the end of the certification year, an employee (on November 3, 1961) filed a decertification petition.

The Kennedy Board (Rodgers and Leedom not participating) refused to grant the decertification petition and gave the union another six months in which to bargain, citing its decision in *Mar-Jac*. At the hearing, the parties stipulated as to the unit treatment of nine of the eleven employees in dispute, one had quit, and the eleventh was excluded as contended by the employer.

The decision leaves a good many questions unanswered, but the Board's formal file in the matter shows that the unit placement dispute arose out of the union's refusal to take a positive position, one way or another, as to placement of the individuals in question. The Regional Director viewed the disagreement between the parties as bona fide and, therefore, suggested withdrawal of the charge. The union elected to follow his suggestion, filed the motion for clarification, and made no further attempt to bargain.

Once more, the majority showed no concern over the

rights of the employees. By July 14, 1962, when the Board's decision issued, the certification was almost two years old. While the parties apparently did not engage in bargaining after the first six months, there is no showing that this was the fault of the employer or that the employer failed to act in good faith. Instead, the lack of bargaining arose out of the intransigence of the union and its election of procedural steps. By filing the decertification petition, at least 30% of the employees demonstrated they wanted a secret ballot election. Why should they be denied this right? As in the *Mar-Jac* case, if they voted for the union, the hand of their bargaining agent would be strengthened. If they voted against it, they would have exercised their right to refrain from concerted activities as the Act provides.

The foregoing cases provide a startling contrast to *Rocky Mountain Phosphates, Inc.*, 138 NLRB No. 35, 51 LRRM 1019. There the Board, on June 30, 1960, certified an independent union as representative of Rocky Mountain's employees. Several months later, apparently because of dissatisfaction with bargaining progress, the employees dissolved the independent and designated Local 375 of the Operating Engineers as their representative. When Local 375 requested recognition on April 6, 1961, (approximately nine months after the certification), the employer refused.

McCulloch, Fanning and Brown found a refusal to bargain in good faith in violation of Section 8(a)(5), because the employer was fully aware that the certified union had become defunct and that Local 375 had been designated as bargaining agent by the employees. They held the employer must bargain, even though the statutory provision (which permits only one election per year) would bar an election. Rodgers and Leedom dissented, finding it improper to place a duty on the employer to determine whether or not the certified representative was defunct where the employees, by moving to set aside the certification, could ask the Board to make the determination. The employer must act at his peril under these circumstances and, if he makes an error of judgment in either direction, he has violated the Act. They pointed out the sharp contrast between the Supreme Court rule in *Ray Brooks v. N.L.R.B.*, 348 US 96, 35 LRRM 2158, holding that an employer should not resolve on its own the bargaining status of the certified representative, and the majority's view here; the latter would force the employer to do precisely what *Ray Brooks* said he should not do.

One final example provides another illustration of the new Board's willingness to place an employer in an impossible situation. After the IBEW was certified as bargaining representative of the employees of Sunbeam Lighting Company of Gary, Indiana, the employees appointed five of their members to act as a bargaining committee. The IBEW representative sat on the committee as spokesman. After several bargaining sessions, the employee chairman informed the IBEW representative that the employees were so dissatisfied with the way negotiations were proceeding that they were going to strike the following day. No strike was held and a few days later the employer presented his "final" contract proposals which the committee was to take back to the employees. The IBEW agent suggested to the committee members that they not reveal the terms of the employer's offer until all the employees were together at a planned meeting. The agent then returned to his office in Chicago, some 75 miles away, and made no further appearances at the plant.

The following morning, the news of the employer's final offer had spread among the employees and, at 10:00 a.m., approximately 75 employees in a unit of 120 walked out of the plant. The IBEW agent was informed of the walkout and told the chairman to arrange a meeting at the CIO hall that evening. Meanwhile, some of the employer's supervisors circulated among the strikers and told them to come back to work or they would be considered as "voluntarily" quitting because they had left the plant without permission in violation of a plant rule. About thirty returned.

That evening, prior to the meeting at the CIO hall, the committee chairman received a telegram from the IBEW agent, stating there would be no further union or negotiating meetings while the unauthorized work stoppage continued. The committee chairman read the telegram to the strikers and they voted unanimously to return to work the next morning. In the meantime, the employer had mailed termination letters to the strikers who had refused to return and, when they appeared at the plant the next morning, they were informed that they had terminated themselves and would not be permitted to work. The employer closed the plant for about a week, and, after another IBEW representative was assigned, the employer agreed to "re-employ" certain of the strikers. The employer's basic contention was that the walkout was a "wildcat strike," that it undermined the bargaining representative, and the strikers were therefore engaged in unprotected activity.

McCulloch, Fanning and Brown held the employer had violated Section 8(a)(3) of the Act by discharging and refusing to reinstate the strikers, since their walkout was a privileged expression of their dissatisfaction with the employer's offer and was for the purpose of strengthening the status of their bargaining committee. Even though less than a majority of the employees participated, the strike was protected and the appearance of all strikers at the plant the following morning satisfied the requirement that they make an unconditional application for reinstatement. *Sunbeam Lighting Co.*, 136 NLRB No. 107, 49 LRRM 1963.

Rodgers and Leedom dissented, finding the conduct unprotected because it tended to usurp the authority of the certified bargaining representative. The union neither called, authorized nor sanctioned the walkout. They pointed out that the effect of the majority decision was to make the five-man employee committee the true representative, despite the IBEW's certification as *exclusive* bargaining agent. They also emphasized the absence of evidence that even a majority of the committee supported the strike. The majority decision penalized the employer for failing to accede to the demands of a minority group, requiring the employer to infringe upon the statutory rights of the IBEW as bargaining agent. Thus, in their view, the employer was forced to choose between a violation of Section 8(a)(5), by bargaining with the employees rather than with their representative, or of Section 8(a)(1) and (3), by discharging strikers who sought to force the employer into the other violation.

Although the Act requires both the employer and the union to bargain in good faith, it is well established neither must concede to any particular demand made by the other. Both the legislative history and court decisions make it clear that the Board has no right to sit in judgment on the substantive terms of collective bargaining agreements. Nevertheless, previous Boards sometimes had difficulty drawing a line between a good faith attempt to reach agreement and the Board's idea of what the agreement should be. It is evident the new Board is having similar trouble.

During the course of 17 negotiating sessions between General Tire and Local 826 of the Operating Engineers, the union's list of items which "must" be included in a contract was reduced from 79 to 26. At the final meeting, the employer offered to compromise 9 of the remaining issues. Fanning and Brown found General Tire had not bargained in good faith and had no intention of entering into an agreement with the union because it first offered a wage scale less than it was currently paying and one less paid holiday. The same attitude was also demonstrated by the company's absolute refusal to any limitation on contracting out work, in their view, and by its refusal of the union's offer of capitulation to the employer's position in return for a check-off of dues. Rodgers dissented, recognizing that the bargaining was hard and long but feeling the substantial number of items agreed upon demonstrated the employer's good faith. *General Tire & Rubber Co.*, 135 NLRB No. 28, 49 LRRM 1469.

It is difficult to reconcile the Supreme Court holding in *N.L.R.B. v. American National Insurance Co.*, 343 US 395, 30 LRRM 2147, that the Act ". . . does not compel either party to agree to a proposal or require the making of a concession . . .", with the *General Tire* case. Certainly the Act contains no requirement that an employer must commence bargaining at the present level of wages and conditions of employment and negotiate in an upward direction only. But when the Board finds an employer's attempt to lower wages or reduce holidays indicative of bad faith, a very substantial limitation on bargaining flexibility has been imposed. There is not even a suggestion that the reverse—an exorbitant demand by the union—demonstrates bad faith. Furthermore, when the Board interjects its judgment as to limitations on contracting out or the merits of the employer's proposal vis-a-vis dues check-off, how can it be said that a party is neither required to agree to a proposal nor to make a concession? If the union demands a limitation on contracting out and the employer must agree, he has been forced to make a concession and the question then becomes the extent of the concession. If the employer makes a proposal and the union agrees if dues check-off is added, a Board ruling that the employer must accept the counter-proposal is compulsion to agree to the proposal.

A requirement that an employer must re-open a portion of a contract previously agreed upon, in effect, also compels him to make a concession. Sixty-three of Equitable Life Insurance Company's 482 debit agents were represented in two separate bargaining units by the Insurance Agent's International Union. Five months prior to the expiration of contracts covering the organized agents, Equitable increased commission rates for unrepresented employees and, following past practice, asked the union for approval to give the same increase to agents in the bargaining units. The agents in one unit accepted the increases but, with respect to the other, the union demanded bargaining as to ". . . increases in compensation, working conditions and other conditions of employment." Equitable advised that it was unwilling to make any other changes during the contract term.

McCulloch, Leedom and Brown viewed the union's demand as a request to bargain on the company proposal. Whether the union would insist on bargaining on a broader basis was speculative. Consequently, the employer created a "take it or leave it" situation, a refusal to bargain in good faith in their opinion. *Equitable Life Insurance Co.*, 133 NLRB No. 158, 49 LRRM 1070. Rodgers and Fanning dissented, pointing out that the union's demand specified bargaining on a broad basis. In any event, since the company had no duty to make the offer and did not undercut the union by making it, they felt there should be no duty to bargain about an offer that need not have been made.

Although Fanning dissented in the *Equitable Life* case, he joined with Leedom in finding a refusal to bargain on the part of an employer who declined to discuss a union demand for a unit which included supervisors. *Great Western Broadcasting Corp.*, 139 NLRB No. 11, 51 LRRM 1266. Rodgers dissented, arguing that the law clearly prohibited inclusion of supervisors and a request to bargain in an inappropriate unit cannot form the basis for a violation of the Act.

Employees of four Ohio refineries of Standard Oil Company (Ohio) were represented by the Oil Workers' Union, three contracts being with local unions and a fourth directly with the International. In the 1960 contract negotiations, the locals adopted a joint program which they considered binding on all unions involved in the negotiations. After several bargaining sessions, each designated certain representatives to sit in on "pilot" negotiations but the employer refused to bargain with these "temporary" representatives on the basis that it would be tantamount to company-wide bargaining and would evidence acquiescence in such a procedure. Individual plant bargaining was continued and, eventually, agreement was reached covering three of the four units. In each instance, however, after negotiations were completed and the contract ratified, union officials refused to sign until agreement was reached at the fourth refinery.

The Board (Rodgers not participating) found the company had failed to bargain in good faith by refusing to negotiate with the "temporary" representatives as they were duly appointed representatives of the employees in the bargaining units. A majority, consisting of Leedom, Fanning and Brown, also found a comparable violation on the part of the unions in refusing to sign the contracts. Their refusal was merely a device, unrelated to any dissatisfaction with the contract terms, intended to increase the bargaining power of the local at the fourth location. Therefore, according to the majority, an extraneous issue was imported into the bargaining after agreement had been reached. *Standard Oil Co., (Ohio),* 137 NLRB No. 68, 50 LRRM 1238.

McCulloch dissented as to the union violation, in essence viewing the union's conduct as a legitimate bargaining tactic. After pointing out the dissipation of bargaining strength flowing from a contract signed at one refinery prior to reaching agreement at others, he declared "the importance of collective bargaining . . . overrides the apparent expansion of the scope of the bargaining unit." As the majority pointed out, however, the issue was not the reasonableness of the union's conduct. Section 8(d) requires "execution of a written contract incorporating any agreement reached if requested by either party." Any attempt to force agreement in another bargaining unit with different contracting parties as a condition to such execution was a clear violation. The Act does not guarantee that unions will be afforded maximum bargaining strength in every situation.

The foregoing cases show an unusual alignment of Board members. Another peculiar split resulted from a dispute between Radio Corporation of America and the International Brotherhood of Electrical Workers. Their contract covered bargaining units in various plants of RCA and provided that new units organized by IBEW locals would automatically be included as part of the national agreement. Local 11 of IBEW won an election among the maintenance electricians at RCA's Los Angeles and Van Nuys plants. After the NLRB certification issued, Local 11 insisted that a separate agreement be negotiated covering the new group. Both the employer and the International Union contended that the national agreement must be applied.

A charge of refusal to bargain brought by Local 11 against RCA was dismissed by McCulloch, Rodgers and Leedom. They found that the national contract was executed by the IBEW of which Local 11 was an affiliate, that the Local's affiliation was explicitly stated in the representation election and certification, and that the terms of the national agreement were sufficiently consistent with the Local's objectives that it sought only minor modifications. *Radio Corporation of America*, 135 NLRB No. 100, 49 LRRM 1606.

Fanning and Brown, dissenting, analogized the case to that of an election in a bargaining unit where a contract is outstanding. There the Board has held a newly-certified union is not bound by its predecessor's agreement. The majority distinguished such cases as involving contracts negotiated by an unsuccessful rival union. According to the minority, even though the parent union considered the local bound because it must conform to the International's constitution and by-laws, Local 11 was not a party to the national agreement, did not negotiate, approve or ratify its terms, and did not now choose to do so. Finally, the minority argued that the national agreement covered industrial units, while this was a craft unit.

Still another example of the random pattern of opinion in these cases is *Hercules Motor Corp.*, 136 NLRB No. 145, 50 LRRM 1021. There the full Board, with Fanning dissenting, found Hercules did not fail to bargain in good faith by refusing to comply with a United Auto Workers' request that a union time-study man be permitted to examine the employer's data pertaining to a grievance over employer establishment of standard hours unit rates. During negotiations on the existing collective bargaining agreement, the union made repeated attempts to incorporate provisions giving the union a broad right to employer data and to investigate such grievances. These demands had been resisted by Hercules and were not included in the contract as executed. The agreement clearly required that all disputes be settled under the grievance and arbitration procedure. The majority decided the policy of the Act—to encourage the practice and procedure of collective bargaining—would be best fostered by requiring that "full play" be given to means chosen by the parties for settlement of disputes, i.e. the grievance procedure.

In a vigorous dissent, Fanning contended that the majority was over-ruling the long line of Board decisions requiring an employer to furnish the union information necessary for the proper functioning of a bargaining agent. The majority answered that the issue presented in *Hercules Motor* was whether the union had a right, under the contract, to grieve about the wage rates in question. This was a dispute for whose resolution the contract specifically provided machinery and, until that dispute was settled in the union's favor, there was no need for the union to have the information sought.

The Kennedy Board might have been expected to adopt a very broad interpretation of the duty of the employer to furnish information to the bargaining agent, including the necessity of providing the union with information such as that demanded here. Perhaps the explanation lies in the fact that McCulloch and Brown seem anxious to strengthen voluntarily adopted means of settling disputes. The *Hercules Motor* decision will further that goal. But, compare their views in *Timken Roller Bearing Co.*, 138 NLRB No. 1, 50 LRRM 1508.

A more important standing for grievance and arbitration procedures also is evident in *Montgomery Ward & Co.*, 137 NLRB No. 41, 50 LRRM 1162, where McCulloch and Rodgers held that the employer did not refuse to bargain with the certified union over the establishment of two new truck terminals, as it had notified the union of its intention well in advance and the union had never requested bargaining but had merely objected to the employer's refusal to apply a contract at an existing terminal to drivers transferred to the new terminals. They found the parties had a specific grievance and arbitration procedure in the contract which both had agreed should be used to settle the dispute but, instead, the union filed NLRB charges. Fanning agreed with the former proposition and would not reach the grievance question, but Brown emphasized that he would dismiss the complaint on the sole ground that the grievance procedure was available.

Although arising out of a discrimination case, *International Harvester Co.*, 138 NLRB No. 88, 51 LRRM 1155, is the clearest demonstration of the new Board's views on the weight to be given an arbitration award. There McCulloch, Leedom and Brown dismissed a complaint which would have had the effect of setting aside an arbitrator's award upholding the discharge of an employee under a union security contract. The arbitration involved an employee whom the union sought to have discharged after he cancelled his check-off authorization and became delinquent in his dues. The plant was located in Indiana, which had passed a "right to work" law during the term of the contract. The grievance leading to the arbitration was filed after the union shop contract expired. When the award (which amounted to a reduction in seniority) resulted in the employee's lay-off, he filed charges against both the union and the employer.

The majority, adverting to Supreme Court opinions strengthening the arbitration process, declared it would voluntarily withhold its authority to decide unfair labor practice charges involving the same subject matter as an arbitration proceeding, unless fraud, collusion, unfairness, or serious procedural irregularities were demonstrated, or the award was clearly repugnant to the purposes and policies of the Act. Rodgers dissented because the grievance was filed after the contract had expired. Fanning also dissented, agreeing with the Trial Examiner that the union had pursued the grievance to arbitration in order to secure the discharge of the employee and the company had complied with the award. The *International Harvester Co.* case indicates that the Board will be most reluctant to exercise its jurisdiction where arbitration provisions of a contract are applicable, and thus will give more weight to an arbitration award than has previously been its policy.

The significance of wide variations in the approach of the various Board members to the foregoing cases lies in the uncertainty which results. During recent years, many employers have been forced by economic necessity into hard bargaining. Such bargaining increases the probability of strikes and, without clear guidelines for good faith bargaining, an economic strike may be converted to the unfair labor practice variety. When this occurs, the employer's opportunity to continue operating by hiring replacements is substantially reduced because of the strikers' rights to oust the replacements when the strike ends. The cases are of little guidance, and no pattern of decisions has developed.

The greater weight given grievance and arbitration procedures may be helpful in some instances. But the lack of a pattern of individual views clouds the true impact of the decisions. Also, the standards announced in *International Harvester* are sufficiently broad and ambiguous to permit many cases to go either way. Again, the employer is faced with a difficult problem in forecasting Board action.

The new Board's indifference to the employer's dilemma in cases such as *Rocky Mountain Phosphates,* where he must determine at his peril an issue which could and should be determined by the Board, is in direct conflict with the Congressional purpose of delineating rights of employers, employees and unions. The same lack of concern for the employer's problem and the Congressional intent is demonstrated by *Sunbeam Lighting.* In neither instance is there any compelling reason for ruling against the employer.

Employees fare no better. The *Mar-Jac* rule utterly disregards their rights in favor of the certified union and, in the process, weakens the strength of a bargaining agent favored by the employees. Employee rights may appear to have been protected in *Rocky Mountain Phosphates,* but the result was to grant bargaining status to an international union without a secret vote. Conspicuously missing in these cases are any examples of rights of unions subordinated to those of the employees.

CHAPTER XIII

REFUSAL TO BARGAIN-CONTRACTING OUT AND PLANT REMOVAL

The decision of the Kennedy Board in *Town & Country Mfg. Co., Inc.,* 136 NLRB No. 111, 49 LRRM 1918, was the forerunner of one of the most controversial interpretations of the law issued by any NLRB. It has far-reaching implications for employers and places an enormous premium on technical competence in threading one's way through the morass of Board rules without being spattered by the mud of alleged bad faith.

Town & Country is a manufacturer of house trailers. Since beginning operations in 1956, the Company had used various arrangements for delivering completed trailers, but minor problems with respect to compliance with ICC regulations were a constant irritant. About July 1959, the difficulties became more serious and it was decided to make deliveries with company-owned trucks operated by employee-drivers. The new arrangement caused considerable dissatisfaction among the drivers, who were terminated as independent contractors and hired as employees. In August of 1959, most of them joined a local of the Teamsters' Union. The employer resisted the organizing drive, but the union was certified as bargaining agent on October 1, 1959. The first bargaining meeting was held October 19 and, as admitted by the business agent, considerable progress was made. At the conclusion of the meeting, the employer agreed to submit a counter-proposal in about ten days.

On October 27, an ICC investigator, who had been asked to look over the new delivery system shortly after its adoption in July but who had been unable to make his inspection earlier, finally appeared at the company office. After a brief investigation, he informed the company general manager that he believed the employer was guilty of more than one hundred violations of ICC regulations and indicated criminal action would be taken. Within a matter of hours, the general manager, seeking to avoid further violations, tentatively decided that the best solution was to use commercial truckers operating under ICC permits and to discontinue company deliveries. A final decision was not made until November 1, but on October 29 the union was notified that such action might be taken and invited to discuss the matter. The union did not press for an immediate meeting, and none was held for about two weeks, although the plan was gradually put into effect, beginning November 1.

The Kennedy Board held that the employer had failed to bargain about the decision to subcontract unit work prior to making such a decision in violation of the good faith bargaining requirements in the Act. The majority also ruled that the economic reasons for the employer's action, i.e., the ICC difficulties, were a mere pretext, the company's true motive being to penalize the drivers for having selected a union as bargaining agent. *Fibreboard Paper Products Corp.*, 130 NLRB No. 161, 47 LRRM 1547, which held that Congress did not intend to compel bargaining concerning basic management decisions (such as whether and to what extent to risk capital and managerial effort) was over-ruled. As a remedy, Town & Country was ordered to resume the delivery system which it had discontinued and to pay back pay to the drivers involved. Also, see *American Mfg. Co. of Texas*, 139 NLRB No. 57, 51 LRRM 1392.

The practical effect of the decision is to require that an employer must bargain with the union prior to taking any step which eliminates work currently being performed by employees represented by the union. An unanswered question is the extent to which he must discuss the situation. If the employer has any duty to talk with the union, it is apparent that it goes further than merely informing the union of the action to be taken.

The theory of the majority members rested upon the principle that the duty to bargain about the decision to contract out was a mandatory subject of bargaining because it involved the elimination of jobs from the bargaining unit, and thus terms and conditions of employment. They did not see the obligation to bargain as imposing an undue burden nor as obligating the employer to agree to anything.

Rodgers and Leedom dissented on the ground that the statutory obligation to bargain is not so broad and all-inclusive as to warrant an inference that Congress intended to compel bargaining concerning basic management decisions. Leedom agreed with the majority that the truck drivers were discharged for discriminatory, rather than economic reasons. In his view, the employer terminated the trucking operation to rid itself of the union. Therefore, the drivers remained employees, and the employer's duty to bargain with them continued. Rodgers dissented from this holding also, as he found the motivation for the conduct to have stemmed from the ICC difficulties. In his view, if the decision to terminate an operation is a management prerogative, a duty to bargain about its effects renders the prerogative meaningless.

The most alarming aspect of the *Town & Country* case is its remedy. Not only was the employer required to bargain with the union about the decision to terminate the trucking operation and pay back pay to employees laid off because of the termination, but it was also required to resume the discontinued operation. This meant buying trucks, reinstating drivers, and risking ICC violations for an undetermined period of time, after which the employer, theoretically, could take exactly the same action which was found improper in the current case.

Several months after *Town & Country* issued, the *Fibreboard* case was reconsidered and the new rule applied. *Fibreboard Paper Products Corp.*, 138 NLRB No. 67, 51 LRRM 1101. McCulloch and Fanning held that failure to negotiate concerning a decision to subcontract maintenance work was a refusal to bargain for the reasons expressed in *Town & Country*. Added emphasis was placed on their view that bargaining about the decision does not restrain an employer from subcontracting. Rodgers, in one of the most vigorous dissents he has written, effectively highlighted the magnitude of the issue involved.

> "We are dealing here," he said, "with a matter of basic import to the economy generally, and one of immediate concern to every person or group of persons engaged in private business in this country—the matter of how far and to what extent, if any, business management is free to make those economic decisions necessary to the improvement, or indeed the survival, of the business concern with which it is identified. More specifically, this case, like the recently issued Town and Country case, poses the question of whether business management is free to subcontract work in the interest of the more efficient operation of its business.
>
> "In Town and Country, the majority has held, and here holds, in effect, that such decision is foreclosed to management; that such decision, if made at all, must be a negotiated decision, satisfactory to the union. For any decision made solely by management and based solely on economic factors constitutes a violation of this law, which violation must be remedied by the agency's ordering the concern involved to reinstitute an uneconomic, outmoded or obsolete operation, and to remit back wages to all former employees 'ad-

versely affected' by such managerial action. This is a drastic penalty."

Unimpressed by the majority argument that the duty to bargain contemplates merely "a prior discussion" which "in no way restrains an employer" from terminating an operation if he sees fit, Rodgers declared:

"If the foregoing social niceties represented all that is involved, one could not object. But the fact remains that by making such management decisions the subject of *mandatory* rather than *permissive* bargaining, my colleagues have, as they well know, thrust the entire question squarely into the area of economic struggle and industrial turmoil where strikes, picket lines, charges, counter-charges, protracted litigation, and many other aspects of economic power possessed by a union are 'protected' by this Board and are, therefore, legally available to a union to compel a complete abandonment by management of its proposal, on pain of suffering irreparable damage to every aspect of its business. . . .

"If this rule of the majority stands, it is difficult to foresee any economic action which management will be free to take of its own volition and in its own vital interest (whether it be the discontinuance of an unprofitable line, the closing of an unnecessary facility, or the abandonment of an outmoded procedure) which would not be the subject of *mandatory* bargaining.

"In the final analysis, the subjecting of such management decisions as this to the ambit of the Board's processes, and particularly to the mandatory bargaining requirements, simply means that short of complete union agreement, any action taken by management must hereafter be taken at its peril.

"The time involved in extensive negotiations and in protracted litigation before the Board, together with the numerous technical vagaries, practical uncertainties, and changing concepts which abound in the area of so-called 'good faith bargaining' make it impossible for management to know when, if, or ever, any action on its part would be clearly permissible. These factors, together with the crushing, burdensome remedy, which this agency will retro-actively impose upon a given enterprise should the National Labor Relations Board determine that the action of manage-ment was (for whatever reason) improperly taken, will serve effectively to retard and stifle sound and necessary manage-ment decisions. Such a result, in my opinion, is compatible neither with the law, nor with sound business practice, nor with a so-called free and competitive economy."

The remedy in the reconsidered *Fibreboard* case corre-sponded to *Town & Country* and included an order to "reinstitute" the maintenance operation which Fibreboard contracted out. Back pay, however, was awarded only from the date of the Supplemental Decision, September 18, 1962, rather than the July 31, 1959, date, when the operation was discontinued. The majority felt "unusual circumstances" existed because of the reversal of its own prior determination that the law had not been violated.

Although *Town & Country* was followed in *Renton News Record*, 136 NLRB No. 55, 49 LRRM 1972, the new Board decided the discontinued operation in question need not be restored. There two newspaper publishers automated their printing operations and closed their composing rooms without prior discussion with the Typographers Union which repre-sented their employees. Fanning and Brown, who constituted the majority of the panel, found the employers were motivated by economic considerations resulting from automation. But, as the effect of automation is of considerable importance to the employees, the employers violated their duty to bargain by failure to discuss the change of operations and its effects with the union.

The majority ordered bargaining about the effects of the change in operations only because the employers were forced to change their methods or go out of business. (Apparently, it is more serious to be forced out of business than to go to jail!) They chose the former, which necessitated participation of other newspapers, not parties to the proceeding. The majority declared the usual order, which requires restoration of the discontinued operation and reinstatement of employees, would have a detrimental effect on other participants and would be punitive rather than remedial as to Renton and the other employer directly involved. Leedom would have found refusal to bargain only in the employers' failure to discuss the *effects* of the changed operation with the union.

The drastic remedy was followed again in *Adams Dairy, Inc.*, 137 NLRB No. 87, 50 LRRM 1281. Adams subcontracted its delivery services to independent distributors and terminated its driver-salesmen who were members of the union. For some years, the employer had utilized independent distributors outside the County of St. Louis, while the driver-salesmen made deliveries within the County. In the course of negotiations, the union regularly sought inclusion of provisions which would guarantee driver-salesmen commissions on customers within their assigned rounds, even though obtained by independent distributors. As an alternative, the union asked for an agreement that the driver-salesmen's routes would not be altered. The employer never capitulated to these demands, but did not discuss with the union the replacement of all driver-salesmen or the discontinuance of delivery operations.

Fanning and Brown held the union had not waived or lost its right to object to the employer's unilateral replacement of the driver-salesmen and the employer, therefore, failed to bargain in good faith when he subcontracted part of his delivery service. Leedom, in agreement with the Trial Examiner, found the employer in violation of the law because of his failure to discuss with the union the benefits to which the drivers would be entitled, but not because he failed to bargain over the economic decision to subcontract. The remedy was to bargain with respect to utilization of independent distributors, to reinstate driver-salesmen to their former (or substantially equivalent) positions, and to pay them back pay—in effect, to restore the operation. Also, see *Hawaii Meat Co., Ltd.*, 139 NLRB No. 75, 51 LRRM 1430.

The harsh remedy of *Town & Country* has also been applied despite bargaining about the decision to contract out or remove a plant. A cooperative dairy which went out of the cheese-making business was ordered to make cheese again after the Board decision in *Marathon-Clark Cooperative Dairy Association*, 137 NLRB No. 91, 50 LRRM 1285. The Teamsters represented the employees in the bargaining unit. At the first negotiating session on a new contract in March, 1961, the employer outlined in detail the company's financial plight and stated that changes, probably including the contracting out of cheese-making operations, were necessary. Meetings continued until June 17, and contracting out was raised at each of them. By June 9, the union had agreed to settle for the old contract, but the employer contended it did not have sufficient information as to its own economic position to make the union a specific offer on a new agreement. The company "point blank" refused a union suggestion that a consultant be hired to make operations more efficient. The union struck on June 17.

Late in April or May, the employer had begun discussions with two cheese-makers about taking over, on a contract basis, the cheese-making operations when its employees went on a strike. These individuals gave up their means of livelihood before any threat of a strike had been made and moved their homes near the employer's plant. As a result, on June 17, they immediately began operating the cheese-making process, first as employees but, on July 1, on a contract basis.

McCulloch, Leedom and Brown disagreed with the Trial Examiner, who found the company motivated by the purely economic intent to avoid entering into a contract except on terms it felt necessary to avoid economic collapse. They found the issue to be whether the employer fulfilled its bargaining obligations under the Act, not whether its actions were reasonable in the light of its economic situation. To them it was evident that the employer's whole course of conduct was dictated by a desire to rid itself of the union, not to explore in good faith the possibility of reaching an agreement. The employer's position that it had insufficient economic knowledge to make any firm offers was inconsistent with its rejection of a union suggestion that an expert be called in to make company operations more efficient. The company's bad faith was also shown by the arrangement to contract out the cheese-making operation and, though it raised the matter at negotiating sessions, it made no effort to bargain over the decision to contract out or its effects. The majority found the whole program of the employer involved stalling tactics to rid itself of the union and the employees it represented. The remedy was to re-establish the cheese-making operation, reinstate strikers and pay strikers back pay.

Though there is no dissent in the case, it is difficult to reconcile the Board decision with that of the Trial Examiner who dismissed the complaint. Without going into detail, the Board decision read as if the employer made no written proposals, while, in fact, it did make such proposals, all of which offered less in benefits than were granted under the contract in force. Also, the Trial Examiner pointed out the consistency in the employer's position on contracting out and the ample opportunity which the union had to discuss the matter. The Board's emphasis on the anti-union bias of the employer's chief negotiator was disclosed by the Trial Examiner to rest on "a couple of isolated remarks in social conversations two or three years in the past" and one facetious remark made about a year previously. Other similar doubts are raised by a careful comparison of the Trial Examiner's and the Board's decisions which, in the light of the drastic remedy of restoring a discontinued operation, seriously reflect on the validity of the decision under the Board's own theory of the case.

An even more drastic remedy was ordered in *Sidele Fashions, Inc.*, 133 NLRB No. 49, 48 LRRM 1679. Sidele had bargained with the Ladies Garment Workers for some eighteen years as a member of an association in Philadelphia. On one occasion, in 1952, Sidele refused to go along with the association contract until the union agreed to a ten per cent wage cut but there was no showing of any other problem with the union. In July 1959, Cahn, owner of Sidele, began construction of a plant in South Carolina to manufacture a cheaper line of blouses than was made at the Philadelphia plant. In June 1960, the association agreed to a new contract which would have cost Sidele almost double its profit of the previous year. Sidele sought special relief from the union, but the business agent insisted the company sign the association contract before any consideration would be given to its special problem. Sidele then decided to move its entire production to the new plant.

McCulloch, Leedom and Brown agreed with the Trial Examiner that the move was economic and not to avoid bargaining, but they decided it was unlawful because made after the company was faced with an onerous wage increase. They found no showing Sidele would be bound by the new contract (even though the union would not discuss the matter until the contract was *signed*), and no showing the union would strike to enforce adoption of the new contract (though that was what had happened in the past). The Board held the move was made, therefore, to enforce acceptance of the employer's bargaining position, a violation of Section 8(a)(3) of the Act, and that the shutdown was a bargaining tactic unlawful under Section 8(a)(5).

As a remedy, McCulloch and Brown ordered reinstatement of the Philadelphia employees at a plant in the Philadelphia area, if operations were resumed there, or in South

Carolina with moving expenses paid. Back pay was ordered until reinstatement was offered at the Philadelphia plant or substantially equivalent employment was found. Thus, back pay would not be tolled by an offer of employment, with moving expenses paid, at the South Carolina plant. Leedom disagreed with this aspect of the remedy.

Member McCulloch terms the remedial problems in such cases as "one of unscrambling the egg." Nevertheless, the remedy seems most drastic, even if this is the goal. Had the employer bargained with the union about the move, he (theoretically) would have been under no duty to agree that the move should not be made, that he pay moving expenses from Philadelphia to South Carolina, or that particular termination benefits be paid to employees who elected to remain in Philadelphia. Having failed to go through the motions of discussing the matter with the union and his statutory duty to the employees being only to provide them an opportunity to hold substantially equivalent positions at the new location, it would appear that a most adequate remedy would have been to require reinstatement in South Carolina with back pay until that time. The foregoing assumes that the employer violated the Act by closing down completely an operation which he believed had become uneconomic because of a union demand, an assumption of doubtful validity under the circumstances. Also, see *Kingsford Motor Car Co.*, 135 NLRB No. 76, 49 LRRM 1555, and *Fine's Nearby Egg Corp.*, 132 NLRB No. 133, 48 LRRM 1547.

The same principle is involved in *Ox-Wall Products Mfg. Co., Inc.*, 135 NLRB No. 87, 49 LRRM 1585. Until 1958, Ox-Wall, a manufacturer and distributor of hand tools, performed its assembly and shipping operations in New York City. These operations were then transferred to a plant in New Jersey but, in September 1960, the employer's tax consultant advised that a move back to New York should be made by April 30, 1961, because of a new tax statute in

New Jersey. The Machinists' Union began organizing the employees in late November, 1960. The Trial Examiner found some interrogation and threats, including threats to move, based on conflicting evidence, most of which was resolved on the "probabilities" in the light of the entire record rather than demeanor. The move back to New York was made on March 31, 1961, when the employer leased inadequate space, which it occupied until permanent space was found in June. Most of the shipping department employees were discharged when the move was made.

Fanning and Brown decided that economic considerations supported a move as of April 30, 1961, but the acceleration to March 31 was motivated by union reasons arising out of a demand for recognition on March 15, followed by the filing of an election petition a few days later. They found that the employer made no serious move to find space until late in March, after the union petition was filed, and that the company precipately moved to inadequate space when it need not have moved until a month later. Leedom dissented, because the employer had admittedly been looking for space since September, 1960, and it would have been unsound business practice to wait until the last possible moment to make the required move.

In a footnote, Fanning and Brown pointedly expressed disagreement with two Courts of Appeals which had held that there is no violation where the preponderant reason for a move or its acceleration is business necessity, including costs which may result from imminent unionization of employees. *N.L.R.B. v. Rapid Bindery, Inc.*, 293 F2d 170, CA 2, 48 LRRM 2658, and *N.L.R.B. v. J. M. Lassing, d/b/a/Consumers Gasoline Stations*, 284 F2d 781, CA 6, 47 LRRM 2277. In any event, they viewed the cases as being distinguishable because the economic problem was not one which could be affected detrimentally by the advent of the union so as to justify an acceleration of the move by one month. Thus, the Ox-Wall move was for discriminatory purposes.

The majority position proves too much. If the advent of the union could not justify the "premature" move of the operation on an economic basis, it would tend to prove the move had nothing to do with union considerations. In other words, if the imminent unionization was of no economic concern, it would show that Leedom was correct in his view that an employer would not wait until the last possible moment before moving, even though he could not get exactly the space he wanted. Other than the possible economic impact, the employer apparently had nothing else to fear from the union. There is no reference in the decision nor seemingly any contention that the employer would have been required to take the union with him, if certified. Thus, in the unlikely event the mechanics of the election process were completed by April 30, the date all agreed a move was necessary, there would have been no practical difference in his position vis-a-vis the union regardless of the status of the organizing attempt.

Little comment is required to highlight the tremendous problems which will follow if the courts uphold the view of the Kennedy Board in the foregoing cases, particularly those which rest on the *Town & Country* rule. To bargain about the effect of a decision to close down a part of a business or to remove an entire plant is one thing. To bargain about the decision itself is far different. Cost factors invariably are a major element in such matters. Disclosure of an intent to move prior to making the actual decision will frequently cause a substantial increase in the cost of the move. Though the NLRB may have little interest in enabling an enterprise to reduce its costs, freedom to add to, take from or reorganize a business is fundamental to the free enterprise system. Many restrictions have been placed on this freedom, one being the protection of employees in their right to act collectively. The Act does not, however, make employee rights paramount over all others and, unless the plant removal is accomplished for the purpose of destroying those rights, the Act should not apply.

Furthermore, if the employer must bargain about a decision to move, the question immediately follows as to whether he must furnish the union cost information on which the decision is based. The Board and courts have required employers to furnish the bargaining agent, on request, a wide range of information necessary to permit the union to bargain understandingly. An employer who claims "inability to pay" increased wages must furnish information to substantiate his claim. Will it not follow that an employer who must bargain about the decision to move his plant or sub-contract, must substantiate his claim to the union where he asserts economic necessity as his reason?

Finally, in *Sidele Fashions,* the majority refuted its own argument that the obligation to bargain about the decision in no way restrains the employer from effectuating it. There, Sidele bargained with the union prior to the move and, when the union would not discuss Sidele's special problem until the employer signed a master contract, the decision to move was made. The Board viewed the move as a bargaining tactic and, therefore, unlawful. In spite of the majority's protestations to the contrary, *Town & Country* and the new *Fibreboard* case force the employer into the same position occupied by Sidele. For example, if an employer bargains with a union about a decision to subcontract, based on economic considerations, the union presumably will disagree. If the union insists upon existing or revised terms and conditions of employment, any unilateral act by the employer can be viewed as a move to force acceptance of the employer's proposal to subcontract the operation in question. In other words, when the employer talks to the union about the decision to subcontract, he stimulates a proposal from the union which forecloses him from acting because, according to *Sidele,* he will have acted to force acceptance of his bargaining position. *Sidele* was decided before *Town & Country,* but there is no indication the majority feels its decision in *Sidele* is incorrect.

It must be kept in mind that, if the Kennedy Board prevails, this bargaining and exchange of information will take place *prior to the decision to move or to subcontract.* And, for the employer who errs, intentionally or unintentionally, the penalty is to move back again—to "unscramble the egg."

The *Town & Country* theory is a glaring example of administrative legislation. The sections of the statute involved here have been a part of the Act since 1935. Plant removal and subcontracting problems have continually been before the Board. The courts have uniformly found no requirement that the employer bargain about the decision to move or to subcontract. Congress has twice enacted major amendments to the basic statute without showing any interest whatsoever in incorporating a theory of violation such as the Kennedy Board has decided is now to be part of the law. Once more, the intent of executive appointees has been substituted for the intent of Congress.

CHAPTER XIV

REMEDIES

The Board has broad power to fashion appropriate remedies where violations are found. The cases discussed in earlier chapters indicate the Kennedy Board's approach to the subject. Not all go as far as the plant removal decisions. But, if the leaders of the New Frontier are puzzled as to their "anti-business" label, they need look no further than the "go back in business" remedy used in *Town & Country* for one of the reasons. Examples are also found in some of the new Board's other theories of the action required to cure an unfair labor practice. Typical is the new Board's ruling that back pay to individuals suffering discrimination will not be tolled during the period between issuance of a Trial Examiner's Intermediate Report, which finds no back pay due, and a Board order reversing the Trial Examiner. *A. P. W. Products, Inc.*, 137 NLRB No. 7, 50 LRRM 1042. As pointed out in Chapter III, the tolling of back pay in such instances had been the rule since the earliest days of the Board, but the Kennedy majority decided that the wrongdoer was benefitting at the expense of the wronged.

Injured employees were given back-pay benefit primarily at the expense of employers, when the Board began adding interest to back-pay awards. The new policy was based on "legal and equitable" principles and viewed as encouraging compliance with Board orders. At the same time, the majority considered the burden upon the wrongdoer as "relatively minimal." Rodgers and Leedom disagreed. The legislative history "clearly" showed Congress had no such intention and, for more than 26 years, the Board (with court approval) reasoned that a back-pay award was limited to compensation for time lost through unlawful discharge. *Isis Plumbing & Heating Co.*, 138 NLRB No. 97, 51 LRRM 1122. Improperly exacted dues and other monies which must be restored to employees are now treated in the same manner and carry interest. *Seafarers International Union*, 138 NLRB No. 130, 51 LRRM 1208.

Employer concern is also warranted by the Board's decision in *San Juan Mercantile Corp.*, 135 NLRB No. 72, 49 LRRM 1549, where employee rights received an assist against employer misbehavior, but at the expense of the Board's good faith. There the employer entered into a settlement agreement, approved by the Board and by a Court of Appeals, wherein it was stipulated that "back pay shall be computed on a quarterly basis in the manner established by the Board in *F. W. Woolworth Co.*, 90 NLRB 289, 26 LRRM 1185." The *Woolworth* formula provided, generally, that back pay should consist of the total amount the employee would have earned in a given calendar quarter but for the discrimination, less his *total actual* earnings during that quarter.

In *San Juan Mercantile*, McCulloch and Fanning distinguished the *Woolworth* case, finding it involved steady employment. They also found it to be well established that, for the purpose of computing total quarterly earnings, the earnings of an employee who has obtained a job (and is thus mitigating the back-pay liability) do not include what he makes on days when the employer who discriminated against him would have had no work for him. Following this rule, they computed back pay on a quarterly basis but did not deduct earnings on days the employer would have had no work. Rodgers dissented because the computation did not conform to the stipulation. The majority was unconcerned about setting aside a formal agreement which it had previously approved in order to provide a more remunerative remedy, dismissing the employer's objection as a delaying action.

The majority's interest in employee rights has also been noticeable where the remedy involved reinstatement of discriminatorily discharged employees but, again, at the expense of employers. In *Art Metalcraft Plating Co., Inc.*, 133 NLRB No. 48, 48 LRRM 1701, McCulloch and Fanning found an employer had not unconditionally offered to reinstate employees a few hours after he told them to "get out" if they wanted a union. He offered to put them back to work, but the employees refused to return unless the employer recognized and bargained with the union. On three other occasions, similar offers were made and refused. The majority decided the employer's offer of reinstatement continued to be conditional until some four months later, when he wrote the employees, offering reinstatement and stating that his policy with respect to union adherence was altered. Therefore, the employer was ordered to pay back pay for the entire period. Compare *Northern Virginia Sun Publishing Co.*, 134 NLRB No. 109, 49 LRRM 1268.

Rodgers dissented, agreeing with the Trial Examiner. He pointed out that discriminatees who reject an offer of reemployment because their employer refuses to recognize and bargain with their union, become unfair labor practice strikers who are withholding their services until their demands are met. As such, they are entitled to reinstatement upon application but not to back pay.

In *Atlantic Maintenance Co.*, 134 NLRB No. 131, 49 LRRM 1367, Fanning and Brown, Rodgers dissenting, ordered back pay for three discriminatees, even though the Trial Examiner found they credibly testified their reason for not accepting the employer's offer of employment was because its pay scale was lower than the union rate of pay. They also ordered the employer to offer reinstatement to one employee who said he would not come back to work as long as a certain sales manager was working for the company, to another who said he would not care to work for the sales manager any longer, and to a third who said he was not coming back because he was leaving the city. Also see, *Hatch Chevrolet Co.*, 136 NLRB No. 26, 49 LRRM 1761; *National Furniture Mfg. Co., Inc.*, 134 NLRB No. 84, 49 LRRM 1234.

The Trial Examiner in *Titan Metal Mfg. Co.*, 135 NLRB No. 22, 49 LRRM 1466, discussing generally the right of reinstatement, declared that an economic striker is entitled to his job unless the replacement is actually employed in the position formerly occupied by the striker at the particular time a striker unconditionally offers to return. Thus, the job is not filled if a replacement has been hired and later was terminated or quit. The issue was not involved in the case and was not supported by the authority cited, *Union Bus Terminal*, 98 NLRB 458, 29 LRRM 1356. Nevertheless, McCulloch and Fanning adopted the Intermediate Report without comment on this issue, though Rodgers noted that it was unnecessary to consideration of the case.

It is not clear whether the majority would follow the Trial Examiner, but that is the implication. It could mean that a striker must be given a permanent preference to his pre-strike job and employers are faced with one more pitfall in dealing with unions.

The foregoing cases demonstrate an assiduous interest in protecting employee rights—the interest noticeably missing in union security matters—at the expense of employers. The new Board's remedies in cases of unlawful employer assistance to a labor organization show the exact opposite. But here it is the interests of unions and employees which must be balanced.

An independent union at *Filtron Co., Inc.*, 134 NLRB No. 158, 49 LRRM 1404, had a bargaining relationship extending over several years. The labor agreement contained certain illegal union security provisions which had been carried over from one contract to another but which the Trial Examiner found were not carried out in practice. Rodgers, Fanning and Brown found unlawful assistance. The majority ordered withdrawal of recognition because the employer assisted the independent through the illegal union security provisions, but Rodgers, like the Trial Examiner would have required the parties merely to cease maintaining and giving effect to the unlawful contract.

Filtron provides an interesting comparison with the *Jervis B. Webb* case discussed in Chapter VII, where Fanning and Brown refused to find a union guilty of a discriminatory hiring arrangement. There they looked closely at the language of the union security clause in the contract, found it lawful, and were unconcerned about an admitted unlawful practice. In *Filtron* they found an employer in violation of the Act because of the contract language but were not interested in the Trial Examiner's finding that the contract provisions were never carried out in practice. The cases, taken together, indicate considerably more attention to form than substance. It seems apparent that violations should have been found in both instances if employee rights were to be fully protected but, if there must be a distinction, an unlawful hiring practice is far more detrimental to the employees than contract language ignored by all. Instead, form was emphasized, the employer found guilty, and the case against the union dismissed.

The same panel found unlawful assistance in *Post Publishing Co.*, 136 NLRB No. 23, 49 LRRM 1768. There the employer furnished an independent union most of its financial support by turning over cafeteria profits of about $600 a year and permitting the union to retain proceeds from a vending machine. Fanning and Brown ordered the employer to withhold recognition until a bargaining agent was certified and to suspend the contract and bargaining relationship with the independent. Rodgers dissented on the basis the unlawful contract did not warrant the drastic remedy ordered, since the unlawful assistance did not give rise to an inference that the union's ability to represent the employees was adversely affected.

Rodgers contrasted the case with *M. Eskin & Son,* 135 NLRB No. 61, 49 LRRM 1551, where McCulloch, Rodgers and Leedom found it unnecessary to require withdrawal of recognition, even though the Board found that clearance by the assisted union (the Teamsters) was required as a condition of employment. Also before reinstatement after a strike, the employees were forced to revoke designations of any labor organization except those in favor of the assisted union, to revoke withdrawals of check-off authorizations to the Teamsters, and to withdraw a representation petition and unfair labor practice charges filed by another union. Rodgers pointed out that the assisted union in the *Post Publishing* case had represented the employees for 38 years without, according to the majority, any criticism or any suspicion of its legitimacy or independent character. Also, contrast *Duralite Co., Inc.,* 132 NLRB No. 28, 48 LRRM 1371, discussed in Chapter VII, where the employer was ordered to withhold recognition from I.U.E. where the assistance found appears no greater than that provided the Teamsters in *M. Eskin & Son.*

It is always tempting, in discussing remedies, to speculate on the correlation between the identity of the wrongdoers and the relief deemed necessary to rectify the transgressions. The question bound to be asked is whether there is any significance in the fact that the assisted union was an independent in the *Post Publishing* case and the rival was the I.U.E., while, in *M. Eskin & Son,* the assisted union was the Teamsters. Also, did the fact that the union in the *Filtron* case was an independent affect the result?

Remedies sometimes lead Board members into doing indirectly what they are unwilling or unable to do directly. For example, McCulloch has expressed the view that Section 10(b), the six-months statute of limitations, does not preclude considering conduct prior to that time for the purpose of framing a remedy. *American Lubricants Co.*, 136 NLRB No. 83, 49 LRRM 1888. Rodgers and Leedom characterized his approach as measuring a "make-whole" remedy, not by the violation found, but by some other violation which might have been found if a timely charge had been filed. In other words, by tailoring a remedy, misconduct beyond the reach of the statute may be brought within its scope.

A different aspect of the same temptation is found in *New England Web, Inc.*, 135 NLRB No. 102, 49 LRRM 1620, where the full Board (Rodgers not participating) found violations of Sections 8(a)(1), (3) and (5), because an employer closed his plant and discharged all of the employees in order to avoid bargaining with the union. The majority members, Leedom dissenting, argued that the proper remedy was to require the employer to bargain with the union, and the most straightforward approach would be to resume the discontinued operations. Since that might not have been feasible, they ordered the employees reinstated "as a group" at other companies found to constitute a single employer. The right of the employees to be represented for collective bargaining could be preserved, in their view, only by group reinstatement.

Leedom looked upon the remedy as an indirect method of accomplishing what the majority said it would not do directly, i.e. ordering the reopening of *New England Web.* The majority felt that any difficulty the employer might encounter in complying with the order stemmed from its own unlawful conduct. Neither the majority nor the dissent expressed any concern whatsoever about employees of the other companies who might have to be replaced to accommodate "the group," though it seems the obvious practical result.

A discussion of remedies would be incomplete without reference to *Employing Bricklayers' Association of Delaware Valley*, 134 NLRB No. 145, 49 LRRM 1377, not because of the importance of the case but to show how far the Board can drift from the substance of labor-management relations. An employers' association was found to have unlawfully assisted the Bricklayers' Union because the association's executive secretary voted in an election for delegates to the union's international convention. The executive secretary, who was a member in good standing of Local 1 of the union, voted over the objection of two local officers. The Trial Examiner found that the selection of delegates to such a convention every two years was too remote from the bargaining function of the local union for any interference or assistance to result.

The full Board, except for McCulloch who dissented, disagreed and found that, because international unions assert influence and control over bargaining powers and functions of locals, a management officer participates in the formulation of a union bargaining policy by voting in such an election. McCulloch felt the participation of one supervisor out of 319 voting members in an election of the type under consideration was too remote.

Chairman McCulloch is to be complimented on his approach in this case. Surely the NLRB has more important uses for its time and effort than to concern itself with such speculative and improbable interference with employee rights.

CHAPTER XV

PROCEDURE

Not all of the Kennedy Board's new rules involve interpretations of substantive law. Modifications in Board procedure, both through case decisions and revisions in Board rules, have substantially altered methods of handling cases. Most important rule changes were the extensive revisions arising out of delegation of the representation case function to Regional Directors, as authorized by the Landrum-Griffin Act, effective May 15, 1961. The delegation, in turn, led to procedural changes through case law, such as *Leonard Wholesale Meats, Inc.*, 136 NLRB No. 103, 49 LRRM 1901 (discussed in Chapter III), where the new Board revised the time for filing a petition for an election in a bargaining unit covered by an existing contract.

A similar development is found in *Ideal Electric & Manufacturing Co.*, 134 NLRB No. 133, 49 LRRM 1316. For many years, the Board limited its consideration of pre-election conduct as a basis for objecting to an election to acts which occurred between the date of the Board's Decision and Direction of Election and the election date. In the *Ideal Electric* case, the Board reasoned that the new delegation and the shorter time lag in processing representation cases made a period between the date of filing the petition and the election date more appropriate than the old rule.

There can be little quarrel with the *Ideal Electric* case

but, several months later, the Kennedy Board felt impelled to take a further step and reach a much more questionable result. This occurred in *Goodyear Tire and Rubber Co.*, 138 NLRB No. 59, 51 LRRM 1070, where the rule in *consent* election cases was also changed to permit consideration of conduct going back to filing of the petition. The majority members found no difference between objectionable conduct occurring under a consent arrangement and a formal directed election. They seemed to feel making a distinction would permit an employer or union to avoid the consequences of its impropriety.

The majority ignored a major reason for employer consent, however, particularly under the current Board, i.e. the assurance past conduct would not interfere with the election. Under the old rule, the employer was certain that no act committed prior to the consent, including conduct of lower ranking supervisors and others of which he was unaware, would be used to set aside an election. He thus was able to police more effectively both his own activity and that of his agents which might lead to objections. With *Goodyear Tire*, this incentive was wiped out and it is now to the employer's advantage to avail himself of the somewhat longer period of delay encountered by insisting that a formal Board hearing be conducted.

At the present time, the Board itself rarely considers a representation case other than as an appeal from a Regional Director's decision. Because an appeal may not be taken as a matter of right, the serious differences of opinion as to the review function developing within the Board are of real significance. In *Austin Ford, Inc.*, 136 NLRB No. 123, 50 LRRM 1001, McCulloch, Fanning and Brown granted review and reversed a Regional Director who had found appropriate a unit of all automotive line mechanics and helpers employed by a retail automotive dealer. The majority decided, in agreement with the employer, that the unit should include all service employees because the mechanics and helpers were not a distinct and homogeneous group which would be appropriate on either a craft or departmental basis. Rodgers dissented, arguing that the Board's rules clearly limited the grounds on which a request for review could be granted, none of which were present. Paraphrasing the rules, he emphasized the Director's findings were supported by the facts and were in accord with Board precedent. No issue of reconsideration of Board policy was involved and no issue was raised as to conduct of the hearing.

While deviation from its own rules appears in isolated cases such as *Austin Ford,* the true incidence of Board irregularity in ruling on appeals is much more difficult to determine. Most such rulings are denials which are neither published or publicized. Review has been granted in only about 3% of the election cases and only a part of the decisions in these cases are distributed to the public. One might assume that any ruling important enough to be reviewed by the Board would also be sufficiently meaningful to be published for future guidance of the public and the Regional Directors. Such is not the case, and the Board is continuing to issue its so-called "short form" decisions. These are a part of the public files of the Board and may be read there. They are not included in the bound volumes of Board decisions and orders and are rarely covered by the labor law services.

When substantial questions of law or policy are involved, or there are compelling reasons for reconsideration of an important Board rule or policy, the public should be informed. Also, it would have a salutary effect if Directors' decisions which were clearly erroneous or showed prejudicial error in the conduct of the hearings were brought to light by means of published decisions. If the delegation is to be successful, the Board has a considerable responsibility to police the decisions of the Directors through the review process and to clarify the handling of delegated cases by exposing any error in procedure or policy which may have occurred.

It is impossible to judge the extent of the problem. In the writer's own practice, a short form unpublicized decision was used in a case of first impression involving the validity of a representation petition filed by a union found to be Communist-infiltrated by the Subversive Activities Control Board (*Diversey Corporation*, 10-RC-5251). The Board may have been correct in its decision that the petition should be processed, pending final review of the SACB order, but both the statute and the question of policy involved were such that the public was entitled to know the Board's interpretation. The same decision included a departure from Board precedent in a finding that separate plants constituted a single bargaining unit under the facts of the case.

Serious problems are also likely to develop because of the Board's increasingly cavalier treatment of the right to a hearing in a representation case, particularly where objections to the election are involved. Since the delegation, objections are ruled upon by the Regional Directors. When objections are filed, a Board agent from the Regional Office investigates, talking to witnesses suggested by both the union and the employer. As the Board agent is the only official who talks to the witnesses, it is apparent that determinations of credibility rest upon his shoulders. The agent makes a report to the Regional Director, which is not seen by the parties but which forms the basis for the Regional Director's rulings upon the objections. Hearings are rarely held. The parties have no opportunity to cross examine the witnesses, do not know what they say and, in many instances, do not know their identity. The Regional Director has no independent knowledge of the facts of the case but must rely completely upon the investigation of the Board agent. It would seem that serious questions of due process are involved but, to date, the Board has consistently upheld the Director's refusal to grant hearings and has shown no concern about the problem. Perhaps a footnote in the *Joclin Mfg. Co.* case, 137 NLRB No. 23, 50 LRRM 1123, reflects the Board attitude when it says:

". . . a party is entitled to a hearing only where such a hearing would serve a useful purpose."

Unfortunately, the Board now makes the sole determination of what is a useful purpose and does so on the basis of the Board agent's investigation.

Problems of Board jurisdiction were substantially reduced by the 1959 amendments which required the Board to continue asserting jurisdiction over all cases meeting the standards then in effect. The only significant difference of opinion was centered on whether the Board's jurisdiction extends to vessels of foreign registry. *West India Fruit & Steamship Co., Inc.*, 130 NLRB No. 343, 47 LRRM 1269, decided by the previous Board, is the leading case. Decisions of the new Board include *Hamilton Bros., Inc.*, 133 NLRB No. 85, 48 LRRM 1740; *United Fruit Co.*, 134 NLRB No. 25, 49 LRRM 1138; *Grace Line, Inc.*, 135 NLRB No. 70, 49 LRRM 1562; *Owens-Illinois Glass Co.*, 136 NLRB No. 32, 49 LRRM 1777, and *Dalzell Towing Co., Inc.*, 137 NLRB No. 48, 50 LRRM 1164. The Kennedy appointees followed the lead of the previous Board and have asserted jurisdiction in most such cases. Rodgers continues to dissent. The question is now before the United States Supreme Court and, curiously enough, the Kennedy administration has entered the proceedings to argue against the Kennedy Board's position.

Of the new Board's procedural innovations, most vulnerable to criticism is its policy on reconsideration. The Board rules contain no provision authorizing motions for reconsideration of a Board decision or ruling. Nevertheless, the Board has uniformly considered such motions when filed and, infrequently, has reversed itself in the process. The Kennedy Board, however, has granted a sizeable number, many in cases presenting controversial issues where reconsideration has resulted in a reversal of precedent or a different outcome in cases of first impression.

It is not unusual for a court or an administrative tribunal to make some changes in existing precedent as the personnel of the adjudicating authority changes. Most common example, of course, is the United States Supreme Court, where many concepts of constitutional law have undergone radical alterations. Nevertheless, rarely have so many changes been made so quickly as by the Kennedy Board; furthermore, it is extremely rare to find a precedent reversed in a previously decided case by any adjudicating authority. Because there are no statutory standards and no time limitations on motions for reconsideration, there seem to be no restraints on the new Board where it wishes to change the result in a given case.

In all fairness, it must be pointed out that granting reconsideration is both logical and proper in some instances. *General Motors Corp.*, 133 NLRB No. 21, 48 LRRM 1659, is an example. The Eisenhower Board dismissed a charge of refusal to bargain filed by the United Auto Workers against General Motors because the company would not discuss an "agency shop" provision as part of a contract in a bargaining unit located in Indiana, which has a "right to work" law. Of the five members, the three who constituted the majority could not agree on a common rationale and the other two dissented. 130 NLRB No. 54, 47 LRRM 1306. Where a majority of the Board is unable to work out a common theory of the law's meaning, both reviewing courts and parties faced with similar cases are in difficulty. Therefore, it is only reasonable that the Board grant reconsideration if greater unanimity can be found. In the *General Motors* case, a common ground appeared but, on reconsideration, the new Board found the law violated. Only Leedom disagreed.

The new Board has seemed most anxious to grant reconsideration where interpretations of the Landrum-Griffin amendments on organizational and recognition picketing were involved. The previous Board had issued a number of major decisions, speaking to these issues for the first time, only a few weeks before the new appointees took office. Reconsideration was granted in most, if not all, of these cases and with few exceptions, different interpretations resulted.

There are two explanations. Most generous to the new Board is that it was endeavoring to clarify the law as promptly as possible in order that parties would know how to conduct themselves and unnecessary complaints would not be issued. The other is that the Kennedy appointees were anxious that no interpretations contrary to their own views should reach the courts. Inasmuch as the new Board substantially weakened the earlier decisions and found very few violations, it is implicit in the latter theory that the Kennedy appointees also sought to forestall issuance of further complaints based on the interpretations of the previous Board. Because of the absolute power of the General Counsel over whether or not to issue a complaint and the impossibility of testing these provisions in any other manner, his treatment of future charges determines whether additional cases presenting similar issues will come before the Board and the courts. Had the Eisenhower Board decisions remained in effect, the General Counsel would have had much greater support for issuing complaints following its interpretations and the courts would have been provided with many more opportunities for review. Now that reconsideration has been granted, the Board law is uniform and, while the General Counsel can disregard the Board's views, he must be prepared to withstand substantial pressure and criticism if he does so.

Perhaps the most questionable of the new Board's reconsidered matters is that of *Fibreboard Paper Products Corp.*,

130 NLRB No. 161, 47 LRRM 1547, originally decided March 27, 1961. As explained earlier, the case held that an employer does not have to bargain about the decision to close down a part of an operation and he does not refuse to bargain in good faith if he acts without discussing the matter with the union. Reconsideration was granted and, as explained in Chapter XIII, the original decision was reversed. 138 NLRB No. 67, 51 LRRM 1101. Although a three-man panel (McCulloch and Fanning, with Rodgers dissenting) signed the new decision, it is apparent that Brown's vote was needed to offset those of Rodgers and Leedom before reconsideration was granted. Yet Brown, then Regional Director in San Francisco, issued the original complaint in the case, raising anew the question of intermingling the Board's prosecuting and adjudicating functions. Regardless of the interest of the new Board in establishing its interpretation of the law, it would be well advised to exercise some restraint in selecting the vehicle for announcing its views.

Reconsideration by a different route appeared in *American Broadcast Co.*, 134 NLRB No. 148, 49 LRRM 1365. There the Guild, a non-affiliated union, won an election in a unit of soundtrack employees, previously represented as a part of a multi-employer bargaining unit. In a representation case, decided by the former Board, the existing multi-employer contract with an affiliated union was held not to bar the election because it contained illegal union security clauses. Bargaining history was not considered in determining the appropriate unit, as prior contracts contained similar unlawful clauses.

When the employer refused to bargain, McCulloch, Fanning and Brown held that it had not violated the law, reversing the previous decision and finding the election should have been barred. The majority said that issues previously raised in a related representation matter will be re-examined in a refusal to bargain proceeding ". . . where the disputed matter involves a legal, as distinguished from a mere policy, issue . . . if we believe our earlier resolution to be incorrect." Rodgers and Leedom dissented. In their view, administrative regularity is undermined by setting aside a unit found appropriate under the policy then in effect.

The majority, in its anxiety to reach a desired result, opened the door to difficulties in future cases. Earlier Boards, with rare exceptions, have refused to review in an unfair labor practice proceeding matters previously decided in a representation case. The Courts have sometimes disagreed but the Board has done its best to discourage any attempt to weaken the representation decision. *American Broadcast* provides some useful language for future litigants. The distinction between legal and policy issues is not easy to draw. It is interesting that the rule should be announced in a case involving contract bar rules, which have no statutory basis but are grounded entirely on policy.

Similarly, concern over a particular result without adequate regard for procedure, is found in *Philanz Oldsmobile, Inc.,* 137 NLRB No. 103, 50 LRRM 1262. Board Rule 102.46 (b) provides that no matter not included in a statement of exceptions may thereafter be urged before the Board. In holding a strike for the purpose of forcing Philanz to consent to a representation election to be a protected activity, McCulloch, Fanning and Brown disregarded findings of a Trial Examiner to which no exceptions had been filed. As pointed out by Rodgers and Leedom, the Trial Examiner found the strike unauthorized and none of the parties had raised the issue. Thus, the majority decided an issue that the parties did not believe was in the case.

One final procedural point is worth mention, though now reported to have been changed. After delegating the representation cases to Regional Directors, the Board established internally a method for processing appeals from the Directors' decisions. A staff of legal assistants handled the requests for appeal, presenting them orally as a rule, to a "member of the month." The Board members alternated in this capacity and, unless the member of the month chose to have the case presented to the full Board, his decision was final.

The system was in direct conflict with Section 3(b) of the statute which permits delegation of Board powers to no less than a three-member panel. Its existence was kept confidential as long as possible but, eventually, began to come to light. When the system was first mentioned in a motion for reconsideration, the Board granted the motion and disposed of the case on its merits. Finally, after a court attack was filed, the system was changed in August, 1962. There are without doubt many certifications in existence which involved appeals denied by a "member of the month" before the procedure was abolished. As of this writing, the validity of such certifications had not been tested in a refusal to bargain case. When this occurs, particularly if in a case where a Director has made a questionable decision, courts may well refuse to uphold the election proceedings.

The Kennedy Board's approach to procedural matters is an accentuation of that of previous Boards, none of which has required strict compliance with its own rules. Nevertheless, the new Board reflects an unusual disregard for procedural regularity which places the agency in an unfavorable light. The "member of the month" system, the eagerness to alter precedent by use of reconsideration, the indifference to broad implications of a changed policy, each indicates an excessive attention to result with inadequate concern for the practical impact on future cases.

CHAPTER XVI

PICKETING FOR ORGANIZATION
OR RECOGNITION

Few Americans would dispute that freedom of association is one of our fundamental rights. Inherent in the right to associate is the right *not* to do so. These rights existed long before any labor legislation had been enacted in this country and are, in fact, among those rights which existed before the Constitution and are protected from Government encroachment by the Bill of Rights. *United States v. Bailes,* 120 F. Supp. 614.

Despite this fact it has been a traditional union tactic to force employees to join a labor organization by picket-line pressure and other coercion exerted against their employers. Both the use and effectiveness of the technique were greatly accelerated by the favorable provisions of the Wagner Act and the tremendous growth of union power which followed. Unorganized employers and employees literally had no protection from such picketing.

The inevitable abuses which resulted stimulated an intensive effort to limit both organizational and recognition picketing in Taft-Hartley. The only specific language adopted was a narrow ban on picketing by one union to force membership on employees who had already voted in an NLRB election for another union. Section 8(b)(4)(C).

However, in setting forth the right of employees to be free not to join a union (Section 7), many legislators thought the broad proscriptions on union restraint and coercion of employees in their exercise of this right [Section 8(b)(1)(A)] would be sufficient to provide some relief. But, for many years, no General Counsel would issue a complaint on this theory. It was not until shortly after the 1959 amendments were enacted and the theory was of no more practical import that the Supreme Court first ruled it would not support a violation. *N.L.R.B. v. Drivers, Local 639 (Curtis Bros.),* 362 US 274, 45 LRRM 2975.

By 1959, there were so many graphic examples of the injustice flowing from organizational and recognitional picketing that it was customarily referred to throughout the consideration of the Landrum-Griffin amendments as "blackmail" picketing. The necessity for relief was so apparent that the only real conflict was the scope, rather than the need, of remedial legislation. The resulting amendments, incorporated in Section 8(b)(7), represented an overwhelming Congressional view that severe limitations were required to eradicate the evil.

Section 8(b)(7) provides that it is an unfair labor practice where a union pickets or threatens to picket and has as an object:

1. to force the employer to recognize or bargain with the union (recognition), or
2. to force the employees to select the union as their bargaining agent (organization).

Such picketing and threats are invalid in three situations:

7(A) where the employees are already represented by another union, whether as a result of an NLRB election or of voluntary recognition by the employer, and there is a contract in effect which would bar an NLRB election;

7(B)   where a valid NLRB election has been conducted within the preceding 12 months, and

7(C)   where such picketing has been conducted without an election petition being filed within a reasonable period of time (not to exceed 30 days).

A proviso to subparagraph 7(C) removes from that proscription picketing or other publicity carried out for the purpose of truthfully advising the public that the employer does not employ members of, or have a contract with, a labor organization, unless an effect of such picketing is to stop pick-ups and deliveries or prevent performance of services at the employer's place of business.

It is important to note the use of "an" and "the" in the statute. Recognition or organization need be only *an* object to bring picketing under the restrictions of the section. In the proviso to 7(C), on the other hand, *the* purpose must be one of truthfully advising the public before it will be excused. Congress went back to *an* in designating the extent of permissible impact on deliveries and services.

The first significant interpretations of the new picketing restrictions were made by the Eisenhower Board but most were hastily reconsidered and reversed after the Kennedy appointees took over. Of these, the most important was *Hotel and Restaurant Employees', Local 681 (Crown Cafeteria)*, 135 NLRB No. 124, 49 LRRM 1648, which involved an interpretation of 7(C). The union began picketing Crown when it opened for business on May 5, 1959, after the employer refused to operate by hiring employees through the union hall and signing a standard union contract. Picketing continued with minor interruptions until January 13, 1960, when it was discontinued as a result of the NLRB charges. At no time did the union file a representation petition. The picketing did not stop deliveries or services, the signs truthfully stated that the employer was non-union, and there was ample evidence that recognition was one of the union's objectives.

In the first *Crown* case, Leedom, Rodgers and Kimball found a violation, as *an* object was recognition and *the* purpose of the picketing was recognition rather than information. The majority reasoned that the legislative intent for the 7(C) proviso was to make it clear that *purely* informational picketing should not be curtailed. Jenkins and Fanning dissented. (130 NLRB No. 68, 47 LRRM 1321)

After the Kennedy appointees took office, the original decision was reconsidered and reversed, and the reasoning of Fanning's dissent adopted by McCulloch and Brown. The new majority argued that there would be no need of the proviso and it would be a contradiction in terms if it applied only where the union was *not* seeking recognition or bargaining. They viewed the function of a legislative proviso as that of exempting from a general proscriptive clause a class of cases which it would otherwise cover. The majority, therefore, declared the proviso should be read to permit picketing which has as its purpose organization or recognition as long as it truthfully advises the public that an employer does not employ members of, or have a contract with, a union.

Rodgers and Leedom dissented, adhering to the views expressed in the original majority opinion. They saw the issue as being one of the effect to be given the publicity proviso where the evidence wholly apart from the picket signs established an object of the picketing to be immediate recognition or organization. In their view, the structure of the statute showed Congress recognized that picketing to advise the public that an employer does not employ members of, or have a contract with a labor organization, necessarily has as *an* object recognition or organization. They found it most significant that the words "an object" were used to bring picketing within the scope of Section 8(b)(7), while "the purpose" was used to bring such picketing within the exception created by the proviso. They believed it follows that informational picketing may be conducted only when there is no independent evidence of a recognition or organization objective.

See also: *Hotel & Restaurant Employees Union, Local 89 (Stork Restaurant, Inc.)*, 135 NLRB No. 122, 49 LRRM 1653; *Retail Clerks, Local 400 (Jumbo Food Stores, Inc.)*, 136 NLRB No. 24, 49 LRRM 1798; *International Ladies Garment Workers (Saturn & Sedran, Inc.)*, 136 NLRB No. 44, 49 LRRM 1803; and Rodgers' concurrence in *Hotel Employees' Union (Marriott Motor Hotels, Inc.)*, 136 NLRB No. 72, 49 LRRM 1838.

The Kennedy Board agrees that the use of the words "an object" means that Section 8(b)(7) bans picketing which has recognition or organization as only one of its objects. *Hotel and Restaurant Employees' Local 535 (Educational Supply Services of California)*, 134 NLRB No. 156, 49 LRRM 1376. Nevertheless, the majority has been unwilling to read "the purpose" in the proviso as carefully. The specific change from "the object" in the general proscriptive clauses of Section 8(b)(7) in earlier bills to "an object" when Landrum-Griffin was introduced shows that a distinction between "an" and "the" was significant to the Congress. Furthermore, the majority theory in *Crown Cafeteria* reconsidered, that a proviso is used only to except conduct which would otherwise clearly fall within a statute, is plainly inaccurate. It is not uncommon to include a proviso in order that possible misinterpretation of the general language will be excluded. The most compelling argument against the majority interpretation of the proviso has been supplied by then Senator Kennedy who, in speaking to the conference report, characterized the proviso as permitting *"purely* informational picketing." The characterization is accurate, as inclusion of the proviso constituted Congressional recognition, out of deference to Senate concern, that there could be picketing for the *sole* purpose of informing the public that an employer did not have a contract with, or employ members of, a labor union. The proviso goes no further.

To digress for a moment, some of the language in the second *Crown Cafeteria* decision is most curious when considered in the light of the new Board's "disclaimer" cases. These arise when an employer files a representation petition because of union organizational acivity and a minority union, which has been trying to force recognition, then disclaims any such object. In the past, it has been well established that a disclaimer must be clear and unequivocal and any current or subsequent inconsistent action by the union will dissipate its effect. In *Crown Cafeteria* reconsidered, the new majority emphasized that picket signs reading "Does not employ members of" or "Does not have a contract with" clearly imply a recognitional, organizational or bargaining objective. The majority also dropped a footnote pointing out that, if informational picketing under the proviso is for recognition or bargaining as distinguished from organization, a routine representation petition would be processed.

But in *Miratti's Inc.*, 132 NLRB No. 48, 48 LRRM 1407, McCulloch, Fanning, and Brown took the opposite approach in dismissing an employer petition because of the union's disclaimer. The disclaimer was accepted despite the fact that the union had attempted for the past three years to secure recognition and a contract, including picketing with signs informing the public that the employer did not have a union contract and by other means. As recently as six weeks before the union's self-serving statement disclaiming any recognitional objective, it had sought recognition by a cross check of authorization cards. On the basis of these facts, Rodgers and Leedom dissented. Also, see *Andes Candies, Inc.*, 133 NLRB No. 65, 48 LRRM 1711; *Jefferson Chemical Co., Inc.*, 134 NLRB No. 162, 49 LRRM 1379.

It is apparent that the very procedure suggested in the

footnote in the *Crown* case was denied to the employer in *Miratti's*. The practical effect is that a union can picket with a "no contract" sign and Section 8(b)(7)(C) will not be violated because the picketing has recognition as an object but its purpose is only to truthfully advise the public that the employer does not have a union contract. On the other hand, the employer petition for an election will be dismissed because the same picket signs do not show a recognition objective.

As additional 8(b)(7) cases have been decided, the inconsistency described above is demonstrated to be merely a by-product of the new Board's attempt to weaken the picketing restrictions until the Congressional purpose has been completely dissipated. For example, at the Oakland G. R. Kinney Store, a union unsuccessfully sought permission from the employer to talk to his employees about joining. On February 3, 1960, the union told the employer it would advertise to the public that the store was non-union and would not meet union conditions. The following day, the union sent a letter to the employer threatening an "advertising" campaign, saying its "exclusive" purpose was to persuade the public not to patronize Kinney. The letter continued:

> "We do not claim at this time to represent a majority of the employees of your store, nor is it any part of the purpose of our advertising campaign to secure a union contract covering these employees. In fact, our union will refuse to enter into any such contract until and unless a majority of your employees at your store voluntarily without any coercion of any kind designate the union as their collective bargaining representative."

Picketing with a sign saying, "This store does not operate under AFL-CIO union conditions—please do not patronize" began February 5 but did not interfere with pickups, deliveries or other services. On February 17, the employer filed Section 8(b)(7) charges and an election petition. Two months later, on April 17, an "expedited" election was held at which all employees voted against the union. Picketing and handbilling continued after the election.

McCulloch and Fanning found *an* object of the union conduct was organization, recognition and bargaining, pointing out that two days before the picketing began union officers asked for permission to talk to employees about joining the union and the letter disclaimed a bargaining objective but only until a majority joined. They found, however, that the language of the picket signs and the handbills conformed to the publicity proviso of Section 8(b)(7)(C) and, since the expedited election procedure could be used only if 7(C) is violated, the election was invalid. Therefore, there was no violation of the Section 7(B) ban on picketing for 12 months after an election. *Department and Specialty Store Union, Local 1265 (Oakland G. R. Kinney, Inc.),* 136 NLRB No. 29, 49 LRRM 1771. Leedom dissented on the basis of *Crown Cafeteria,* pointing out that the majority relied on independent evidence to establish that organization was "an object" of the picketing but ignored the same evidence in concluding "the purpose" was informational.

The new Board's inconsistent consideration of "all the facts and circumstances," highlighted by Leedom in *Oakland G. R. Kinney Co.,* is a curious position for a Board whose approach to decision making is "empirical." Perhaps it, too, is a by-product of the nullification of Section 8(b)(7). Another example is *Carpenters District Council of St. Louis (Vestaglass Inc.),* 136 NLRB No. 78, 49 LRRM 1880, where McCulloch and Fanning, with Rodgers dissenting, evaded the issue of the object of the picketing and dismissed the case on the basis of the publicity proviso, looking only at the picket signs and handbills and refusing to consider such surrounding circumstances as the testimony of a union picket that he was told he would be picketing until the company "kicked in or signed up."

Any doubt as to the majority position was removed by *Local 125, Window Cleaners' Union (Atlantic Maintenance Company)*, 136 NLRB No. 105, 49 LRRM 1939. Rodgers and Leedom concurred in finding a violation and added they would also find certain picketing unlawful because of other evidence showing its purpose was not publicity. The majority members pointedly responded that they would not agree with the implication that "surrounding circumstances" might render unlawful picketing that conformed to the language and intent of the proviso in other respects. Also see *IBEW Local 3 (Jack Picoult)*, 137 NLRB No. 138, 50 LRRM 1410; and compare Brown's approach in the employer free speech cases where he insists upon looking at statements in the context of other conduct. *The Rhyne Co., Inc.*, 134 NLRB No. 74, 49 LRRM 1302.

After the recent decision in *Hotel & Restaurant Employee Union (Fowler Hotel, Inc.)*, 138 NLRB No. 114, 51 LRRM 1180, it may be questionable whether the surrounding circumstances issue is of importance anyway. In the *Fowler Hotel* case, McCulloch and Brown found picketing excused by the publicity proviso even though the picket sign read: "ON STRIKE FOR RENEWAL OF OUR UNION CONTRACT" followed by the union name. Rodgers and Leedom dissented. They could not see how a picket sign which on its face stated its purpose as the renewal of a contract could be deemed limited to the purpose of advising the public that the employer did not have a union contract. (Fanning concurred in finding a violation but on other grounds.) If such language can be read as mere publicity, it seems doubtful that the majority would glean anything from surrounding circumstances which would work to the detriment of the union.

While the foregoing cases made serious inroads on Section 8(b)(7), it was not until *Barker Bros. Corp.*, 138 NLRB No. 54, 51 LRRM 1053, issued that the broad scope of the

new Board's disagreement with Congressional intent was
fully revealed. If *Barker Bros.* does not ". . . complete the
virtual nullification of the Congressional purpose in enacting
Section 8(b)(7)(C)," as Rodgers and Leedom pointed out,
it falls very little short of that goal.

It was admitted that "an" object of the union's picketing
at *Barker Bros.* was recognition and that it had been carried
out over a 12 week period at approximately 18 of the employer's retail stores. Furthermore, it was undisputed that
the picket signs were not truthful in that they stated the
employer was "NON-UNION" when, in fact, non-selling
employees were represented under contract with the Teamsters and Building Service Unions. Finally, the majority
found that deliveries and services had been stopped or delayed on more than five occasions. The actual number, according to the dissent, was probably in excess of fifteen.

The Kennedy majority specifically found that the picketing
was for *the* object of forcing or requiring recognition. As
Rodgers and Leedom pointed out, the evidence demonstrated
that the union's picketing was not *informational* which, in
itself, removed the protection of the publicity proviso. Moreover, the majority's own finding of *the* object would seem
to preclude a finding that *the* purpose was informational.
The majority did not see fit to discuss the point. Also, the
majority members disregarded the falsity of the picket signs
for several reasons. They thought it "unreasonable" that a
union seeking recognition should be required to assume the
burden of informing the public that the employer had contracts with other unions and they declared there was no
"intent to deceive the public" and no evidence that the public
was deceived. The dissenters merely pointed out the untruth-
fulness of the signs but they might have emphasized that
nothing in the language of the proviso or its legislative history
indicated Congress intended to excuse falsity regardless of
the intent to deceive.

The majority members' principal discussion in *Barker Bros.* centered on their view that the picketing was excused because it did not have the effect of interfering with deliveries or services. They decided the Board's task was one of striking a balance between labor's interest in communicating its ideas to the public by picketing and management's desire to be insulated from the coercive effects of such conduct. They believed a literal reading of the statutory language would ". . . do a disservice to Congress . . ." and render illusory the union's right to inform the public; that a "quantitative" test of number of deliveries or services not performed was an "inadequate yardstick"; and that the more reasonable test was in terms of the actual impact on the picketed employer's business. They admitted some interruptions but found no proof of any actual interference. In addition, they placed the duty on the General Counsel to prove that the picketing, in fact, interfered with, disrupted or curtailed the employer's business. Having failed to anticipate such a duty would be assigned to him, the General Counsel lost his case and the complaint was dismissed.

The dissenters argued that the majority, without citing any legislative history or persuasive authority in support, in effect said ". . . Congress did not intend the result which would obtain if the plain and unambiguous language were applied as Congress wrote it." They felt the majority sought ". . . to make the statute mean what it does not say, and say what it does not mean." Congress gave no indication whatsoever that it intended the Board to strike a "delicate balance" between labor and management. Instead, the dissenters declared that Congress struck its own balance by writing the proviso as unambiguously as possible and ". . . all that remains for this Board, *like it or not,* is to apply the law which Congress has given us."

Further cases will be required before the majority's theory of how much interference with deliveries or services is necessary to meet the standard of interference, disruption of curtailment of the employer's business which the Kennedy Board substituted for the statutory test of "an effect." In *Electrical Workers Union, Local 429 (Sam Melson, General Contractor)*, 138 NLRB No. 57, 51 LRRM 1065, the refusal of subcontractors' employees to cross the picket line for a three week period satisfied the majority's yardstick. The same result obtained where the employer was forced to change his source of supply. *San Diego County Waiters' Union (Joe Hunt's Restaurant)*, 138 NLRB No. 55, 51 LRRM 1063. But "one service stoppage" and a "temporary service delay of a few hours" did not cause sufficient disruption. *Retail Clerks Union (Hested Stores Co.)*, 138 NLRB No. 56, 51 LRRM 1061. Rodgers and Leedom emphasized in *Hested Stores* that the one service stoppage consisted of a refusal by an electrician to perform service which *was not performed during the duration of the picketing*. The temporary delay involved a refrigerator repairman. As pointed out in their dissent ". . . refrigeration being what it is, virtually any delay in effecting a refrigeration repair would necessarily have a serious impact . . ."

When the publicity proviso (which applies to Section 8(b)(7)(C) only) is not available, it might be assumed that the majority members would be forced to follow the literal language of Section 8(b)(7)(A) and (B) or the closely related Section 8(b)(4)(C). The latter section was the Taft-Hartley ban on rival union picketing of employees represented by a certified bargaining agent.

Shortly before the Kennedy Board took control, a panel consisting of Leedom, Rodgers and Jenkins found a Section 8(b)(4)(C) violation in *Local No. 41, Hod Carriers' Union (Calumet Contractors Association)*, 130 NLRB No. 17, 47 LRRM 1253. The Christian Labor Association was the certified bargaining representative for employees of Calumet members. In the representation proceeding leading to certi-

fication, the Hod Carriers and seven other craft unions inter-
vened to contest the bargaining unit, while at the same time
disclaiming any interest in representing the employees involved. From late October, 1958, until June 5, 1959, the
Hod Carriers picketed a construction site where an employer
member of Calumet was working. The picket signs contained no specific demand for recognition or bargaining but
stated that the "prevailing rate of pay and conditions are
not being met." The signs emphasized that they were addressed to the public only. The Eisenhower Board followed
the established rule, and held that one of the objects of the
picketing was clearly to force the employer to meet the prevailing rate of pay and conditions for the area, constituting
an attempt to force itself on the employees as their bargaining
agent and a violation of Section 8(b)(4)(C).

The decision was issued on February 10, 1961, and on
April 26, after the Kennedy appointees took office, the union
requested reconsideration. It was granted and McCulloch,
Fanning and Brown reversed the earlier case, dismissing the
complaint and holding that the union's admitted objective—
to require the employer to conform to standards of employment prevailing in the area—"is not tantamount to, nor does
it have an objective of, recognition or bargaining." In their
view, a union may be concerned about a particular employer
undermining area union standards and may be willing to
forego bargaining provided subnormal working conditions
are eliminated (133 NLRB No. 57, 48 LRRM 1667).
Rodgers and Leedom dissented for the reasons expressed
in the original decision.

The same principle was followed in *Automobile Workers'
Union (Fanelli Ford Sales, Inc.)*, 133 NLRB No. 163, 49
LRRM 1021, and in *Houston Building and Construction
Trades Council (Claude Everett Construction Co.)*, 136
NLRB No. 28, 49 LRRM 1757, although both arose out
of Section 8(b)(7) charges. Another example is *Hod*

Carriers' Union, Local 107 (Texarkana Construction Co.), 138 NLRB No. 10, 50 LRRM 1545, where, in addition, the majority disregarded evidence of several discussions pertaining to "using union men."

To digress again, despite the importance of the Calumet decision and its reversal of precedent, the majority provided no explanation of its thinking and was satisfied merely to repeat Member Fanning's short dissent in the *Industrial Chrome Plating Co.* case, 121 NLRB No. 1298, 42 LRRM 1559. There Fanning took the approach that, though there might be some justification for arguing that picketing by an outside union when another union has newly won a Board certification is an unwarranted harassment, ". . . this is an argument that must be addressed to Congress." In the *C. A. Blinne* case, discussed below, the new majority relied heavily on the proposition that Congressional silence in reenacting statutory provisions indicates approval of past Board interpretations. The principle followed in the first Calumet decision was the law of the matter at the time the 1959 amendments were added, Section 8(b)(4)(C) was not altered, and additional picketing restrictions were added, yet the *C. A. Blinne* theory of Congressional approval through silence is not even mentioned in the second Calumet decision.

When Calumet reconsidered is viewed in the light of an employer's duty to bargain, its illogic is more fully exposed. The form of a demand makes little difference in establishing an employer's duty to bargain. Writing on a placard paraded in front of the employer's place of business is as much a demand as a statement made at the bargaining table. The employer refuses to bargain when he will not discuss any bargainable issue and, furthermore, he refuses to bargain if he unilaterally makes changes in wages, hours or terms and conditions of employment without consulting the bargaining agent, regardless of a demand. Thus, if the Calumet employer had acceded to the Hod Carriers' demands,

as listed on their picketing signs, he would have been guilty
of a refusal to bargain with the certified union and, possibly,
unlawful assistance.

The Board's great concern over the right of a union to
publicize an employer's alleged undermining of area standards once again misconstrues the purpose of the Act. To
eliminate obstructions to the free flow of commerce, the
Congress has encouraged collective bargaining and protected
workers in their full freedom of association, self-organization
and designation of representatives of their own choosing. It
has not seen fit in this Act, though it has in other statutes,
to provide specific means of protecting area wage standards.
The employees of Calumet had exercised their free choice
in an NLRB election and had reached an agreement with
their employer through free collective bargaining. To read
the Act as then permitting another union to obstruct the free
flow of commerce by a picket line, in complete derogation
of the freedom of choice of the members of the Christian
Labor Union and of the collective bargaining which they had
successfully accomplished, is a self-evident arrogation of the
Congressional authority to establish policy.

An extreme example of the Kennedy Board's refusal to
find an object of recognition or organization and thus no
violation, is *Teamsters' Union, Local 200 (Bachman Furniture Co.)*, 134 NLRB No. 54, 49 LRRM 1192. The Teamsters demanded recognition March 24, 1960, and filed an
election petition a few days later. The union, after losing
the election by a vote of 4 to 3, filed objections which were
over-ruled and a certification of results issued. Charges of
unfair labor practices occurring prior to the execution of
the consent agreement, filed with the objections, were settled
by an informal agreement participated in by the union.
About two weeks later, the Teamsters began to picket at
the employer's store with a sign reading "BACHMAN
ADMITS UNFAIR LABOR PRACTICES. UNFAIR

LABOR PRACTICES VIOLATE FEDERAL LAW." Most of the employees in the bargaining unit worked at a warehouse five miles from the scene of the picketing. The union business agent testified the decision to picket was made after a discussion with other union officials about losing elections, for the purpose of "letting people know about the employer's activities."

McCulloch, Fanning and Brown refused to find the picketing in violation of Section 8(b)(7)(B) because the picketing was not for recognition, *the employees having sought union membership rather than being solicited.* Also, the union did not picket prior to the election when it legally could have done so and it made no overture which would tend to impugn its asserted purpose. Rodgers and Leedom dissented, pointing out the vigorous prosecution by the union of its election petition aimed at recognition, followed by picketing after the election was irrevocably lost and it could not otherwise compel recognition. To disregard such clear evidence of recognition and accept the union's assertion that it was picketing solely to protest the employer's unfair labor practices and did not have any object of recognition "strains credulity to the breaking point" in their view. There is, of course, no publicity exemption to Section 8(b)(7)(B) and the majority was, therefore, faced with the alternative of finding a violation or the absence of *an* object of recognition or organization.

Another example of the "missing object" technique was used by the majority to avoid application of Section 8(b)(7) in *Local 344, Retail Clerks' Union (Alton Myers Brothers, Inc.),* 136 NLRB No. 118, 49 LRRM 1969. The union began picketing July 10, 1958. A Board-conducted election was held December 12, 1958, at which the union was overwhelmingly defeated, 17-2. The union's objections to the election and a motion for reconsideration were denied and, finally, on April 24, 1959, a certification of results issued. The union continued its picketing until enjoined on November 28, 1959, after a Section 8(b)(7)(B) charge was filed. During the unfair labor practice hearing, the union secretary-treasurer testified that the Retail Clerks abandoned their efforts to organize the employees in June, 1959, and thereafter merely sought public support against the company's non-union standards. Nevertheless, late in September, 1959, the union sent a letter to other local unions in the area in which it said it had been picketing for organizational purposes since July 10, 1958. The Kennedy majority accepted the word of the union agent that the object of the picketing had changed in June, 1959, and ruled that the September letter should be disregarded because it was written more than two months before Landrum-Griffin became effective (but after the law was passed).

The incongruous result when the majority strains the interpretation of "an object" to the extent found in *Alton Myers* is that the restrictions on picketing after a lost NLRB election are less stringent than if no election has been held. In the 7(C) cases, where the majority can dismiss on the "informational" theory, it has not always bothered to determine whether the picketing is for organization or recognition (*Vestaglass, Inc., supra*). Where picketing is excused on informational grounds there must be no interruption in deliveries and services but, in the 7(B) cases, the union is free to create such interruptions when the majority is forced to dismiss on "object" grounds in order to avoid finding a violation.

Perhaps the most extreme view is implied by the dissent of McCulloch in *Ladies' Garment Workers Union (Coed Collar Co.)*, 137 NLRB No. 181, 50 LRRM 1473, where the majority found 8(b)(7)(B) violated by union picketing after a lost election with only a two day hiatus. There, even though the union clearly was seeking recognition up to the day it lost the election and it then claimed it was picketing to protest unfair labor practices but did not even change part of its signs, McCulloch found ". . . it difficult to conceive of what more the Union could have done to comply with the newly-enacted statutory provisions short of permanently abandoning its picketing . . ." This seems an overly pessimistic view of conduct available to the union but, in any event, the Act contains no guarantee of a union's absolute right to picket. Instead, there would rarely appear to be a more appropriate time to protect the *employees* from the coercive effect of a picket line than immediately after they have expressed their free choice as to a bargaining agent in a secret ballot election conducted by NLRB.

In a line of cases beginning with *Hod Carriers, Local 840 (C. A. Blinne Construction Co.),* 135 NLRB No. 121, 49 LRRM 1638, another reconsidered decision of the former Board, the majority found still another way to devitalize Congress' attempt to restrict organization and recognition picketing. After the employer refused a union demand for recognition, the union commenced picketing for three announced objectives: (1) recognition of the union, (2) payment of the Bacon-Davis scale of wages, and (3) protest against Blinne's unfair labor practices in refusing to recognize the union and in threatening to transfer, and transferring, one employee. Three weeks later, unfair labor practice charges were filed by the union, part of which (including a refusal to bargain charge) were dismissed by the Director about six weeks after commencement of the picketing. After the dismissal, the union filed a representation petition. The employer, meanwhile, had filed a charge alleging violation of Section 8(b)(7)(C) because the union had picketed more than thirty days without petitioning for an election. The Regional Director obtained a settlement of the union's charges, subsequently approved by the Board, as to the employer threats and transfer of the one employee, and a complaint issued against the union on the 8(b)(7)(C) charges.

In the original decision (130 NLRB No. 69, 47 LRRM 1318), Leedom, Rodgers, Jenkins and Kimball found the Act violated, rejecting one union argument, among others, to the effect that it would be unfair to apply Section 8(b) (7)(C) because the employer's unfair labor practices deprived the union of fundamental rights, i.e., that it was entitled to recognition because it represented a majority of the employees in the bargaining unit. Thus they held there was no merit in the theory that unfair labor practice charges are a defense to a Section 8(b)(7) charge. The Eisenhower Board emphasized that Congress had specifically rejected such a view and found that only a meritorious charge of employer assistance to a rival union would be such a defense. Fanning, dissenting, argued that complex legislation such as this must be viewed in the spirit as well as the substance of the law. He could find nothing in the statute or legislative history which indicated Congressional disregard for established Board standards to assure free and uncoerced election results. He, therefore, felt that the Board's practice of staying election proceedings if meritorious charges have been filed should be applied to expedited elections. He disregarded the legislative history argument, which was built around the amendments to Section 10(l) of the Act, because the amendments were intended to refer only to Section 8(b)(7)(A), in his opinion. There is nothing in the statutory language to support his limited view.

In the new majority's reversal of *Blinne*, three separate views were expressed by the Board. McCulloch and Brown agreed with the result in the first case (a finding of violation), but treated the question of concurrent unfair labor practice charges against the employer while expedited election proceedings were pending in a different manner. In their view, no action should be taken on an election while meritorious unfair labor practice charges are pending against the employer and, until a valid election is held, the union's right to picket for recognition, bargaining or organization should not be inhibited. Their theory apparently is that the unremedied unfair labor practices prevent a free expression by employees as to a bargaining agent and there is no mandate by Congress to compel holding an election under such circumstances. They found a violation in the *Blinne* case, however, because the refusal to bargain charges were without merit.

Their theory sounds reasonable but it proves too much. The McCulloch-Brown approach amounts to a holding that, if an employer is charged with coercing his employees, a union should have an equal opportunity to coerce them, also. Because an employer's unfair labor practices have not yet been remedied, it does not necessarily follow that picketing must be permitted. Once again, it is the employees' right of free choice in selecting their bargaining agent which should be protected, not the right of the union to force organization or recognition by picketing. It would seem apparent that free choice can be exercised more effectively if the employer's unfair labor practices are cured and an election held without the economic pressure of a picket line on the employees during the process.

Fanning concurred in the second *Blinne* case, but would not have found a violation on the theory that the union relied on the established Board practice of requiring a union to elect between processing a representation petition and a refusal to bargain charge. Noting that a union cannot go to an election and, having lost, maintain a refusal to bargain charge, *Aiello Dairy Farms*, 110 NLRB No. 1365, 35 LRRM 1235, Fanning felt *Aiello* would require approval of a continuation of that practice in the Section 8(b)(7)(C) cases. Compare Brown's and Fanning's views in *Franz Food Products of Green Forest, Inc.*, 137 NLRB No. 35, 50 LRRM 1143, where they over-ruled *Humko, A Division of National Dairy Products Corp.*, 123 NLRB No. 310, 43 LRRM 1419.

The extreme to which the majority would extend its

concept that a meritorious refusal to bargain charge is an adequate substitute for filing an election petition in Section 8(b)(7)(C) cases is demonstrated by *Typographical Union, Local 285 (Charlton Press)*, 135 NLRB No. 123, 49 LRRM 1650, another reconsidered case. There McCulloch, Fanning and Brown found the union did not violate Section 8(b)(7), even though it neither filed an election petition nor a refusal to bargain charge. The union was excused by the fact that the charge would have been barred by the six months statute of limitations and that the union could not have filed because it chose not to comply with the Communist affidavit sections of the Act then in effect. Rodgers and Leedom dissented, following the views expressed in *Blinne*. Compare, *International Typographical Union (The Greenfield Prtg. & Publ. Co.)*, 137 NLRB No. 49, 50 LRRM 1156.

One more technique to debilitate Section 8(b)(7) was used by the new majority in *Laborers' Union, Local 383 (Colson and Stevens Construction Co., Inc.)*, 137 NLRB No. 149, 50 LRRM 1444. The Carpenters' and the Laborers' Unions, operating through the Phoenix Building and Construction Trades Council, picketed construction jobs where Colson and Stevens were working in order to obtain the company's signature on a "master agreement." The Carpenters' picketed for 30 days, the maximum allowable reasonable period under Section 8(b)(7)(C). Subsequently, the Laborers picketed for 26 days. No election petition was filed. The majority refused to find a violation of Section 8(b)(7)(C) because neither union's picketing exceeded 30 days. Rodgers and Leedom dissented because "a realistic appraisal" led them to the conclusion that the two unions, through the Joint Council, were acting in concert in support of their demands.

The organizational and recognition picketing cases are a telling commentary on the unwillingness of the new Board to carry out the Congressional intent. Much as the Board may dislike the approach of Congress or may disagree with the statutory provisions, the Board must apply the law as it is, not as the Board members would like it to be.

Even the most casual reading of the legislative history of Landum-Griffin shows that a major objective of the amendments was to protect employees from the abuses of union power. Beyond question, union attempts to force organization and recognition through picket lines was one of the evils Congress intended to eliminate insofar as possible without interfering with the union's right of free speech. But can it be argued seriously that the Congressional intent is being implemented when the statute is read as providing no relief where the union says its picketing is informational and the Board will not look at "surrounding circumstances" to ascertain the "truth of the assertion"? Or where "truthful" is defined as "untruthful but with no intent to deceive"? Or where "an effect" is read to mean "proof of interference, disruption or curtailment of the employer's business"? Or where a refusal to bargain charge is considered a defense, even though Congress specifically rejected this contention? The answer to each question must be an unequivocal "No."

The practical result of the picketing cases is that a moderately resourceful union representative should now have little difficulty in advising his union how to picket and yet comply with Section 8(b)(7) as amended by the Kennedy majority. And once more Congress must face the seemingly impossible task of finding words which the Board will accept as meaning what they say.

CHAPTER XVII

SECONDARY BOYCOTTS

Since the arrival of the Kennedy Board, the secondary boycott provisions of the Act have been a prolific source of split decisions. Surprisingly, McCulloch has joined with Rodgers and Leedom on a limited number of issues to make portions of the law more effective, but the divided opinions demonstrate a determined dilution of the Congressional intent by the new majority. As in the picketing cases, the recent enactment of the Landrum-Griffin amendments simplifies the task of assessing the direction of the Board's interpretations.

Limitations on secondary boycotts first became a part of the Act when Taft-Hartley was passed in 1947. The restrictions were stated in terms of proscribed *methods* to accomplish proscribed *objects,* both of which had to be infringed before the law was violated. As the statute was interpreted, the forbidden methods went no further than union inducement of certain types of employees, acting as a group, to strike or cease performing work. The improper objectives were construed more broadly, most common being the typical secondary boycott, i.e., to force an employer or other person not to do business with, or handle the products of, the employer with whom the union had a dispute—the primary employer.

The history of the 1947 Act makes it abundantly clear

that Congress intended to place broad restrictions on secondary activities. Senator Taft's classic remark, to the effect that the secondary boycott provisions were broadened because no Committee witness had succeeded in explaining the difference between good secondary boycotts and bad secondary boycotts, is frequently noted. Nevertheless, the NLRB and the courts have consistently construed the statutory language very narrowly, leaving many loopholes in the law. It was these loopholes which the Landrum-Griffin amendments were designed to close.

The 1959 Act substituted the words, "individual employed by any person" for the word "employees" to broaden the proscribed methods of boycotting and close the loopholes which permitted union pressure on single employees, supervisors, and railway, municipal and agricultural employees [Section 8(b)(4)(i)]. Also, in order to reduce direct union pressure on neutral *employers,* a ban on threats, restraint and coercion of any *person* was added to restrictions on inducement of employees [Section 8(b)(4)(ii)].

The unlawful objectives, on the other hand, were left largely unchanged except for an added proscription on forcing any employer or self-employed person to enter into an agreement prohibited by Section 8(e), i.e. a "hot cargo" contract. Also, a proviso was incorporated excusing conduct designed to publicize, truthfully, by means other than picketing, that a ". . . product or products are produced . . ." by an employer with whom a union has a primary dispute *and* are ". . . distributed . . ." by another employer. The proviso applies only as long as the publicity does not cause employees, other than those of the primary employer, to refuse to handle goods or perform services at any place away from the primary employers' premises.

In one case after another, the new Board has narrowed the impact of the Act's proscriptions on secondary activity. More often than not, the conflict between the neutral employer's right to be free from industrial strife and the union's right to exert economic pressure has been unbalanced heavily in favor of the union. Some of the decisions of the Eisenhower Board, as it interpreted the new amendments in its closing days are also open to criticism. Despite the broad intent of the original secondary boycott provisions and the well-documented goal of the 1959 amendments, Congress has been singularly unsuccessful in convincing the Board, regardless of its membership, that it wants secondary boycott activity stopped.

The interpretations of the "publicity" proviso are an appropriate starting point, as they clearly illustrate the task faced by Congress. As in the organization and recognition picketing cases, the plain language of the statute has virtually disappeared. The well-publicized *Teamsters' Union, Local 537 (Lohman Sales Co.)*, 132 NLRB No. 67, 48 LRRM 1429, was the lead case. The union called a strike at Lohman, a wholesale distributor of candy and tobacco products after an impasse in bargaining for a contract covering Lohman's drivers. As a part of its pressure on the primary employer (Lohman), the union approached the owners of four drug stores and asked them not to buy from that company. One owner was threatened with the distribution of handbills, and handbills were passed out at two of the stores. They stated that the Lohman employees were on strike and that the tobacco and candies on sale in the store were distributed by Lohman, although the stores, in fact, bought similar products from other wholesalers. The handbills urged that no tobacco and candies be purchased. Several appeals were also made to employees of the drug stores not to buy or order Lohman products.

The full Board agreed that the appeals to employees violated Section 8(b)(4)(i)(B). With Rodgers dissenting, the Board also held that the distribution of the handbills to consumers in front of the stores buying from Lohman was proper. The majority recognized handbilling might constitute restraint and coercion, but viewed the activity in *Lohman* as protected by the proviso of Section 8(b)(4), which permits, as noted above:

> "publicity, other than picketing, for the purpose of truthfully advising the public . . . that a product or products are produced by an employer with whom the labor organization has a primary dispute and are distributed by another employer . . . "

as long as such publicity does not induce the withholding of services at the secondary employer's premises. The majority found that the handbills were truthful, as they were "substantially accurate," even though the stores did not purchase *all* the items listed from Lohman.

The Board also found the publicity proviso operated, even though Lohman, the primary employer, was a distributor rather than a manufacturer of tobacco and other commodities. They read the words "product or products . . . produced" in the statute to include distribution of products. Legislative history was used as the basis for the decision on the unusual theory that the absence of any history showing Congress intended to permit publicity solely with respect to manufactured products, and not to products distributed by wholesalers, proved no distinction was intended. Rodgers dissented, declaring that in the absence of legislative history the Board must turn to the plain language of the statute. He then, most effectively, demonstrated that the statutory language supported the distinction.

The theory used by the majority in *Lohman* has been followed in a number of cases with increasingly questionable results. In *Radio and Television Engineers, Local 662 (Middle South Broadcasting Co.),* 133 NLRB No. 165, 49 LRRM 1042, the union struck radio station WOGA, picketing the station and an automobile agency from which remote broadcasts were made. The union also circulated to its members, to WOGA advertisers, and to the public a leaflet asking that business not be given to merchants still advertising over WOGA. A list of such advertisers was included.

The majority held that the radio station produced a product by its advertising of the automobiles, thereby becoming a producer of automobiles. The automobile dealer distributed the product, i.e. apparently the automobiles produced by the radio station, and was thus a distributor. Consequently, the leaflet was protected by the publicity proviso and the picketing was lawful under the "common situs" doctrine. Rodgers dissented for the reasons given in *Lohman* and was unable to resist suggesting that it would "come as something of a surprise not only to WOGA, but to General Motors, Ford, Chrysler and other automobile manufacturers" to learn that WOGA was a producer of automobiles.

A television station joined the ranks of "producers" in *AFTRA San Francisco Local (Great Western Broadcasting Corp.)*, 134 NLRB No. 141, 49 LRRM 1391, where it was found to produce not only automobiles, but bread, gasoline and beer. Also, see *Local 968, Teamsters' Union (Schepps Grocery Co.)*, 133 NLRB No. 134, 49 LRRM 1011.

The limitation in the proviso to Section 8(b)(4), that it applies only when a "product or products are produced" by the party with which the union has its dispute and only when such product or products are "distributed" by a different employer (the secondary employer), has continued to be highlighted by Rodgers' dissents. The majority has found it necessary to explain in detail its concept of production but, for some reason, has ignored the distribution requirement of the statute. The primary employers in *Electrical Workers, Local 712 (Golden Dawn Foods)*, 134 NLRB No. 73, 49 LRRM 1220, were subcontractors doing electrical and refrigeration work at a supermarket. Their difficulties with the union arose out of the fact that they employed either members of another union or non-union workmen.

At the entrance to the supermarket parking lot used by customers, Local 712 distributed handbills asking that the supermarket not be patronized because electrical and refrigeration work was done by persons other than members of Local 712. McCulloch and Fanning found the handbilling protected by the proviso, citing *Lohman Sales*, but without further explanation. Their theory must have been that the electrical and refrigeration services were products produced by the primary employers. They made no mention of the fact that these services also must be distributed by another employer, the supermarket in this instance. Rodgers dissented because neither primary employer produced anything, providing services instead, and "certainly by no stretch of anyone's imagination can it be said that there is *distribution* by another employer of the results of their labors." Also, see *Electrical Workers' Local 73 (Northwestern Constr. Co. of Washington)*, 134 NLRB No. 46, 49 LRRM 1131, and *Teamsters, Local 901 (Editorial "El Imparcial," Inc.)*, 134 NLRB No. 83, 49 LRRM 1224, and *Local 154, Typographical Union (Ypsilanti Press, Inc.)*, 135 NLRB No. 96, 49 LRRM 1605.

It will be recalled that the handbills in *Lohman* were only "substantially" truthful. The majority's lenient approach to truth is demonstrated in other cases as well, although the proviso requires that the publicity be for the purpose of "truthfully" advising the public. In *Wholesale Delivery Drivers Union, Local 848 (Servette, Inc.)*, 133 NLRB No. 152, 49 LRRM 1028, the union handbill listed a number of products distributed by Servette, the primary employer, and asked that they not be purchased. The handbills were untruthful in that all of the stores where the handbilling took place did not purchase all of the items listed from Servette. Leedom, Fanning and Brown felt it was sufficient that each store purchased at least one of the items listed. Rodgers dissented.

The standard of truth and accuracy required in handbills is in marked contrast to that required of an employer during a union organizing drive (see Chapter V, Free Speech) but is similar to that used in applying the publicity proviso of Section 8(b)(7)(C) (see Chapter XVI). It is a well-established principle of law that provisos are narrowly construed, and it would seem to follow that a restrictive interpretation of the truthfulness of the handbill would be proper. On the other hand, the employer right of free speech during an organizing drive is based both on the Constitutional principle of free speech and on specific language assuring the right in Section 8(c) of the statute. The Board's narrow construction of employer speech and broad reading of the publicity proviso reverses the usual rule of statutory interpretation.

Another balancing of interests in favor of unions at the expense of neutral employers is found in the ambulatory picketing and "common situs" cases. The latter classification refers to the well-established policy of permitting a union, within strict limitations, to picket a site common to more than one employer if the union has a dispute with only one employer. In *Electrical Workers, Local 861 (Plauche Electric, Inc.),* 135 NLRB No. 41, 49 LRRM 1446, Plauche was an electrical contractor in Lake Charles, Louisiana, who had a collective bargaining agreement with Local 861 terminating July 27, 1960. Although meetings had been held, no new agreement was reached because the standard union contract was not acceptable to Plauche and the union would not vary any of its terms. In carrying out a subcontract for work to be performed at U. S. Tire Engineers, Plauche employees reported each morning and evening at their employer's office, were dispatched by truck to the job, and reported back in the evening. On occasion, an employee would return to the office during the day to pick up a tool or materials. In order to obtain its demands for a new contract from Plauche, the union picketed U. S. Tire Engineers, clearly limiting its dispute to Plauche, but did not picket the Plauche office. The union also picketed a Ramada Motel construction site, when Ramada refused to replace Plauche with a union contractor.

McCulloch, Fanning and Brown found no violation of Section 8(b)(4), reversing *Brewery and Beverage Drivers Union (Washington Coca-Cola Bottling Works, Inc.)*, 107 NLRB No. 299, 33 LRRM 1122. There, the Eisenhower Board unanimously held unlawful picketing at stores of Washington Coca-Cola customers, both when its trucks were at the stores and at other times, where the union's object was to sever the business relationship between the primary employer and its customers. The majority members regarded *Washington Coca-Cola* as imposing a rigid rule that picketing at a common situs is unlawful when the primary employer has a regular place of business in the locality which can be picketed. They argued that various Courts of Appeals have refused to accept such a rule and also that it was improper in the light of the Supreme Court's criticism of per se rules. They declared they would not automatically find unlawful picketing at a site where primary employees spend practically their entire working day because the employees may report for a few minutes at the beginning and end of each day at the primary employer's regular place of business.

Rodgers and Leedom dissented, quoting *Washington Coca-Cola* at length to demonstrate that it did not involve a per se rule but was a balancing of the dual Congressional objectives of preserving the right of the union to bring pressure on offending employers in primary labor disputes and of shielding unoffending employers and others from controversies not their own. Picketing at the premises of secondary employees was recognized in *Washington Coca-Cola* as allowable only when there was no other way in which the union could picket the primary employer's employees.

They emphasized that the theory of the exception, and the standards which such picketing must follow, presumed that the union's appeal was limited to the primary employer's employees. When the reason for the exception was absent and the union had an opportunity to direct its inducement to such employees at their employer's premises, the only reasonable inference was that inducement occurring at another situs was, in fact, directed at the secondary employees working there. (This seems particularly true where, as in *Plauche Electric*, the union did not even picket the primary employer's office.)

The majority also stated that, in partially over-ruling *Washington Coca-Cola*, it was not "unmindful" of the reference to that case in the 1959 amendments. It dismissed the reference, however, as not precluding Board re-examination of the decision, as the Court of Appeals which enforced *Washington Coca-Cola* did not rely entirely on the Board's rationale. The majority noted that the legislative history also cited *Pittsburgh Plate Glass Company*, 110 NLRB 455, 35 LRRM 1071, approvingly and that case substantially limited, if not squarely conflicted, with *Washington Coca-Cola*.

Such an argument is an excellent demonstration of the reason for the Board's continuing difficulties with Congress. The conference report, cited by the majority, was the most authoritative legislative history on the Landrum-Griffin Act. That report clearly approved the *Board* decision in *Washington Coca-Cola*, not any Court modification, as an authoritative statement of existing law. Senator Goldwater was one of the conferees and his approving reference to the same decision (cited by the majority) was not challenged by any other conferee.

While the Kennedy Board may read *Pittsburgh Plate Glass* as substantially limiting or in conflict with *Washington Coca-Cola*, that is not the view of Congress. Otherwise, the two cases would not have been listed in the Conference Report without explanation. Congressional recognition of the necessity of citing both cases is demonstrated by the Board's misapprehension of their meaning. *Pittsburgh Plate Glass* emphasized that the *Washington Coca-Cola* doctrine was *not* a per se rule. In the *Pittsburgh* case the Eisenhower Board refused to adopt a finding of the Trial Examiner to that effect and found it inapplicable to the factual situation because the primary employees were at their employer's premises only twice a day at most ". . . and sometimes not at all." The practical result of the *Plauche* case has been adoption of a per se rule to the opposite effect, i.e., the Board now automatically finds such picketing lawful. Also, see *Plumber and Pipe Fitters' Union, Local 471 (Wyckoff Plumbing)*, 135 NLRB No. 49, 49 LRRM 1489; *Hotel Employees Union, Local 568 (Leonard Shaffer Co.)*, 135 NLRB No. 53, 49 LRRM 1523; and *Local 730 Teamsters (C. R. Sheaffer & Sons)*, 136 NLRB No. 88, 49 LRRM 1910.

In any event, if Congressional approval of *Washington Coca-Cola* had any weight, it was effectively dissipated by *United Plant Guard Workers (Houston Armored Car Co.)*, 136 NLRB No. 9, 49 LRRM 1713. There the employer transported currency from banks and picked up money or deposits at customers' places of business and transported them to banks or other depositories. When contract negotiations broke down, the union picketed Houston's place of business where Houston employees entered and left about six times a day. Also, the union followed the Houston trucks and picketed the premises of 69 customers while the trucks were there, at times going on to the property of the customers. Fanning and Brown with Rodgers dissenting, found that, as the picketing was conducted only for the duration of the trucks' stay and it otherwise conformed to common situs picketing standards, the evidence did not support the Trial

Examiner's finding that the picketing at customers' premises was unlawful.

In *Steel Workers, Local 5895 (Carrier Corp.)*, 132 NLRB No. 17, 48 LRRM 1319, the union picketed the premises of a railroad located adjacent to the company's plant where the union had called a primary strike and was picketing six or seven entrances. The railroad property was separately owned and was not used by customers or *Carrier* employees. The Board majority likened the railroad's gate to a separate gate of a single employer and held that, because the services performed by the railroad were services rendered in connection with the normal operations of the primary employer, the Act was not violated. The Board considered the effect on the railroad to be incidental and dismissed the separate character of the railroad property with a mere "we do not consider this fact to be material."

Rodgers dissented, arguing that the majority holding directly contravened the 1959 amendments which clearly were intended to extend the secondary boycott provisions to railroads. The majority's approach effectively thwarted that intent because it permitted a union to involve a railroad directly in the union's dispute with the primary employer. He found it unrealistic to say that, when a union goes on the property of a secondary employer for the sole purpose of inducing its employees and coercing the secondary employer, it is primary activity. See *Local 545, Operating Engineers (Syracuse Supply Co.)*, 139 NLRB No. 50, 51 LRRM 1372, for another example of the new Board's preoccupation with protection of the union in its primary dispute and its concept of the impact on the neutral employer as "incidental."

Carrier Corp., Lohman Sales, Plauche Electric, and the cases which followed are unusually clear demonstrations of the new Board's methods of debilitating the secondary boycott restrictions. In each instance the neutral employer was forced to withstand union attacks on his business in order that the union might place greater pressure on another employer. Less obvious techniques bringing about the same result are also found among the boycott cases.

Under Taft-Hartley the terms "induce or encourage," which remain unchanged in the Landum-Griffin amendments, were construed as broad enough to include every form of influence and persuasion. While the new Board has maintained the view that inducement or encouragement need not be successful in order to be improper, it has begun to find that conduct formerly thought to be inducement or encouragement falls short of this mark. Probably the best example is *Upholsterers Union, Local 61 (Minneapolis House Furnishing Co.)*, 132 NLRB No. 2, 48 LRRM 1301. There McCulloch, Fanning and Brown ruled that secondary picketing of retail stores, with signs ostensibly urging prospective customers not to buy certain products, was not "per se" inducement or encouragement within the meaning of Section 8(b)(4)(i) of the Act.

The Upholsterers had picketed retail furniture stores with signs containing the following legends:

> "Help us keep our jobs—BUY MATTRESSES MADE LOCALLY BY UPHOLSTERERS LOCAL 61 AFL-CIO"

and

> "Buy union made upholstered furniture made by Upholsterers Local 61 AFL-CIO."

The majority members, relying on a newspaper article, found there was no inducement of store employees to engage in a work stoppage, and no such stoppage was likely, in view of the union's advance publicity that there would be no strikes or suspension of pickups or deliveries at picketed stores. They also felt the legend on the picket signs, the contents of leaflets distributed at the picketed stores which appealed to the consumer public and not the store employees, and the absence of picketing at truck entrances or those used exclusively by store employees demonstrated the picketing was not directed at the employees. *Perfection Mattress & Spring Co.*, 129 NLRB No. 1014, 47 LRRM 1121, was over-ruled.

Rodgers and Leedom would have followed the *Perfection Mattress* case. In their view, a picket line necessarily invites employees to make common cause with the picketing union irrespective of the literal appeal of the legends on the picketing sign. Also see, *Local 760, Teamsters Union (Tree Fruits Labor Relations Committee, Inc.)*, 132 NLRB No. 102, 48 LRRM 1496; *Plumbers and Pipefitters Union, Local 519 (Babcock Co.)*, 137 NLRB No. 46, 50 LRRM 1219; *Service and Maintenance Employees Union (William J. Burns Intl. Detective Agency, Inc.)*, 136 NLRB No. 34, 49 LRRM 1793.

In Minneapolis House Furnishing Co. the full Board held that the picketing described was a violation of Section 8(b)(4)(ii) of the Act. There the new Board members agreed with the previous view, as expressed in the *Perfection Mattress* case, that peaceful picketing for an objective proscribed by Section 8(b)(4) constitutes coercion and restraint of an employer within the meaning of 8(b)(4)(ii) because it is in the nature of economic retaliation against the employer who fails to comply with the union's demand. Legislative history was relied upon as showing a clear intent that such picketing was not to be permitted.

But, while the Board has indicated that a violation of 8(b)(4)(ii)(B) will be found where a union makes an *unqualified* threat to picket a secondary employer's premises in order to force it to cease doing business with the employer with whom the union is involved in a labor dispute, it is clear that the majority is reluctant to find the threat to be unqualified. *General Drivers Union, Local 886 (The Stephens Co.)*, 133 NLRB No. 134, 49 LRRM 1013. There Leedom, Fanning and Brown found an unqualified threat when the union wrote a letter to secondary employers that it intended to picket such employers to inform all union members and the general public of the facts of the strike with the primary employer. A second letter, however, backed away slightly and said that if any picketing of Stephens, the primary employer, took place in the vicinity of the secondary employers' places of business it would be conducted in strict conformity with the Board standards for such picketing. This letter, Fanning and Brown found, showed an intent to engage only in lawful picketing and was therefore not improper. Leedom disagreed as he felt there was no possible way in which the union could picket in the vicinity of the customers' premises without violating the law.

Fanning and Brown, with Leedom dissenting, also found no threat where a business agent told a general contractor that he would give a subcontractor until 8 o'clock the next morning to "straighten out" the use of two independent contractors whom the union wanted to displace with union men. The general contractors' understanding of the nature of the comment as being a threat rather than a notification was shown by his immediate effort to have the subcontractor get rid of the independent contractors unsatisfactory to the union. *Local 83, Teamsters' Union (Marshall and Haas)*, 133 NLRB No. 116, 48 LRRM 1791. Also, see *Electrical Workers Union, Local 38 (Hoertz Electric Main. Co.)*, 138 NLRB No. 17, 50 LRRM 1560 and *Roofers Union, Local 47 (Atlas Roofing Co. Inc.)*, 134 NLRB No. 35, 49 LRRM 1180.

By adopting a ruling of the Eisenhower Board the new members maintained another limitation on the 1959 amendments. In *Local 505, Teamsters' Union (Carolina Lumber Co.)*, 130 NLRB No. 148, 47 LRRM 1502, the preceding Board held "any individual employed by any person," did not have its literal meaning but included supervisors who were more nearly related to rank-and-file employees than to management. Factors to be considered in determining whether a particular person was such an individual [and, therefore, could not be induced within the meaning of Section 8(b)(4)(i)] were listed as: organizational set-up of the company; authority, responsibilities and background of supervisors; their working conditions, duties and functions on the job involved in the dispute; and their salary or earnings, perquisites and benefits. The *Carolina Lumber* rule was approved by the new Board, without dissent, in *Sheet Metal Workers, Local 299 (S. M. Kisner & Sons)*, 131 NLRB No. 147, 48 LRRM 1226, where a corporate officer was found to be a managerial representative and not an "individual." The effect of these decisions was to open once more a loophole which Congress was specifically trying to close, i.e. the limited view of persons who may not be induced.

Another technique of the new Board is its resolution of questions of independent contractor status or employer-employee relationship. In *Local 83, Teamsters' Union (Marshall & Haas)*, 133 NLRB No. 116, 48 LRRM 1791, Yuma Builders Supply had a subcontract to supply ready mixed concrete which Marshall & Haas was using in the construction of a drainage and irrigation channel for the Department of Interior. Yuma contracted with two men, Drake and Nooney, to deliver the concrete from Yuma's plant. They were paid on a cubic yard basis and were free to operate in any manner which they desired, including full control over the equipment which they furnished, hiring of helpers, hours and other conditions of employment. Fanning and Brown found no violation when the contracts of Drake and Nooney were terminated immediately after the union business agent gave Yuma 24 hours to "straighten out" by getting rid of them. The majority reasoned that Drake and Nooney were employees, the nature of their work being like that of other Yuma employees. They were not doing business with Yuma because they performed part of a continuous operation, loading in succession at the Yuma plant and driving to the construction site where each unloaded in turn like four drivers employed directly by Yuma. Leedom dissented because of the absence of any showing of the "minute and comprehensive control" which the Board ordinarily requires before it will find that an individual is an employee.

When a non-employee relationship would result in dismissal of a secondary boycott complaint, however, the new Board has been more willing to find the necessary status. *Television and Radio Artists Union (L. B. Wilson, Inc.)*, 133 NLRB No. 72, 49 LRRM 1060. Compare *Site Oil Co. of Mo.*, 137 NLRB No. 145, 50 LRRM 1364, for the majority's view of independent contractors in a refusal to bargain case and *A. S. Abell Co.*, 137 NLRB No. 36, 50 LRRM 1131, an interference case.

Questionable handling of the employer-employee relationship, resulting in dismissal of another secondary boycott case, is found in *Teamsters' Union Local 107 (Sterling Wire Products Co.)*, 137 NLRB No. 150, 50 LRRM 1403. There Sterling discharged three drivers November 20, 1958 and changed its delivery method to use common carriers, including Fees, Inc. Fees hired the three drivers and took over the employer's trucks. The drivers continued to operate from the Sterling plant although they, at times, delivered products of other customers of Fees. Sterling was not the only customer of Fees at which Fees' drivers were stationed. November 30, 1960, Sterling terminated its arrangement with Fees and Fees discharged the drivers. They began picketing Sterling but made no request that Fees reemploy them.

McCulloch, Fanning, and Brown found no violation of the Act, reasoning that Sterling was a "co-employer" of the drivers who had been transferred to Fees' payroll. The transfer was a mere formality and right of control had been retained by Sterling. Rodgers and Leedom dissented, agreeing that certain instructions were given to the drivers by

Sterling, but contending that these amounted only to routine directions which any shipper would give his carrier. The majority also found that the present dispute was a continuation of that which arose in 1958 but the minority pointed out that that dispute had been settled when Sterling made its original agreement with Fees. At that time Fees employed the drivers and brought them under its union contract, which was a part of a multi-employer agreement with the same local union. The minority viewed the decision as holding that an enterprise may not sever a business relationship with another without being subject to picketing by the other's employees.

The question of whether or not a secondary dispute exists has caused a division of opinion on the new Board, resulting in McCulloch joining with Rodgers and Leedom in some instances to find violations. One example is *Local 1066, International Longshoremen's Association (Wiggin Terminals, Inc.)*, 137 NLRB No. 3, 50 LRRM 1056. There Wiggin operated a marine terminal, Bay State ran a stevedoring service, and Renault imported automobiles. For some time Renault had its cars unloaded by Bay State and hauled on trailer trucks about twenty miles from the port. The process required several days to unload a ship. Commencing June 28, 1961, Renault leased space at Wiggin in order to drive newly unloaded cars directly from the dock, using Wiggin employees. The union objected to Wiggin and Renault but not to Bay State. Renault agreed to guarantee the union five days pay after the vessel was unloaded but later withdrew from this arrangement. When Wiggin said the problem was up to Bay State, the union "slowed down" and Renault reverted to the old procedure of using trailer trucks.

McCulloch, Rodgers and Leedom found the union's primary dispute was with Renault and its objective was to force Bay State to cease doing business with that employer.

Fanning and Brown dissented on the theory that the primary dispute was with Bay State, but the majority countered that the facts showed the union looked to Renault to satisfy its demands. The test is one of purpose, not of effect. Also see *Local 5, Plumbers Union (Arthur Venneri Co.)*, 137 NLRB No. 100, 50 LRRM 1266; *Painters Union, Local 1778 (Frank Musny, d/b/a S&M Glazing Co.)*, 137 NLRB No. 25, 50 LRRM 1170; *Longshoremen's Union, Local 19 (J. Duane Vance)*, 137 NLRB No. 13, 50 LRRM 1090; and *Teamsters' Union, Local 282 (Acme Concrete & Supply Corp.)*, 137 NLRB No. 137, 50 LRRM 1374.

Brown's concern with the primary nature of the dispute is also evident in his dissent in *International Longshoremen's Association (Board of Harbor Commission)*, 137 NLRB No. 117, 50 LRRM 1333, where he argues that, if the power to resolve the dispute is the "touchstone" of a primary dispute, even a primary strike is unlawful where the primary employer cannot grant a wage increase because he cannot pass it on to customers. He believes the crucial factor in determining which employer is primary is the fundamental character of the dispute. The majority looked upon this as a failure to distinguish between a situation where an employer has no legal power to take a particular action and a situation where he possesses such power but finds it not economically feasible to exercise it. Also, see *Local 282, Teamsters' Union (Precon Trucking Corp.)*, 139 NLRB No. 92, 51 LRRM 1441.

In at least one case, Fanning has disagreed with McCulloch, Leedom and Brown (Rodgers did not participate) as to the scope of the order in a secondary boycott case. *Bakery Drivers' Union Local 484 (Sunrise Transportation)*, 137 NLRB No. 98, 50 LRRM 1289. There the union, which had struck a bakery, was found to have violated the Act by inducing the primary employees to cease handling products scheduled for delivery by a common carrier because the objective was to limit the bakery's right to subcontract only to employers who had agreements with the contracting union. The majority issued a broad remedial order because the carrier involved did business with other employers, not all of which were members of a multi-employer association with which the union had a contract, and also because the union viewed its dispute with the carrier as an industry problem. Fanning would have limited the effect of the order to the members of the association, even though the record disclosed a proclivity on the union's part to spread the dispute widely.

The Kennedy Board's interpretation of the secondary boycott provisions, as revised by Landrum-Griffin, fully justify the concern of the Congressmen who introduced those amendments. When it is recognized that Congress' intent in Taft-Hartley was to ban *all* secondary boycotts, and the Landrum-Griffin Act was designed to correct the Board's circumvention of that intent, the new Board's persistence in reopening the loopholes must be frustrating indeed to the Congress. One of the major Taft-Hartley defects was the Board's narrow interpretation of employees who could be unlawfully induced. Congress' remedy was to substitute "individual employed by any person" for "employees." Yet the Board now decides Congress did not mean what it said but intended to add lower level supervisors only. Had this actually been the Congressional purpose, it seems obvious that more restrictive language would have been used. Another loophole which the 1959 amendments were specifically designed to close, was the Board's elimination of railroad employees from the secondary boycott protections. Yet the new Board has merely shifted its theory in railroad boycott cases by attempting to spread the umbrella of "common situs" over adjoining railroad property, once more permitting pressure on railroad employees in most cases. In other instances, no violations have been found because definitions of independent contractor or employer-employee relationship vacillate. Inducement, encouragement, and threats have become more difficult to prove. And the publicity proviso, added to make certain that the more restrictive provisions of the amendments did not completely foreclose union publication of certain disputes, has been distorted beyond recognition.

Regardless of the Board's view of what the law should be, Congress made its intent clear. Neutral employees and their employers were to be protected from all secondary boycotts. Interpretations which deny that protection thwart the will of Congress and usurp its policymaking function.

CHAPTER XVIII

HOT CARGO CONTRACTS

Another area of restriction on union activity added by the Landrum-Griffin Act in 1959 was the outlawing of "hot cargo" contracts. Section 8(e) now provides that it is an unfair labor practice for a union and an employer to enter into:

> "any contract or agreement, express or implied, whereby such employer ceases or refrains or agrees to cease or refrain from handling, using, selling, transporting, or otherwise dealing in any of the products of any other employer, or to cease doing business with any other person. . . ."

except for certain agreements in the construction and garment industries. The language is very broad and, read literally, it outlaws both specific contracts and some traditional union practices, such as commitments to honor the union label. The question, as might be expected, is whether or not the new Board has construed the statute as literally as written.

In the first major Kennedy Board interpretation of Section 8(e), the full Board held the act of entering into or making an unlawful hot cargo contract was sufficient to establish a violation, regardless of whether an attempt was made to enforce the agreement. *American Feed Co.*, 133 NLRB No. 23, 48 LRRM 1622. The union involved was the Teamsters and the unlawful provision excluded from the employees' duties any requirement that they handle or work on goods coming from or going to the premises of an employer with whom the union had a controversy.

The unanimity found in the *American Feed* case did not continue, but, surprisingly, McCulloch has joined with Rodgers and Leedom to constitute a majority in a number of instances. Thus, they found a contract violative of Section 8(e) under which an employer association agreed that, whenever the employer members found it feasible to subcontract work coming under the jurisdiction of the union, preference would be given to shops or subcontractors approved by or having contracts with the union. The contract became effective August 15, 1959, before the enactment of Landrum-Griffin, but was held by a mediation panel to be binding after Section 8(e) became operative. *Machinists' Union, District 9 (Greater St. Louis Automotive Trimmers & Upholsterers' Ass'n.)*, 134 NLRB No. 138, 49 LRRM 1321. The majority did not decide whether, generally, subcontracting clauses which seek to preserve jobs or job rights of employees in the unit are unlawful. The agreement in question was read as allowing subcontracting but only to persons approved by the union. The majority felt this was different from a prohibition against an employer handling non-union products. Fanning and Brown would have dismissed the complaint. They viewed the contract, though unlawful, as not having been "entered into," since it was already in existence when Section 8(e) was adopted.

In a companion case involving the same employer and an almost identical contractual provision but a different union, the Teamsters, the full Board also found the agreement unlawful but again split on whether the Act had been violated. In this case, the contract had been signed more than six months before the unfair labor practice charge was filed and, also, before Section 8(e) became effective. The Teamsters subsequently tried to enforce the agreement, however, by urging the employer not to subcontract work to shops being struck by the union. Fanning and Brown would have found no violation because "Entering into an agreement requires a mutuality of assent to be bound," which was not established by showing the efforts of one party to enforce the agreement. McCulloch, Rodgers and Leedom found the contract unlawful, however, relying on the union attempt to enforce and the employer's compliance with the union demand. A contrary result would permit a union to obtain such a provision and, if it took no action for six months, the contract would become binding. *Teamsters' Union, Local 618 (Greater St. Louis Automotive Trimmers & Upholsterers Ass'n)*, 134 NLRB No. 139, 49 LRRM 1326. Also, see *Dan McKinney Co.*, 137 NLRB No. 74, 50 LRRM 1225; *Teamsters' Union, Local 890 (San Joaquin Valley Shippers' Labor Committee)*, 137 NLRB No. 75, 50 LRRM 1229.

The rule that reaffirmation of the "validity" of a hot cargo contract is included within the meaning of the statutory phrase "to enter into" and the agreement is, therefore, a violation of Section 8(e) was more clearly established in the McCulloch-Rodgers-Leedom majority in *Los Angeles Mailers' Union, No. 9, I.T.U. (Hillbro Newspaper Printing Co.)*, 135 NLRB No. 107, 49 LRRM 1659. There, Hillbro, on September 1, 1960, entered into a contract with Pacific Neo-Gravure, under which Pacific was to print and deliver to Hillbro (which publishes the *Los Angeles Examiner*) a weekly television supplement to the Sunday edition. The existing labor agreement between Hillbro and the union provided that the employer should not require employees to process material received from, or destined for, shops in which an authorized strike or lockout involving a subordinate union of the I.T.U. was in progress. A dispute arose between Pacific and I.T.U., which represented Pacific's mail room employees, over whether the I.T.U. or the Bookbinders' Union should perform certain duties involving the tieing of bundles. On September 2, the I.T.U. Business Manager told Hillbro that it was "heading for trouble" because Pacific was assigning the disputed work to members of another union. He also said his union would consider itself "locked out" (making the contractual provision described above operative), in which case members of I.T.U. would refuse to handle the television supplement for Hillbro. After Hillbro informed the union that it considered the contractual provision unlawful under Section 8(e), the union gave Hillbro formal notice that a strike or lockout was in progress at Pacific.

McCulloch, Rodgers and Leedom found the provision unlawful and the union's conduct to threaten, restrain or coerce within the meaning of Section 8(b)(4)(ii). Also, they found the object of the conduct was to force the employer to "enter into" an unlawful hot cargo agreement within the meaning of Section 8(b)(4)(A). The language of Section 8(e), as well as its legislative history, indicated to them that Congress was intent upon banning absolutely all forms of hot cargo consensual arrangements. Thus, the phrase "to enter into" a hot cargo agreement was not intended to have the restrictive meaning of similar phrases in contract or real property law and included "reaffirmation" of an existing hot cargo clause.

Fanning and Brown agreed that the contractual provision was unlawful but would have found no violation of Section 8(b)(4)(ii) because the union's object was not to force Hillbro "to enter into" any agreement. "Entering into" is not "enforcing" and, if Congress had meant "enforce," it would have said so. They also argued that enforcement of the contract would be a violation of Section 8(b)(4)(B) and there was, therefore, no justification for straining the language of Section 8(b)(4)(A). The majority noted that conduct frequently violates more than one section of the Act, e.g. all Section 8(a) violations are also interference, restraint and coercion within the meaning of Section 8 (a)(1).

The same split of opinion is found in *Lithographers' Union, Local 45 (Lithographers' and Printers' Ass'n.)*, 137 NLRB No. 179, 50 LRRM 1449, where "reaffirmation" was found when the employer advised the union it opposed action challenging the legality of the contract. The employer also would not disavow any part of the contract after certain employers in the association took steps to set aside the unlawful portion of the agreement.

In one of the most significant Section 8(e) cases, the usual Kennedy Board majority was reunited. *Teamsters' Union, Local 546 (Minnesota Milk Co.)*, 133 NLRB No. 123, 49 LRRM 1001. Minnesota Milk and the Teamsters had a contract which required that no product should be sold for resale to peddlers or so-called "independent" milk men. The employer sold products to a man named Hillyer, and Hillyer was given a specific area (formerly served by one of the employer's regular drivers) where he was to resell the products at his own price, the difference representing his only compensation. Hillyer rented a truck from the employer but no other criteria of employee relationship was present. The Teamsters threatened to strike until Hillyer was made a regular employee and joined the union.

McCulloch, Fanning and Brown decided that Hillyer was an employee and not an independent contractor, since he distributed products in the same manner as the employer's regular drivers and, except for the right to fix his own price, his right of control over his method of doing business was not substantially greater than that exercised by the regular drivers. Therefore, Section 8(e) was not violated when the union forced the company to terminate the arrangement. The majority also found the contractual provision not violative of Section 8(e), as it was "too vague" to be susceptible of construction or interpretation and the ambiguity was not cured by the evidence of its operation and administration.

The majority then specifically disagreed with a statement of the Trial Examiner to the effect that the legislative history showed Congress clearly intended that Section 8(e) outlaw not only traditional hot-cargo clauses but all similar clauses which directly or indirectly required an employer to cease doing business by contract, subcontract, or in any other manner with any other person.

The majority said:

> "We find no justification in the statute for so sweeping a generalization. With respect to contracts and agreements prohibiting an employer from the contracting or subcontracting out of work regularly performed by his employees we shall examine each such contract or agreement as it comes before us. The language used, the intent of the parties and the scope of the restriction vary greatly in such agreements and each must meet scrutiny in terms of the statutory restraint on its own."

Rodgers and Leedom dissented by commenting that they, also, did not believe Section 8(e) should be interpreted to bar all agreements prohibiting the subcontracting of work. They found the contract in the *Minnesota Milk Company,* however, to be unlawful, as it explicitly provided that certain work should be done only by "regular employees of the company or members of Local 546." It also prohibited wholesaling of products to others "unless they pay dues" to the union. The clear purpose of the clause was to limit the class of persons with whom the employer might contract to members of the union or those who paid dues.

The reluctance of both the majority and the minority to read Section 8(e) broadly is inconsistent with the majority language in the *Hillbro* case, where emphasis was placed on the Congressional intent of banning *all* forms of hot cargo consensual arrangements. The language of Section 8(e) is very broad. It bans entering into any agreement, express or implied, where the employer agrees to refrain from dealing with any other employer. An agreement not to subcontract fits within the literal language of the statute. There is no suggestion in the legislative history that the Section is not to be read literally. Here again, regardless of whether the Board members agree with the language used by Congress, their function is to enforce the Congressional policy, not what they think that policy should be.

It is apparent that Section 8(e) is now supported by a most insecure foundation. Retirement or replacement of either Rodgers or Leedom might lead to a new appointee who would agree with Fanning and Brown on the meaning of "enter into." If so, the hot cargo contract ban would be substantially weakened, and the Congressional intent, as in the picketing and boycott areas, further circumvented.

CHAPTER XIX

JURISDICTIONAL DISPUTES

A final chapter dealing with specific cases must be included to round out our discussion. In this instance, however, while some criticism is directed at the Board generally, the primary use of the divided opinions is to highlight a problem which must be resolved by Congress.

The 1947 Act included provisions both to halt strikes arising out of jurisdictional disputes [Section 8(b)(4)(D)] and to resolve the disputes themselves [Section 10(k)]. For many years, the NLRB confined itself in the latter area to determining whether the employer's assignment of work violated any Board order or certification or any contract between the employer and the striking union. If not, the strike was halted by the Board on the ground that it was in violation of Section 8(b)(4)(D). In 1961, the Supreme Court held that the Board's policy was incorrect and that it was required to determine the underlying jurisdictional dispute on its merits and to make an award of the disputed work. *N.L.R.B. v. Radio Engineers Union (CBS)*, 346 U.S. 573, 47 LRRM 2332.

The first determinations following the *CBS* case are now beginning to come down, and it is already obvious that the problems are going to be manifold. *Local 107, Teamsters Union (Safeway Stores, Inc.)*, 134 NLRB No. 130, 49 LRRM 1343, one of the first, is an illustration. There Local

107 had represented Safeway drivers employed at its Wilmington, Delaware, meat processing plant for some 10 years. At the end of 1959, the three drivers who comprised the Wilmington unit were discharged and the work previously done by them assigned to drivers at Safeway's Landover, Maryland, and Kearney, New Jersey, plants. The employees at these plants were represented by Teamsters Locals 639 and 660, respectively. The employer filed jurisdictional dispute charges when the Wilmington plant was picketed by Local 107.

The case first came to the Board prior to the CBS decision. At that time, a panel consisting of Rodgers and Leedom, with Fanning dissenting, decided that Local 107 was picketing to force re-assignment of the work and, as it had no claim to the disputed work arising out of a Board order or certification or a contract claim, its conduct was unlawful. After the CBS decision, Safeway petitioned to re-open the proceeding and to determine in accordance with the principles laid down in CBS which of the employee groups was entitled to the work. The Board granted the request, and Local 107 repeated its argument that no jurisdictional dispute existed as its strike was to protest Safeway's termination of the collective bargaining relationship and its refusal to sign a new agreement.

On reconsideration, McCulloch and Brown agreed with Local 107's contention but on a different theory. They understood the Supreme Court in CBS as not only rejecting the type of determination which held that a striking union was not entitled to disputed work but, also, as holding that Section 8(b)(4)(D) and Section 10(k) require that two or more employee groups must claim the right to perform the work. They said it was implicit that the sections must resolve conflicting claims by rival groups and could not be used to arbitrate a dispute between the union and the employer where there were no such claims. Here, there was no real competition because Local 107 was merely attempting to retrieve jobs for its members which had been assigned by Safeway to others. Fanning concurred on the ground that the Local 107 strike was in protest against Safeway's unilateral action in eliminating jobs of its drivers.

Rodgers and Leedom dissented. *CBS* did not require that the plain wording of Section 8(b)(4)(D) be ignored. It did not hold that there must be competing claims between rival groups of employees but, instead, specifically pointed out that, in accord with Board precedent, there could be jurisdictional disputes between unions and unorganized groups as well as between two or more unions. They stated that the former could arise only where an employer assigned work to an unorganized group and a union contested that assignment. That the union or group to whom the work is assigned need not actively assert a right to the work is well established in their view. Also, see *Local 331, Teamsters Union (Bulletin Co.)*, 139 NLRB No. 117, 51 LRRM 1490.

The majority view appears to eliminate application of Section 8(b)(4)(D) to disputes involving unorganized employees, as they rarely specifically make the type of claim or oppose the union position in the manner contemplated by the majority.

McCulloch and Fanning also held that there was no dispute within the meaning of Section 8(b)(4)(D) in another case which they viewed as not involving competing groups. *Local 272 Sheet Metal Workers Union (Valley Sheet Metal Company)*, 136 NLRB No. 136, 50 LRRM 1017. Local 272 put pressure on members of a sister Local, No. 104, by making them sign a document acknowledging existence of an international union rule that not more than two men could be sent on a job in another local's jurisdiction and threatening them with union discipline if they disobeyed the rule. When three Local 104 members went into Local 272's jurisdiction to perform a job, the Local 272 business agent obtained their signatures on the document described above, whereupon one of the three left. Later the same day, the Local 272 business agent advised the employer that he intended to live up to the two-man rule and that the employer could obtain additional journeymen from Local 272 if he wished. The employer said he would have to have more than two men and agreed "under protest" to hire them from Local 272.

McCulloch and Fanning found there was no jurisdictional dispute because no competing groups disputed the work assignment. Local 104 had agreed to abide by the two-man rule, and was thus not pressing for the disputed work. They viewed the whole arrangement as being the kind of settlement of a jurisdictional dispute which the Act encourages.

Leedom dissented because Local 272 forced Valley Sheet Metal to assign the work to that Local rather than to employees who were members of Local 104. He did not read the statute as requiring that employees to whom the work is assigned must actively seek it. It is sufficient that they are doing the work. He felt the majority holding extended the *Safeway Stores* case because there the majority viewed the dispute as one created by the employer. In Leedom's opinion, the decision in *Valley Sheet Metal* adopted the principle that the majority will defer to the unions involved to ascertain whether there is a jurisdictional dispute and will thus deny an employer the benefits of Section 10(k).

In another case, no jurisdictional dispute was found by McCulloch, Fanning and Brown because they saw no cause to believe that the competing unions resorted to prohibited methods in pressing their claim for work assignments. *International Association of Machinists (Carling Brewing Company)*, 136 NLRB No. 120, 49 LRRM 1952. The dispute arose over the employer's assignment of maintenance and repair work on certain equipment in its Atlanta brewery. Both the Machinists and the Firemen and Oilers Union had represented separate groups of employees in the plant, beginning in 1958. Thereafter both unions granted the same work assignments and there was a long history of attempts to settle the question, including submission of the disputes to vice presidents of the international unions. The majority found there was no evidence that the IAM voiced a direct threat to anyone or made any statement that could be construed as coercion or restraint in connection with the disputed work.

Rodgers and Leedom dissented, pointing out that the Firemen had advised the employer it would take such action as deemed necessary if the company tried to assign the work to the IAM. The employer was left with the clear impression that this meant strike action, and the Firemen made no contrary contention in the case under discussion. The IAM had filed a brief with the Board in a related case where it said it would strike if it could not get relief otherwise. In a letter to both unions, the employer advised it was filing the instant Section 8(b)(4)(D) charges "in order to prevent threatened work stoppages." Neither union denied that it threatened strike action.

In the first case where the Board issued affirmative work assignment determinations in accordance with the *CBS* decision, it emphasized that it would not formulate general rules to be followed. In *International Association of Machinists, Lodge No. 1743 (J. A. Jones Construction Company)*, 135 NLRB No. 139, 49 LRRM 1684, the Board said:

> "The Board will consider all relevant factors in determining who is entitled to the work in dispute, e.g., the skills and work involved, certifications by the Board, company and industry practice, agreements between unions and between employers and unions, awards of arbitrators, joint boards and the AFL-CIO in the same or related cases, the assignment made by the employer, and the efficient operation of the employer's business. This list of factors is not meant to be exclusive, but is by way of illustration. The

Board cannot at this time establish the weight to be given the various factors. Every decision will have to be an act of judgment based on common sense and experience rather than on precedent. It may be that later, with more experience in concrete cases, a measure of weight can be accorded the earlier decisions."

In the *Jones* case, the job of operating electric overhead cranes in a machine shop was given to Electricians rather than Machinists. The Board found there were no outstanding equities in favor of either group. They, therefore, gave substantial weight to the long-standing rulings of the parent federation of both unions, the AFL-CIO, that the operation of electric cranes is Electricians' work, particularly where, as here, the employer had assigned the work to Electricians. For typical factors relied on in other cases, see *Operating Engineers, Local 66 (Frank P. Badolato & Son)*, 135 NLRB No. 140, 49 LRRM 1633, and *International Association of Machinists, Lodge 681 (P. Lorillard Company)*, 135 NLRB No. 141, 49 LRRM 1693.

The three cases cited above were full Board decisions without dissents. Subsequent determinations demonstrate, however, that such unanimity will not prevail. A three-way split appeared in *International Longshoremen's Association (Union Carbide Chemical Company)*, 137 NLRB No. 85, 50 LRRM 1254, where Leedom and Fanning held that employees in a production and maintenance unit at a chemical plant, currently represented by a Metal Trades Council, were entitled to load and unload ships at the employer's container dock rather than members of the Longshoremen's Union. They viewed the ILA claim as based primarily on its general jurisdiction over loading and unloading of ships. They emphasized, however, that ILA members had never worked directly for the employer, and no general cargo was handled at the container dock. Employees then handling the work in question had skills similar to ILA members, job classifications at the dock were substantially identical with unit classifications in the contract with the Trades Council and, if the disputed work were assigned to ILA, its members would work on an intermittent basis. Rodgers concurred in the result only. Brown dissented and would have awarded the work to the ILA, disagreeing with the majority's factual analysis. It, perhaps, should be noted that the employer had assigned the work to the Trades Council, but all members, except Rodgers, were careful to point out that the employer's assignment of disputed work is not dispositive in a jurisdictional dispute. Despite this language, the Board has not yet ordered an employer to assign work to an "outside" union.

The moving of crates of glass at construction sites was the subject of a long-standing jurisdictional dispute in Houston, Texas. Crated glass was brought to construction jobs by truck. In some instances, the crates were raised by cranes to the floor level where the glass was to be installed, and in other instances the crates were moved by hand from the trucks to temporary hoists or elevators. The crates were then raised to the designated floor level and again moved by hand to the installation area. The crates were eventually opened by outside glaziers who installed the glass. The work in dispute was the moving of the crates from the point where they were deposited by cranes or left the hoist to the installation location.

The dispute came before the Board in two cases. In the first, *Glaziers Local No. 1778, Painters Union (Binswanger Glass Co., Inc.)*, 137 NLRB No. 101, 50 LRRM 1305, Binswanger had contracts with Local 1778, which represented outside glaziers in one unit and, in another, "inside" glass handlers who fabricated and handled glass at local warehouses and transported it in trucks to construction sites. When Binswanger assigned the disputed work to the glass handlers, Local 1778 threatened to picket unless outside glaziers were used, though it represented both groups. The threat was subsequently carried out.

The full Board determined that the disputed work belonged to the glass handlers, as the training and skills utilized by outside glaziers bore little relationship to the work of hoisting and moving crated glass. Also, area glass contractors had historically assigned such work to glass handlers or laborers without serious dispute. A prior award of the Joint Board for the Settlement of Jurisdictional Disputes was found not determinative because it was made upon consideration of a dispute between the Glaziers Union and the Hod Carriers Union, rather than between the outside glaziers and glass handlers.

The companion case, *Glaziers Local 1778, Painters Union (Pittsburgh Plate Glass Company)*, 137 NLRB No. 115, 50 LRRM 1307, arose when Pittsburgh began work on the Humble Oil Building. The company obtained laborers from the Hod Carriers to move the crated glass from the hoists or cranes to the point on the various floor levels where it was to be installed. Local 1778 protested use of the laborers and on two occasions picketed the project to force Pittsburgh to assign the work to outside glaziers.

Rodgers, Leedom and Fanning determined that, in this instance, the disputed work belonged to either the glass handlers or the laborers, whether represented by the Glaziers Union or by the Hod Carriers Union. Their reasoning was substantially as in the *Binswanger* case, although here they found past practice had failed to prove consistent and widespread assignment of the work to either group. The Joint Board award was disregarded again because it was made upon consideration of a dispute between two unions rather than a dispute between outside glaziers and all other non-skilled categories, and because the language of the award expressly limited its determination to the job involved in the *Binswanger* case.

McCulloch and Brown dissented, feeling the Hod Carriers acquiesced in the Joint Board decision and that the majority view disregarded the *Binswanger* decision. Also, they believed an award which allows the employer to determine which of two competing groups shall be assigned work, i.e. inside glaziers and laborers, fails to decide a controversy.

From the foregoing cases, the impracticality of NLRB determining jurisdictional disputes begins to be demonstrated. *Teamsters', Local 406 (Snow White Baking Co.)*, 137 NLRB No. 163, 50 LRRM 1399, is another illustration. McCulloch, Rodgers and Leedom held that the work of delivering bread to two retail stores, which sold bread under their own label, belonged to inside employees then performing such work rather than to driver-salesmen represented by Teamsters, who delivered bread to all other stores. Fanning and Brown dissented. The conflict between majority and minority is entirely one of fact necessitating long and detailed analysis of established work practices, applicable contracts, industry practices and historical union approach. Guidelines for future decisions are difficult, if not impossible, to find.

Perhaps an even better illustration is *Newspaper and Mail Deliverers Union (New York Times Co.)*, 137 NLRB No. 157, 50 LRRM 1347, where the Board was required to determine a dispute as to the union entitled to straighten out newspapers on a conveyor belt. Ordinarily, Mailers performed all work up to and including a wrapping operation and also operated a tieing machine when the papers were destined for suburban delivery. When papers were bound for city delivery, a Deliverer operated the tieing machine. As the newspapers moved along the conveyor belt, it was sometimes necessary to straighten or "jog" the stacks immediately before they reached the wrapping machine. The dispute was limited to this straightening which consisted solely of patting the sides of the bundles by hand and only to such times as a Deliverer was at the tieing machine. To determine that the Mailers were entitled to "pat the sides of the bundles" instead of the Deliverers required two days of Board hearings, hours of analysis and study by Board legal assistants, and sufficient attention from the Board members to issue an eleven-page decision detailing the factors which resulted in their determination.

In addition to the mechanical problems of processing the jurisdictional dispute cases under the *CBS* rule, the Board has already been drawn into a serious dispute which the Industrial Unions and Building Trades Unions have never been able to resolve themselves—the conflict over new construction and repair at industrial facilities where industrial unions represent production and maintenance units. The first case where the issue was clearly brought to light was *Akron Building Trades (John G. Ruhlin Construction Co.)*, 137 NLRB No. 159, 50 LRRM 1426. There four Board members (Brown not participating) determined that work on a plant addition that had been reserved by Goodyear Tire and Rubber Company, an industrial employer, for performance by its own employees, represented by the Rubber Workers, should continue to be performed by them. The Building Trades claimed the work for construction unions on the ground that it violated the Miami Agreement between the Building Trades and Industrial Unions governing such work. The Board decided that Goodyear's assignment of work to its employees conformed to past practice and the work assignment provisions of Goodyear's contract with the Rubber Workers, both of which pre-dated and post-dated the Miami Agreement. They noted that the Miami Agreement was unclear and the parties had not been able to resolve their disagreement under the procedures which it provided.

Now that NLRB must make an award of the work, in accordance with *CBS*, the incentive to stimulate a jurisdictional dispute has increased substantially, particularly for a union which does not have the work but can present a colorable claim. The potential caseload is tremendous. The flow has already begun and the filings are increasing. It is patently ridiculous to pretend the Board has any particular expertise justifying an authoritative determination of who should tie a bundle of newspapers or move a crate of glass from one point to another. It is absurd to think the Board members can give their personal attention to work assignments ranging from three Safeway truck drivers in Wilmington, Delaware, to a single sheet metal worker in South San Francisco. They simply do not have time to study and comprehend the factual background required to apply jurisdictional dispute tests, such as those outlined in the *J. A. Jones Construction Co.* case. This conclusion is a reflection on neither the Board nor its staff. The job is simply too large for a single centralized authority. If the statute remains unchanged, the only practical solution will be for the Board to "rubber stamp" the determinations of a corps of unknown legal assistants, who reach their conclusions on the basis of testimony from witnesses they have never seen.

Furthermore, application of the *CBS* rules has resulted in one of the most significant steps toward compulsory arbitration of labor disputes which has yet transpired in this country. Member Brown, speaking of the impact of *CBS*, said,

> "Therefore, the Board is now required to perform a task not previously accomplished by any public agency in the United States—to engage in what amounts to compulsory arbitration of inter-union disputes."

While Brown was careful to speak of "inter-union disputes," the statute, by its terms, is not limited to disputes between unions.

Desirable as compulsory arbitration may seem to those who are more interested in halting an interruption of work than in the substance of a dispute between the parties, the concept is anathema to representatives of both labor and management.

If the principle of compulsory arbitration is adopted in jurisdictional disputes, with NLRB as arbiter, a ready-made system is established to which can be added national emergency disputes, national defense installation work stoppages, and, gradually, less serious issues.

Odd as it may seem, the whole problem stems from a legislative accident. When the differences between the Taft and Hartley Bills were being reconciled by a Senate-House Conference Committee in 1947, prior to passage of the Taft-Hartley Act, major compromises had to be made by both bodies. The Senate Bill contained authority for the Board to arbitrate contract disputes but the House conferees were very much opposed to arbitration. As a result, the Senate provision was dropped but, according to one of the principal drafters, the conferees overlooked the fact that this made Section 10(k) superfluous. As long as the Board followed the rule that an assignment of the work did not have to be made, the oversight created no major problems. The *CBS* case effectively closed that chapter of Board history.

The only solution to the current problem appears to be through legislation. Because of the compulsory arbitration aspect, it should follow that both management and labor would agree that a change must be made. Whether their ideas as to specific language will also coincide is more debatable. From the standpoint of simplicity and effective business management, an amendment which gave controlling weight to employer assignment of the work is the solution. It is doubtful whether unions will be willing to yield that much authority to employers if they can devise some means to have a voice in the decision. In any event, they are faced with a difficult choice. The post-*CBS* system, with its compulsory arbitration characteristic and unpredictable results, would seem to be less appealing to a strong union than outright employer assignment.

Regardless of the problems, a change must be made if the

NLRB is not to become hopelessly bogged down. Because of the common interest of labor and management, it would be encouraging to see a joint effort toward a workable solution. Action is required promptly before a crisis develops and an impractical scheme is generated by pressures of the emergency.

CHAPTER XX

SUMMATION OF THE NEW FRONTIER NLRB

Experience over the years has shown that objective, balanced criticism of the Board has produced results. The writer has endeavored to maintain such a standard in the presentation of the Board's divided opinions, letting the cases and the reasoning of the members speak for themselves to the greatest possible extent. Nevertheless, maintaining objectivity after immersion in the flood of inconsistencies apparent in the cases discussed is a formidable task. No claim of perfection is made and, in any event, the reader may make his own judgment.

Irrespective of one's philosophy or predilections, and regardless of the objectivity of any analysis, the new Board's divided opinions provide an impressive basis for the conclusion that the Kennedy majority is undermining the purpose of the statute, frustrating the intent of Congress, and demoralizing major areas of labor-management relations. These are strong words but, once more, the cases speak for themselves.

As pointed out earlier, the basic method adopted by Congress to eliminate the burden on commerce growing out of industrial strife was to protect the right of employees to select or reject a bargaining representative without interference. Encouragement of collective bargaining was a second means. Throughout the years as the statute has been amended, Congress has consistently increased the reach and mode of employee protection. At no time since the original Act was passed in 1935 has Congress seen fit to add to the scope of collective bargaining or to re-emphasize its importance. And, neither in the 1935 law nor its amendments has Congress provided any statutory protection to labor organizations as such. Their rights flow from the protection afforded their members. Today, the public, employees, and employers are clearly the intended beneficiaries of the law as written.

Despite this background, the new Board has persistently undercut employee freedom of choice and protection whenever in conflict with the growth of labor unions. The organizations whose rights are derivative have been favored over the source of those rights. The agents have been given precedence over the principals.

Apparently, the Kennedy majority believes employers and their employees have diametrically opposed interests. As Justice Brandeis said:

> "Don't assume that the interests of employer and employee are necessarily hostile—that what is good for one is necessarily bad for the other. The opposite is more apt to be the case. While they have different interests, they are likely to prosper or suffer together."
>
> (Mason, Brandeis, p. 141)

During an organizing drive, the overriding interest of both employer and employees is identical, i.e. neither wants to injure the business, the livelihood of both. Both have an important stake in assuring that the employees understand the impact of unionization on the success of the business. The employer bargaining attitude, the possibility of lost business, strikes, replacement of strikers, all are significant factors which the employees must weigh in making their choice. But the new Board persists in viewing cases dealing with union organizing as involving a conflict between an employer and his employees, apparently assuming the employees will choose the union unless unlawfully influenced. The new Board has zealously striven to make sure employees will not be coerced, intimidated, or even influenced by remarks of their employer. Highly restrictive limitations have been placed on employer expression, even to the extent of foreclosing factual statements of legal position, assuring that the employees will be exposed to a minimum of anti-union information. In other words, employees have been carefully shielded from the light of the full story of unionism by a screen designed to hide harsh realities and let pass only exaggerated union promises. A policy which gives an employee but one side of the story, regardless of whether engrafted on a speculative theory of employer coercion, is a poor substitute for an employee's right to facts from which he may make his own choice.

Throughout the history of the Act, except for a brief period during the Eisenhower Administration, the Board has pressed relentlessly to limit employer speech. Both the courts and Congress have endeavored to curb the Board's excesses. By enactment of Section 8(c) Congress told the Board as specifically as possible, that even employers were entitled to the Constitutional right of free speech. The 1959 amendments did not detract from this concept in any way. Yet the Kennedy Board has now usurped Congress' policy-making function, administratively enacted its own concept of the Constitutional guarantee, and declared it will enforce its decrees through a case-by-case approach which defies the most careful attempt to comply. The result is a return to policies specifically rejected by Congress and a substantial aid to the growth of unions.

Standing alone, the new Board's decisions on employer interference through polling, interrogation, discharges and discipline show great concern for the individual employee.

But, when considered in context with rulings on union security, it becomes obvious that they merely demonstrate the status of employees on the new Board's preference list—a long step above employers and the public but well below international unions. One union security case showed the new Board unwilling to protect non-union employees from paying discriminatory hiring hall fees, even though it was proved they were paying more than union members. In other divided opinions, the new Board uniformly avoided finding unlawful hiring contracts or practices, going so far as to uphold a contract *even though the union's answer to the complaint admitted the illegality.* In the dues tender cases, where the choice lies between protection of the employee who has fulfilled the literal requirements of the statute and aid to the union in enforcing its union security agreement, the new Board has ignored the statute and supported the union. In each instance, union goals were found to outweigh employee guarantees of freedom from union coercion.

More proof of the Kennedy Board's preference for unions over employees, is found in its willingness to deny employees their right to a secret ballot election. A Board order to bargain with an uncertified union, on the theory that an uncoerced election cannot be held, is a most extreme remedy. It nullifies the employee's fundamental right—the exercise of his freedom of choice—and substitutes the Board's judgment. The employee is told, in effect, "The Board knows what you want better than you do yourself." The fact that all employees are not fully qualified to make an intelligent selection has no greater application here than in political elections. Congress gave the employees the choice—no one else.

A strong argument can be made that such a remedy should never be used. Even serious employer misconduct can be corrected. But such an extreme need not be considered to evaluate the Kennedy Board's approach. The *Pinellas* employees lost their vote because of two or three employer mistakes made early in the campaign and never repeated. The *Snow & Sons* employees were victims of Board imposition of a union (which misrepresented the meaning of authorization cards signed by the employees) because *the union* refused to wait for an NLRB election, and despite the fact their employer did not engage in interference, restraint or coercion.

In these cases, the new Board simply avoided the issue of employee rights and placed its emphasis on whether or not the employer refused to recognize the union in order to dissipate its majority. Most employers have precisely this aim in mind when a union starts to organize and every effort which they make to persuade their employees not to join is an attempt to dissipate the union's majority. Most avoid unfair labor practice charges because of their own experience or that of their counsel. Neither statutory law nor moral precept precludes such an approach.

Employees are protected against employer interference, restraint and coercion. There is nothing whatsoever in the Act which says that an employer may not try to persuade his employees they are better off without a union if he stays within these limits. Congressional approval of this policy has been demonstrated time and again. It cannot seriously be argued that Congress intended employers should be powerless to resist a union organizing drive. The enactment of Section 8(c) is sufficient rebuttal in itself. But an employer's right to resist, be it no more than the right to speak freely, is meaningless if it cannot be used to convince his employees of the disadvantages of union membership—to reduce employee enthusiasm for the union—to dissipate the union's strength, not unlawfully, but by presenting the *facts* of unionism to the employees.

Therefore, the controlling question should be "Can the employees exercise a free choice in a secret ballot election?"

not "Has the employer refused to recognize the union in order to dissipate its strength?" If an election cannot be held because of improper employer conduct, let the conduct be corrected—by injunction if necessary—and the vote then taken. In some instances, the vote will be delayed. But, again, nothing in the Act guarantees that the election must be conducted at the peak of the union organizing drive. It should be held when the employees can exercise a free choice, not necessarily when the climate is most favorable for a union victory.

The clearest disregard of the rights of employers and the public is found in the secondary boycott cases. Although prevention of such union pressures protects the employees of secondary employers, there is abundant legislative history to demonstrate that the provisions were added to free neutral employers and the public from the burden of disputes not their own. The same source shows that Congress intended to place very broad restrictions on secondary activities of unions. When the Board, in the years that followed, developed one "loophole" after another in the restrictions, the Landrum-Griffin Act was passed to close the gaps. Regardless of the possible legitimacy of earlier doubts as to the meaning of the language used, there could be no mistaking the intent of Congress in 1959. The entire history of the development, drafting and adoption of the amendments proved Congress wanted secondary boycott activity brought to a halt.

Because the restrictions were designed to protect employers and the public, it would logically follow that any seeming ambiguity in the law should be resolved by looking at this intent. Certainly, the background of the amendments provides no justification for avoiding the literal meaning of language used in order to permit secondary conduct. Yet the Kennedy Board has refused to honor the Congressional will. Its concern once again has been for the union and its right to exert the maximum amount of economic pressure on the employer with whom it has a dispute. In the eyes of the new Board, when a choice must be made between the neutral and the union, the union is heavily favored.

Again, the cases tell the story. Under Taft-Hartley only groups of employees were protected from unlawful inducement. In 1959, Congress sought to include *all* neutral employees under the same umbrella. But the Board, unwilling to read the language as written, amended the Congressional version to provide that "all" added only single employees, minor supervisors, agricultural and municipal employees. Other employees continue to be excluded and, disregarding explicit legislative history, the new Board, for all practical purposes, eliminated neutral railroad employees from the meaning of "all" by evolving a new theory to permit pressure on their employers.

Board redrafting of the "publicity" proviso is a still more flagrant disregard of the rights of neutrals. The statutory language plainly applies only where the publicity concerns a product or products *produced* by the primary employer and *distributed* by another. "*Produce*" means "to make, bring forth, create." Yet, the Kennedy Board has wholesalers making candy, radio stations bringing forth automobiles, and refrigeration repairmen creating refrigerators. The requirement of distribution has been ignored. The result is that the statutory protection for employees, employers, neutrals and the public is being sacrificed for the benefit of unions, the very organizations for whom protection was not provided and whose activities were the specific target of Congressional action.

As stated before, in the Wagner Act Congress made it clear that encouragement of collective bargaining was one method of lessening industrial strife. In implementing this encouragement, however, the new Board has confused bargaining with the growth of union power. Union growth is neither synonymous with encouragement of collective bargaining nor with bargaining which lessens industrial strife.

Indications of this principle are found in the new Board's approach to bargaining unit questions where the decisions show greater fragmentation of bargaining units to be in the offing. Examples are the Board's acceptance of union positions on appropriate units, even though only a portion of the employees are sought. Another is its willingness to adopt policies which substantially increase the probabilities of residual groups, unrepresented in some instances but members of rival unions in others. Fragmentation invariably produces conflict and rivalry within a plant. While the statute provides for separate units where desired by the employees, there is no requirement that they be cultivated by the Board in the absence of employee interest or merely to make it easier for a union to gain a beachhead.

Similar conflict with the statutory purpose appears in the good faith bargaining cases. Few factors discourage true collective bargaining more quickly than to have the government sit down at the bargaining table. No reflection is intended or cast on government efforts at mediation, fostering discussion between management and the union. Nor is criticism intended of government efforts to establish the rules of the contest. But the vice appears when government, directly or indirectly, imposes the terms of the settlement. Time and again, nationally publicized negotiations have proven the mere probability of government pressures on either party to accept a particular demand to be fatally disruptive of bargaining on the issue in question. Therefore, any indication by the Board that it will exert its power against either the union or the employer because of failure to accept the other's demands, strikes at the very heart of collective bargaining. Yet this is what the Kennedy Board has done in the *General Tire* case, when it unquestionably said to the employer, "You must give the union, at a minimum, a checkoff of dues and a limitation on contracting out."

But one step away are the plant removal and subcontracting cases. When an employer must bargain about the *decision* to move or subcontract, the Kennedy Board cannot be expected to approve his mere announcement to the union of an intent to act. If he must bargain, he must discuss union proposals and make counter-proposals in good faith. When he does so under Board pressure, he has been forced to change his position and the union has won a concession, regardless of its extent, with the aid of the Board. The same flaunting of Congressional will seen in the foregoing example is found in the interpretations of the 1959 amendments restricting organizational and recognition picketing. The statutory language has been bent and twisted by the Kennedy Board until it is virtually unrecognizable. *"An* object" has become *"the* object." "Truthful" has become "no intent to deceive." Failure to "perform any" services now means "substantially disrupt" the business.

Many additional illustrations might be repeated to demonstrate the basic conflict between the Kennedy Board and the Congress. At this point, they would be merely cumulative. The new Board's own decisions afford full proof of the wide divergence between the legislative intent and the Board's application of the statute. The final result is a statute, revised administratively both in intent and substance, which reflects the views of executive appointees instead of the elected representatives of the people. Irrespective of the validity of Chairman McCulloch's argument that the President should influence agency direction through the appointive power, it is fundamental to our system of government that our laws are enacted by the legislative, not the executive, branch.

CHAPTER XXI

THE CASE-BY-CASE APPROACH IN PRACTICE

By this time the reader will have formed his own opinion of both the validity of the case-by-case approach to decision-making and its application by the Kennedy Board. In their first announcements of the policy, both McCulloch and Brown were unhesitating in their full acceptance of the theory. McCulloch voiced a word of caution after early public reaction, however, noting a per se approach to all problems had not been abandoned. But he plainly emphasized his faith in the empirical method. The language of the decisions, if not the results, reflect continued acceptance of the theory.

The announcement of the case-by-case policy, as much as its application, has had a demoralizing impact on labor relations. The reason is simple. No longer can labor or management be certain of either their rights or their obligations. Neither can predict accurately the validity of its conduct. Both know that labor has fewer restraints than before and that management has more, but the shift is so broad and sweeping that only general guideposts remain.

The new Board's many changes of precedent alone would be enough to create a major upheaval in labor-management relations. When coupled with continued emphasis on a case-by-case approach, parties find themselves not only speculating on the meaning of the new rule but, also, on whether it will be followed if the facts of the case are slightly different. Perhaps the concern is unwarranted, but there would be little point in the new Board continuing to reiterate its policy if fixed rules are to be followed.

The manner in which the case-by-case method has been applied illustrates the difficulties facing the parties, particularly an employer. Use of the approach has been emphasized in the free speech area but already a set of per se limitations on employer activity is evolving. Thus, speech which violates Section 8(a)(1) "automatically" interferes with an election. Employer remarks must not only be truthful, with a high degree of accuracy required, but also must be supported by substantial evidence. An employer in the retail business, who speaks to his employees on company time and property, must provide an "equal opportunity" for the union to communicate with his employees. An "equal opportunity" doctrine for all employers may be in the offing.

The bargaining order cases are another example of case-by-case applied. Here again, a per se rule is developing which amounts to Board imposition of representation on employees if the union has authorization cards from a majority and the employer commits an unfair labor practice after the union demands recognition. This rule is not yet final and not yet uniformly applied. Nevertheless, it will result if *Pinellas* and *Snow & Sons* are followed.

Most faithful adherence to the new policy is found in union security cases. When non-union employees paid more for use of the hiring hall than did union members, the facts would seem peculiarly well suited to a per se rule, but case-by-case exonerated the union. "Looking at all the facts" enabled the union to avoid liability in the delinquent dues cases, despite a statutory per se rule limiting discharge solely to instances of "non-tender" of dues.

When the foregoing examples are viewed together, a strong argument can be made that case-by-case is more of a device than an approach. Surely the technique is missing in an absolute ban on polling of employees during an organizational drive, or in uniformly finding the small size of a plant sufficient to establish employer knowledge of union activity, or in requiring an employer in every instance to bargain about a decision to remove all or part of his plant. Each example would afford an excellent opportunity to apply the new members' announced policy. There are obviously situations where a poll does not interfere with employee union activity. Organizing can frequently be done more unobtrusively in a small plant than a large one. Fewer individuals know the secret, and less time is required. The Board should have no authority whatsoever to inject itself into a management decision to close an operation unless based on union considerations. It follows that the only proper approach to plant removal cases is to determine whether, under all the circumstances, union animus provided the underlying reason.

Use of the empirical theory is even more suspect when considered in connection with the requirement that a certified bargaining agent have a full twelve months in which to bargain, regardless of the surrounding circumstances or the desires of the employees. The basic twelve-month rule is justifiable. It provides a clear and easily followed guideline for all concerned. But to add together periods of bargaining, deduct interruptions (regardless of whether the employer is at fault), and insist upon a full twelve months in every instance, as was done in *Mar-Jac* and *Lamar Hotel*, does nothing but protect the union itself. It is of no assistance to the employees, who could strengthen the union's hand by a renewed vote of confidence, and does not encourage realistic collective bargaining. When contrasted with the Kennedy Board's willingness to forego the twelve-month rule where its enforcement would work to the disadvantage of the union,

as was true in *Rocky Mountain Phosphates,* but one conclusion follows. The New Frontier Board's choice between
per se and case-by-case depends far more on result than on
principle.

It is in the representation cases that the validity of the
case-by-case method is most vulnerable to criticism and has
its most demoralizing effect. Bargaining unit questions are
peculiarly ill-adapted to the approach. Unless the Board
turns to an "extent of union organization" test (as charged by
Rodgers in *Knoxville News-Sentinel Co., Inc.,* 138 NLRB
No. 91, 51 LRRM 1143), which has been specifically rejected by Congress, unit issues must be determined by arbitrary rules. Impressive language and esoteric arguments may
be expounded at length but, in the final analysis, abstract
factors which defy evaluation are totaled to outline the scope
of the bargaining unit. The result is an arbitrary judgment.
It is far simpler for the parties to operate, unions as well as
employers, if unit rules can be determined ahead of time.
When they can be identified, conflict is reduced and litigation
is kept at a minimum. When standards are known only to
the Board members, the parties have little alternative except
to pass the dispute along to the Board. If truly significant
results were then obtained, perhaps the new approach could
be justified. Instead, however, the Kennedy Board would
merely substitute an unknown for a known result, one as
arbitrary as the other.

Chapter X explained the background of the authority to
delegate representation cases to the Regional Directors. It
seems self-evident that authority can be successfully delegated
only if well-defined standards are available for the use of the
recipients. Such standards existed when the 1959 amendments were passed. The case-by-case approach of the new
Board is effectively eliminating them.

Many other examples could be used. The foregoing sufficiently illustrate the point. The case-by-case approach to

decision-making is not being uniformly followed. Where used, its most impressive consequence has been a major disruption in the framework of the government regulation within which labor-management relations are conducted. Its purported use has been as troublesome as its actual application. The net result has been an increase in industrial strife, directly contrary to the purpose of the statute.

CHAPTER XXII

IS THERE A SOLUTION?

The questions raised by the Kennedy Board's conception of its function are distinguishable from historical problems of NLRB only in degree. As Board members have changed, there have been constant variations in interpretation of the law. Not since the first days of the Board, however, have the changes been so drastic and not even then was the intent of Congress so plainly circumvented. Stated another way, the new Board's conduct has demonstrated more clearly than ever before the necessity for some revision in the system of enforcing our basic labor law. A conplete discussion of recommended solutions is beyond the scope of this volume. Nevertheless, a brief comment to highlight the major considerations is warranted.

The oldest and most drastic approach is that which has been urged since the Wagner Act was passed, i.e. repeal of the statute in its entirety. From the employer viewpoint, this may well have been the most desirable solution during the years shortly after the Act became effective. The tremendous growth of unionism in the early 1940's, however, eliminated the theory as a practical solution from the standpoint of both employers and employees. The power of large international unions today far surpasses that of virtually all employers. Employees are obviously in an even weaker position. If the statute was repealed, the Federal labor law would be wiped out and State law would take over. In most states, the union's power to force its demands on employers, employees and the public would be substantially enhanced.

A more realistic change is presently being vigorously pressed by some employer groups. Their approach, similar to a proposal which had substantial support in the Labor Law Section of the American Bar Association, is to transfer the Board's jurisdiction over unfair labor practices to the United States District Courts. The Board would continue to handle representation matters. This view is grounded on the theory that Federal judges are more carefully selected than NLRB members, are less susceptible to political pressure, and would be more likely to apply the law equitably and administer it impartially.

General Counsel Rothman, in a speech before the Associated Industries of Cleveland, September 20, 1962, reviewed other suggested changes in the enforcement system. While he was more concerned with handling the mounting caseload of the Board, his suggestions are of interest. One plan was essentially like that of Reorganization Plan No. 5, which Congress refused to adopt in 1961. It contemplates the delegation of decisional authority to Trial Examiners in unfair labor practices and hearing officers in jurisdictional disputes. Board review of their initial decisions would be made discretionary. A second proposal was to add three-man boards, created on a geographical basis, which would pass on cases handled by Trial Examiners assigned to each area. Review of the decisions of the three-man boards by the full Board in Washington would also be discretionary.

The plan deemed most satisfactory by Mr. Rothman was the creation of three-man boards, operating on a geographical basis, which would hear and determine unfair labor practice cases. Again, review would be discretionary. In his view, the latter system would foster greater respect for the law, give the parties a sense of more direct participation in its development, provide more uniform administration, and permit greater use of pre-trial procedures encouraging settlement.

The pressing need in the law of labor-management relations, as fully demonstrated by the Kennedy Board, is for certainty of result. The complexities of modern labor-management relationships and the intracacies of current labor laws, in themselves, provide a super-abundance of instability without being accompanied by fluctuating interpretations of the law. Employers must know, as precisely as possible, what they can say to their employees and what they can do during an organizing drive. Unions must know the limits of their secondary or organizational picketing activity. Both must know clearly the boundaries of union security and definite standards for bargaining units. The clarity of the line drawn is fully as important as its position.

Consequently, if light is to be thrown on the obscurity of current labor law and similar problems avoided in the future, the solution must include a system which will provide greater certainty of result. As indicated above, Mr. Rothman's suggestions were not intended to, and do not, provide any particular assistance in this direction. Solutions which are designed to alleviate the problem of increased caseload tend to concentrate on the symptoms rather than on the root of the evil.

The Board's caseload was relatively stable from 1947, when Taft-Hartley was passed, until 1957. In the following two years, the case intake increased dramatically. Although never publicly acknowledged and not widely known within the agency, the bulk of the increase resulted from a change in the method of keeping statistics. After Landrum-Griffin became effective in late 1959, another rise occurred, and in recent months case intake has again gone up sharply. It seems apparent that much of the current increase is a result of the new Board's reversal of well-established precedents and emphasis on the case-by-case approach. As long as the new Board insists upon a policy which makes it increasingly difficult to determine the law applicable to a given set of facts, the Board will be called into an abnormally large number of disputes.

Transfer of unfair labor practice jurisdiction to the courts closely attacks the basic problem but has serious drawbacks. With a large number of district court judges interpreting the law, it seems likely most issues will have to be decided by appellate courts before reasonable certainty is assured. Because of the wide variety of issues, the process will take many years and there will be substantial variations in approach during the interim. The Supreme Court, even with the Board as focal point of interpretation, is still resolving ambiguities in the 1935 Act. Unless the present General Counsel system is continued, another drawback will stem from the unmeritorious cases now disposed of administratively by the General Counsel at a minimum cost to the parties. Only about 15% of the charges filed have merit and roughly 5% are litigated. If but a substantial portion of these cases were processed by the District Courts, it would place a tremendous burden on the Courts and be most expensive to the parties. Finally, representation cases would continue to be handled by the Board, and certainty is as badly needed there as in the unfair labor practice area.

The arguments supporting a transfer of jurisdiction to the Federal Courts must be answered if conditions are to improve. More careful selection of adjudicating members, less susceptibility to political pressure, and greater interest in applying the intent of Congress are needed. It has been suggested that significant progress could be made within the framework of the present system without use of more drastic means. One simple but effective step would be to provide longer terms for Board members—perhaps even life appointments. In any event, terms which would assure that not more than one or two members would be appointed during a presidential administration would be a most effective way of reducing susceptibility to political pressure and to philosophical variations in the Board's expertise. In addition, greater authority to Trial Examiners (but only if appointed with more selectivity) could be used to free the Board to concentrate on more important cases. This, in turn, would assist in reducing the size of the Board members' staffs and would allow the Board members themselves to participate more actively both in deciding cases and writing opinions.

Another badly needed reform—one which would be helpful in clarifying the law, even though no other changes were made—is to provide court review of the General Counsel's refusal to issue a complaint in an unfair labor practice case. At present, his authority in this regard is absolute. When the Board misinterprets the law, particularly by narrowing its scope as the Kennedy majority is doing now in the secondary boycott and organizational picketing areas, a General Counsel who adheres to the Board's approach effectively forecloses an injured party from securing relief. If review of his refusal to act were available, it would both allow a persistent party to force action in a meritorious case, encouraging the General Counsel to follow court rather than Board interpretations of the law, and make a court the final authority in all cases.

Still another suggestion which has been made is to provide for concurrent jurisdiction in the courts and the NLRB. Because of the greater expense to the charging party who prosecutes his own case, most matters would continue to be presented to the Board. However, in those areas where the Board misinterprets the law, or the General Counsel refuses to act, the injured party would have a means for obtaining relief. Also, the mere fact of a choice of forums should have a restraining effect on the Board.

As indicated earlier, it is beyond the scope of this volume to discuss solutions in depth. The foregoing are suggestions only and would require careful study and, undoubtedly, many refinements. The important factor in any solution, however, is to provide certainty. The "delicate perceptiveness necessary to achieve justice," suggested by Chairman McCulloch, is a highly desirable quality, but it must be exercised within the framework of reasonably explicit rules which carry out the intent of the legislative authority—Congress—not the intent of the members of the NLRB. As Justice Holmes said:

> "The tendency of the law must always be to narrow the field of uncertainty." (*The Common Law*, p. 127)

CHAPTER XXIII

CONCLUSION

At this point, the reader will have made his own judgment as to the validity of the criticism of the new Board. Once more let it be emphasized that vigorous disagreement with the Board's views must not be confused with personalities. All five Board members are men of conviction but they are not unusual. Scores of replacements could be found who would reflect the identical philosophy of each. Thus, it is futile to attack the members personally or to expect that a change of faces would have a profound effect on the interpretation of the law under the present administration.

It has been the declared intent of Congress, reflecting the conviction of an overwhelming majority of the people in our country, that our labor laws should protect the individual freedom of American workingmen and women. To carry out this objective, we must be concerned with more fundamental problems than the personalities of NLRB members.

If we would rid ourselves of the misconception, which at times has approached the mesmeric, that there is something sacred about a labor organization as such, we would take a long step toward true protection of individual freedom. Unions are merely another form of human organization, better than some but worse than others. Like other human institutions, each union is no more interested in the public good, in the welfare of our country, or in the preservation of individual freedom than is permitted by the totality of interests, prejudices, integrity and intelligence of its members, reflected in its leaders.

Thus, the standard against which union conduct must continually be tested in applying the statute is that established by Congress—freedom of choice for the individual.

CASE REFERENCES

DATE DUE

DEC 1 0 1993	